OLDER THAN TIME

For many years a freelance journalist, Allegra Taylor is the author of *I Fly Out With Bright Feathers: The Quest of a Novice Healer*; *Acquainted With the Night*, a book on death and dying; *Prostitution: What's Love Got To Do With It?*; and *Healing Hands*. She is married to documentary film-maker Richard Taylor and they have six grown-up children, two of whom they adopted while living in Nigeria and one in Kenya. They also have four grandchildren.

OLDER THAN TIME

A Grandmother's Search for Wisdom

Allegra Taylor

Aquarian/Thorsons

An Imprint of HarperCollins*Publishers*

The Aquarian Press
An Imprint of HarperCollins*Publishers*
77-85 Fulham Palace Road,
Hammersmith, London W6 8JB
1160 Battery Street,
San Francisco, California 94111-1213

First published 1993
1 3 5 7 9 10 8 6 4 2

© Allegra Taylor 1992

Allegra Taylor asserts the moral right to
be identified as the author of this work

A catalogue record for this book
is available from the British Library

ISBN 1 85538 152 4

Phototypeset by Harper Phototypesetters Limited,
Northampton, England
Printed in Great Britain by
Mackays of Chatham, Kent

To my grandmothers
Ethel Way Moore
Sara Tennenbaum

To my children's grandmothers
Patricia Hamilton Honig
Kathleen Bellamy Taylor

and to my grandchildren
Julian, Maddison, Jake and Harrison

With love

Living is not the same as going shopping, nor is it the same as making a nest in which to escape the sufferings of one another. Living has something to do with Eros, with love of life and with the love of other's lives. Here lies wisdom.

MATTHEW FOX, *Original Blessing*

The best time in life is always now because it is the only time there is. You can't live regretting what's past, and you can't live anticipating the future. If you spend any amount of time doing either of those things you'll never live at all.

GERMAINE GREER, *The Change*

CONTENTS

ACKNOWLEDGEMENTS

I couldn't possibly have written this book without a great deal of kindness, help and hospitality. To all those friends and relations who put me up and put up with me and to all the women who have shared their lives with me, I am forever in your debt.

I would particularly like to thank Rivka Buncel and her daughter Sari in Israel; Helen Higgs, Carol Qirreh and Mark Gorman of Help the Aged, London; Anne Benedict in New York; Annabel Ove, the Afro-Caribbean Institute and its Project Director Hazel McClune in Jamaica; Peter and Tammy Minot, Jane Lockard, Frances and John Cutter and the San Carlos Apache Tribal Office in Arizona; India and Laughing Water in Montana; my cousins Peter, Hugh and Michael Stubbins and their families; Cecelia Hurwich in San Francisco; Kaoilani Hulama in Hawaii; Dorice Reid of the Cook Island Tourist Authority and Ewan Smith, Managing Director of Air Rarotonga in the Cook Islands; Deb and Laugharne in New Zealand; Diana McCudden in Australia; Maj Gen R. S. Pannu (Rtd.) and Sam Oomen of HelpAge India; Ngodup Dorje and the Tibetan Women's Centre, Rajpur; The Tibetan Homes Foundation at Happy Valley, Mussoorie; Rasheeda and Anees and family and Madhu and Gopi Mehta in Bombay; Haku and Vilu Shah in Ahmedebad; The Brahma Kumaris of the World Spiritual University, Mount Abu; Shelley Bovey in Glastonbury; Lynne Reid-Banks in Devon; my new-found cousins Janka Hochland and Malka Me-Zehav; Sister Iona of the Community of St John the Divine and Modupe Brownlow, two wise women in London; Erica Smith who commissioned the book and encouraged me and Kelly Davis who edited it with great sensitivity.

A special thanks to Anna Humming Earthworm Hawthorn in Wales from whom I learned such a lot about the nature of magic at her beautiful Mother Nature summer camp and, most of all, my love and thanks to my husband Richard, the father of my children and grandfather of my grandchildren who believed in me and was there when I came home.

The author and publishers would also like to thank the following for permission to reproduce copyright material: Eleanor Ahuna, for an extract from her unpublished journals; Beacon Press, Boston, for an extract from *Grandmothers of the Light* by Paula Gunn Allen, copyright © 1991 by Paula Gunn Allen, reprinted by permission of Beacon Press; Bear & Company Publishing, New Mexico, for an extract from *Original Blessings* by Matthew Fox, copyright 1983, Bear & Co. Inc., and for an extract from *Medicine Cards* by Jamie Sams and David Carson, copyright 1988, Bear & Co. Inc., PO Box 2860, Santa Fe, NM 87504; Faber and Faber Limited, London, for extracts from 'Little Gidding', 'East Coker' and 'Choruses' from "The Rock"' by T.S. Eliot, in *Collected Poems 1909-1962*; Hamish Hamilton Ltd, London, for an extract from *The Change* by Germain Greer, copyright © Germaine Greer, 1991; HarperCollinsPublishers, London, for an extract from *The Absent Mother* by Alix Pirani (first published by Mandala, 1991); Asphodel Long for an extract from *Generations of Memories: Voices of Jewish Women*; Na Kane O Ka Malo Press, Honolulu, for an extract from *Man, Gods and Nature* by Michael Dudley; Penguin Books Ltd, Harmondsworth, for an extract from *Indian Summer* by James Cameron (first published by Macmillan, Penguin Books 1987), copyright © James Cameron, 1979; Random House, Inc, New York, for an extract from *Arizona* by Larry Cheek (first published by Compass American Guides, Inc); Vaine Rasmussen for her poem 'A Book and a Pen', published in *Mana: The South Pacific Journal of Language and Literature*, Vol 5 No 1, 1980; Rabbi Sheila Shulman for an extract from her essay entitled 'A Radical Feminist Perspective on Judaism' (*European Judaism*, Vol 21 No 1, summer 1987); and Rinchen Dolma Taring for an extract from her book *Daughter of Tibet*, published by Wisdom Publications, London.

Every effort has been made to contact owners of copyright material. The author and publishers would be grateful for information regarding the whereabouts of any copyright holder not mentioned above, and will gladly acknowledge them in further editions of this book.

INTRODUCTION

By one of those remarkable synchronicities that seem no accident I first became a grandmother on 31st October, All Hallow's Eve, the holy day of Hecate, Greek Goddess of the Underworld, the Mother of Witches, the Crone. Hecate, is the archetype of the wise old woman, the Hag, who knows how to work magic and commune with spirits, who watches over our dreams and inner visions. She represents the power of the older woman in her menopausal phase – initiate and seeker of wisdom.

Nobody likes the word 'crone'. It has such horrible connotations. All my young-looking, middle-aged friends shudder with distaste at the prospect. We are all influenced by the scary stereotype of the toothless, crooked, warty-faced, whiskery, evil old witch but is there another way to perceive her? Is there a way we can look forward to her arrival and welcome her?

Hecate symbolizes the quest of the spirit, the courageous one who journeys in the darker realms of the psyche. She is the truth-teller, the spider woman, the weaver of webs. She is a traveller seeking transformation. She stands at a crossroads symbolizing a time of decision and renewal. Old age is surely a time to learn about magic, about healing powers, divination and prophecy. A time to walk the mystical path with practical feet.

Both my grandmothers died before I was born. I have grown

up bereft, with no role models from our youth-worshipping culture to help me age with wisdom, confidence and power. All my life I have felt this loss acutely and now I am a grandmother myself.

When I held my baby grand-daughter in my arms for the first time and smelt her newborn, musty smell and knew I would die for her, the spirit of the grandmother awoke. I wished it could be like it is in fairy tales when all the fairy godmothers are invited to a table with golden platters and one by one they bestow their spiritual gifts upon the baby.

My friend Jeannie phoned by chance that day and I was lamenting this lack of ritual which dulls our age when it occurred to us that, of course, there was nothing to stop us inventing our own celebrations. We resolved to create a ceremony that would fill the gap. I invited two other older women friends to join us, and the baby's other grandmother, Wynn, completed the gathering.

The death of the old and the birth of the new. For us as much as for the baby it was a rite of passage. We each held the tiny girl in our arms and kissed her and blessed her. It was a time of great love and tenderness - infinitely potent. We had reclaimed something of incalculable value - the collective power of the older woman. It was the most beautiful feeling of continuation, of passing on priceless treasures, of having an active, useful, unique role to play, of letting go of the last phase of our lives and moving proudly and vitally into the next.

That was when the idea for this book first came into my mind. It would take the form of a search for the wise, courageous old woman I want to become. A quest, in many parts of the world, for the crone in her many guises. I wanted to discover her, reclaim her, invent her, celebrate her.

In antiquity (and in those present-day societies where she is recognized as a valid image and not a useless object), the older woman had a unique function. She commanded respect and her advice was sought. Her community looked up to her and took her seriously. As Barbara Walker points out in her book, *The Crone*, it was the medieval metamorphosis of the wise woman into the wicked witch that transformed her cauldron from a sacred symbol of regeneration into a vessel of poisons. It also changed the word 'crone' from a compliment to an insult and established the stereotype of malevolent old womanhood that still haunts older women in Western society today, along with a legacy of fear, lack of confidence and lack of identity. Because she was past childbearing age the old woman became the ideal scapegoat: 'too expendable to be missed, too weak to fight back, too poor to matter.'

The terror of the Inquisition reigned for 500 years. In relatively permissive England alone, 30,000 witches were tortured and killed between 1542 and 1736. Witchcraft laws were still on the statutes until 1951. There is a growing recognition in the West that most 'witches' were, and still are, none other than midwives and herbalists; wise women who preserve in their collective unconscious the remnants of an older religion based on worship of nature and the feminine principle.

The Inquisition outlawed the ancient wisdoms of women and cut them off from their own spiritual vision. Denied any form of spiritual authority until 1992, when the Church of England synod finally granted them the right to become priests (not priestesses, mind you, and still serving the Father rather than the Mother), women have little confidence in their own mystery, power and magic except as youthful sex objects.

In Britain and America today, in the wake of the women's movement, the New Age movement and the ecology movement, there is a gathering groundswell of interest in women's wisdom, drawing on ancient pagan traditions, European folk traditions and Native American traditions. I wanted to explore this revival and the way it is helping older women reclaim their intrinsic worth. I wanted to go on a personal voyage of discovery to visit and learn from grandmothers in various parts of the world. I wanted to talk to old women about their experiences and listen to their wisdom, insights, secrets, stories.

In the past few years three more of my own grandchildren have arrived and I am learning to invent my role. Now that my energies are no longer directed towards giving birth, rearing my own children and caring for my individual family I am ready to connect with the eternal.

Paracelsus said that witches taught him everything he knew about healing. I am seeking, in the myths and symbols which are my inheritance, an affirmation of those mysterious qualities which have somehow become downgraded and made risible as 'old wives tales' and 'feminine intuition'.

The archetype of the Crone - in Barbara Walker's words, 'the old woman who acknowledges no master' - has been my guide on this long, dark, labyrinthine spiritual journey. She represents precisely the kind of power women need to find in order to counteract the war-mongering, empire-building, rapacious, patriarchal power that has brought our planet to the edge of extinction.

Of course there are many wise women to be found at home so why travel abroad? My reasoning was this: because we live in a death-denying, youth-worshipping society, it is very hard to grow old with zest and confidence. I wanted to travel to such cultures as the Polynesian, Caribbean and Indian where old age is venerated. The journey, in itself, would be a test. Would I be able to cope with unfamiliar situations? It would be an initiation, a rite of passage - learning to befriend the loneliness and the darkness wherein lies our 'unknowing knowledge', as Meister Eckhart put it.

I was of a mind to set the journey in motion and follow where it led. Precisely because I was keen to trust the intuitive, right-brained mode of being, to give myself time to dwell in the empty spaces between things, I made as few plans as possible. I wanted the journey to be non-linear, non-rational, fluid (all the criticisms usually levelled against 'a woman's way of doing things'), with room for surprises, tangents and chance encounters. A dance along an unknown path.

I was already beginning to realize how much I depend on

the pathways other people have already made, how hard it is for me to go into unknown territory and how frightened I am of becoming lost. Danger lies outside the fireside circle but also untold riches. There can be no gains without risks. There's something about modern life that makes us think we can learn everything painlessly, *quickly*, greedily - get a video, have a briefing, hire an expert - but I wanted to take time, to see things from a different perspective, to allow my perceptions to alter slowly, to let the unexpected slip in between my heartbeats. I would have to go away from everything I know.

While musing on all this, trying to justify what seemed like a chaotic muddle, I happened to pick up a copy of Matthew Fox's *The Original Blessing* and turned by chance to this quote from Jung:

> The art of letting things happen, action through non-action, letting go of oneself . . . became for me the key opening the door to the way. We must be able to let things happen in the psyche. For us, this actually is an art of which few people know anything. Consciousness is forever interfering, helping, correcting, negating, and never leaving the simple growth of the psychic processes in peace.

So perhaps I didn't need to justify anything after all. It was all right to 'let things happen'. In the end the quest became like a river. Once I had launched myself it just carried me along. I encountered some ancient traditions and occult wisdoms which have been repressed, forgotten, condemned. I met women in the 'Third World', women of the 'New Age'. I met ordinary women and rare ones, artists and prophets, housewives and mystics, rich and poor, educated and illiterate. I blew all my publisher's advance on a round-the-world ticket. Anyone else doing a similar journey would have seen other things, met different people. Each person's adventure would be unique. This is the story of mine.

As is always the way, no sooner do you become interested in something new than it keeps on turning up in your life. Shortly before I set off on my journey, a friend, knowing that I was wanting to meet wise old women, offered to introduce me to an English village witch. Until recently I had always rather scoffed at the image of modern witches. My local 'New Age' shop has a whole section on the occult, complete with pointed hats, bottles of All Night Long Oil and love potions (mostly imported from California). It is much frequented by young women with long black fingernails and weedy, would-be wizards with plastic shopping bags. But beyond the fancy dress and the longing for a magic wand to make your dreams come true lies a deeper enchantment. Through all the centuries of persecution it has lain low but never completely disappeared.

Paddy Slade, the seventh child of a seventh child, has a Double First in English and Medieval History from Cambridge. She lives on a war widow's pension in an ordinary little pebble-dash council house at the end of a muddy country lane near Bath. I don't know what I expected but it wasn't the sensible, humorous, ordinary-looking country-woman in a woolly cardigan who opened the door to me. The only clue to her profession was a sticker in the window of her car parked in the drive saying, 'My other car's a broomstick', and a small plaque by the front door saying, 'Never mind the dog. Beware of owner.'

Paddy is a hereditary witch. Her mother and grandmother before her were witches and the knowledge has been passed down in her family for many generations. Her sitting-room and kitchen are like any other pensioner's with photos of grandchildren on the mantelpiece and the smell of rhubarb crumble wafting from the oven but upstairs in the spare bedroom she has created a temple and this is where the magic rites are performed. She also loves to be able to work outside in the garden or some other natural setting such as a field or a sacred grove. For a big community occasion, like a seasonal rite, she hires the village hall. She is accepted by all the locals (excèpt her next door neighbour who is a Jehovah's Witness) as the village witch.

I spent a lovely day with Paddy enjoying her company and her wisdom.

'There's so much magic right here in these islands,' she said. 'It's all to do with "spirit of place". We can dig down into our own past and find the magic that's there. The magic is in the stones and in the springs. It is in the trees and in the earth. That's what we have to find again.'

I wanted to know how the malevolent stereotype of witches had become so prevalent. 'Pure propaganda!' said Paddy. 'Old women were such easy, defenceless targets, especially if they had a little bit of property that could be confiscated. The Church was incredibly greedy and twisted. The infamous *Malleus Malleficarum* (the Inquisition's handbook on witch-finding, written by two Dominican monks) sanctioned any amount of torture in order to extract confessions from the accused.'

Witchcraft, according to Paddy, mostly consisted of midwifery, herbalism and laying out the dead. Because it was to do with life and death it was seen as usurping the power of the all-male priesthood. And because it was to do with healing it was seen as usurping the role of the all-male medical profession. Women were not allowed to study medicine and could be accused of witchcraft if they were seen to gather two different herbs! Witches, like the shamans of other cultures, were the repositories of ancient wisdom, symbolically riding the transforming powers of the elements, disappearing into different dimensions. None of this could be tolerated by the Church which fought back by literally putting the fear of God into people. Hundreds and thousands of witches, mostly old women, were tortured, hanged and burned at the stake. Even those who escaped execution were crushed by the fear which exists to this day.

'Witchcraft,' she went on, 'grew out of worshipping the goddess and although the Church did a good job of crushing it they never entirely wiped it out. My family have been witches as far back as we can go. They were country people from Kent - lived in the same place since the year dot. My mother taught me the earth was female, giving life in the way a woman gives birth and was to be cherished. People came to my mother before they'd go to the doctor - for herbal remedies, for advice, for healing.'

Now Paddy's mission is to spread the word that witchcraft is a respectable profession and not to be looked on as some aberration. 'I think of myself as a teacher rather than a healer,' she said. 'That's what I wanted to do ever since I was quite small. Now it has become urgent to put the record straight. Witchcraft is *not* about worshipping the devil. It never was. Satanism is really a manufactured idea, a refined, effete, upper-class pornography. It's a very male thing, the idea of devil-worship, and certainly these cults do exist today. A lot of it is to do with paedophilia. Admittedly, the witches' god was horned but that's because he was Pan; he was Herne the Hunter; he was a fertility god - the ram, the stag, the goat - nothing to do with the devil. Why should the devil have horns anyway? Witchcraft, in its proper sense, has always been the craft of the wise. I call myself a witch because that is what I am and because I hesitate to call myself a wise woman. I don't know that I've achieved wisdom yet.'

We talked about the ways in which older women can begin to reconnect with their power. 'People are going to have to dredge up from their own deep residual memories what has been there all along,' said Paddy. 'Unfortunately women like my grandmother are dead now so I can't ask her but I learn a lot talking to any older woman - chair-bound, crippled. So much of wisdom comes from experience, from being a witness, from happiness and sadness. It travels via tendrils and networks as it always has done. We have begun to come out of the woodwork and *own* our power. Owning it is very important.'

As for rites, Paddy says, we have to reinvent them. She has created rites for the seasons and the festivals, rites for the land and the new moon. She has created a beautiful healing rite to reconsecrate the womb of a woman who has been the victim of rape. 'We, as women, must help with our wisdom, our tenderness and our love to heal the emotional burden the victims of such an outrage carry.'

A lot of magic surrounds rites of passage. As the village witch, Paddy is frequently asked by local people to help them mark a special occasion. 'People come when they are at transitional stages in their lives,' she said. 'We have done a purification for a house, a blessing for an infant. We did a beautiful rite for a young girl who had just started menstruating, and recently a lot of older women have been asking for a post-menopause rite to mark the transition after the childbearing years are over. There's so much fear about losing femininity and usefulness but I *know* that this is the time when we blossom and come into our own - the time when we can move into a celebration of our unique gifts and pass on things of value. The archetype of the crone, the grandmother, the wise woman should be welcomed into our lives. She is a very strong, sure woman. She is the way-shower, the lamplighter, the teacher - passing on the last of her knowledge.'

'I am a pagan in the true Latin sense of the word,' says Paddy. '*Paysan*, peasant, country-dweller, rustic. You can be a pagan without being a witch but being a witch presupposes a frame of reference which is to do with the old religion, the nature gods and the goddess. Your whole life is lived in reverence twenty-four hours a day. It informs everything you do.'

I asked Paddy if there was a rite for the protection of travellers as I was shortly to be leaving on my great round-the-world pilgrimage. There was. She lent me a white robe which she had run up from some sheeting and she wore a yellow silken one. The idea is to take off your everyday clothes and leave them outside the room along with your everyday persona and your watch so that you are in a space outside time. We went into the inner sanctum, the upstairs room painted to resemble a stone circle.

Paddy mixed a special incense from mastic, benzoin, red sandalwood, cardamoms, frankincense, oil of lavender, mercury and lemon rind to burn in a little charcoal brazier and gave me a thistle - the most protective of all herbs - to take with me. She lit some candles and called upon the god and the goddess. She invoked the forces of nature: the powers of the elements and of the four directions. She said, 'We ask a blessing this day upon Allegra who is setting forth on her travels. We ask a blessing on the work she does, on the words she speaks and the words she writes. We ask for the strength of fire to sustain her, we ask for the stability of earth to go with her and to keep her on her path, we ask for the love of water and the intelligence of air to keep her heart and her mind open.' She turned to me. 'State your case.'

'Umm, err, I am about to leave on my journey to speak with wise old women from different cultures. I ask that I will have the courage, the understanding and the humility to deserve the confidences that I will be given. May I use them wisely and write well. This is what I ask.'

Then we drank some grape juice ('fruit of the vine') and ate some 'bread of the earth' cut into little five-pointed stars. Paddy gave thanks. The circle was then closed, we disrobed and stepped back into our ordinary selves in ordinary time and space. A lovely casserole and baked potatoes had been cooking slowly in the oven and we were both pretty hungry.

What moved me most about my encounter with Paddy was the generosity of her creed. It is so enabling and respectful. The American writer Starhawk has written wonderfully about this in her book *Dreaming the Dark*. Witchcraft and magic are based on a world view of 'immanence', a pantheistic conception of the Divine being present throughout the universe, of spirit and transformative power being embodied in the natural world. It is a set of tools, a philosophy of harmony with nature. It is about power from within rather than power over.

Two weeks later I flew off to America.

CHAPTER ONE

Leaving Home

Home is where one starts from. As we grow older
The world becomes stranger, the pattern more
complicated
Of dead and living.

T.S. Eliot, 'East Coker'

On 14th March 1992 my mother would have been eighty. It
was also ten years since she died. I chose this day to leave
on my round-the-world crone quest as it seemed auspicious
and I wanted to honour her on her birthday and ask her
blessing. I had been looking forward to this moment for
months and been packed for weeks but in the last few days
leading up to departure I became increasingly faint-hearted.
Psychosomatic ailments assailed me from every direction: sore
throat, bad dreams, aching body, upset stomach, headaches
and, on D-day, a streaming cold. My body was saying, 'You
don't want to do this. Stay home!'

The ride to the airport felt like the road to exile. It was
eight years since my last trip and I guess it becomes harder
and harder to leave home as you get older. I kept thinking
of the babies' faces and the fact that I'd be missing my
littlest grandson's first birthday. I burst into tears when
I hugged my husband Richard goodbye and went all through
the security check and duty-free with tears spilling
uncontrollably down my cheeks - all ludicrously at odds with

my seasoned traveller, Rohan gear, image.

I gave myself a worse headache and had to ask the flight attendant for some aspirin. The in-flight movie, *Stepping Out*, made me cry as well. Tap-dancing routines always do. They bring back all my unfulfilled childhood longings to be Cyd Charisse. And now I'm a grandmother and I'll never be a dancer and I'm overweight and my children are grown-up. And here I was leaving home like some restless adolescent to do what I never did when I was young.

Everything safe, everything I loved, was at home but an indefinable desire for adventure, to be in a place of not-knowing between the old and the new, coupled with the need to be the one who was missed for a change, had set all this in motion and it now had a relentless momentum of its own. I knew that if I didn't go I could spend the rest of my life hiding from myself, not confronting the fear, not acknowledging the coping strategies that limit me, the addictions that bind me. After months of planning, the yearned for and dreaded day had arrived. Would I find out how to be a wise old woman? Had I hurtled into this too soon – before I had finished being a young woman? I cried halfway across the Atlantic looking like a silly middle-aged frump – puffy face, bloodshot eyes. I didn't feel glamorous like I used to. Last time I travelled alone I didn't need glasses, strange men made gallant gestures, I had sex appeal on my side. This time I felt invisible.

I finally stopped blubbing and snivelling, slept for a bit and woke up just as we landed at JFK. It was early morning, the sun was shining and a brisk, cold wind was blowing. The Manhattan skyline looked just as it should. As you drive into the city from the airport, suddenly there it is. New York, New York! I had three days and only one person I wanted to see so I decided to just wander around Manhattan and use the time as a buffer zone between my real life and this fantasy life of international traveller and wisdom-seeker.

As I plodded the streets, occasionally glimpsing my bundled-up, sensibly shod reflection in shop windows, I wrestled with more thoughts on growing older. It's hard, when you've always been 'attractive', to know when to let go, or rather, when to stop relying on it. Once, when I was in my twenties, I missed my flight from Dominica to St Lucia. As I stood there looking forlorn a man offered to give me a lift in his private plane. That would not happen today. I'm on my own.

Anyway, I read in the paper that at the Museum of Modern Art someone had invented an Age Machine. The idea was to sit in front of a computer screen and map out your face which then aged twenty-five years before your eyes. I wanted to see what I would look like at seventy-six so I walked down Broadway to have a go. The finished effect was disappointingly like the theatrical make-up for a school play – lots of heavy black lines pointing downwards from the corners of my eyes and mouth. A bad-tempered, scowly person stared back at me. The outcome was the same for each person who tried it. Surely character and personality, racial differences, degree of happiness and state of health play a greater part in the final physiognomy than the computer-calculated effects of gravity and skin elasticity. I didn't believe that disagreeable old bag could be me. All rather a waste of time but it kept my mind focussed on the topic of ageing.

I wrote in my diary:

This new stage of growth is frightening because I don't know where it will lead or what I have to lose to get there. I feel exposed and vulnerable, yet I know that the only way to soar is to jump into thin air. After a terrifying period of free-fall the warm currents will hold me aloft. Nobody can tell me about it. I can only trust the process itself.

In a back street I passed a little shop which specialized in the 'occult'. I went in. It was a depressing place – surly assistants, everything dusty and tatty. They sold mostly props and accoutrements for the satanic, manipulative sort of magic. Lots of black candles shaped like penises and books on Aleister Crowley. There was a pornographic flavour to it, with rituals to do with gaining power over rather than living in harmony with the world and its creatures. Poor goddess, I thought, your needs are not being met. The occult and magic are still tainted with the evil that men do. Even more important to bear witness to the beauty and spirituality of real witchcraft.

Magic is *art*. It has to do with forms, with structures, with images that can shift us out of the limitations of everyday reality, with visions that can hint at new possibilities. Magic is also *will* - action, passion, choices, directed energy. Having integrity as a witch means recognizing that you can make choices, that your choices have consequences and that you are personally responsible for those changes.

Shops like this are full of books of spells and incantations: how to get your lover back, how to get revenge, how to win, and so on. These are traps waiting for hungry, angry people who are longing to make their lives different without taking responsibility. But magic is not about having power over people, it is about calling forth your own power from within. Like any other technique, magic can, of course, be misused but it's not very effective in the long run, hence its association with self-deception and charlatanism. The first principle of magic is that all things are interconnected, all is relationship. You can't do any lasting magic without love. We cannot cause change without changing ourselves.

I rode the elevator to the top of the Empire State building, took the ferry to the Statue of Liberty and walked in Central Park. I marvelled at the amazing vulgarity of the Trump Tower, I felt pretty damn brave riding the subway (which was full of perfectly normal people and not the crazed addicts and serial killers we are led to believe), I went to Grand Central Station which is like a cathedral and a kosher bakery rolled into one, selling every type of muffin - my favourite American food. Blueberry ones, carrot and oatbran, cinnamon and apple, raisins, cornmeal, cherry and hazelnut. I chose 'Glorious Morning' with a bit of everything and ate it with a cup of coffee on the train to Brewster North where I met up with my darling cousin Michael.

My worldwide network of strategically placed cousins is, I concede, a great bonus. It was his mother-in-law, Cara Caldwell Watson, I had come to New York to see. A woman who finally realized her dream, at the age of sixty-five, to be a theatre director. A woman who, having raised five children and been a Presbyterian minister's wife, found the courage and the energy to take such a step.

I first met Cara when she came to England a few years back to do the LAMDA (London Academy of Music and Dramatic Art) Summer School course on Shakespeare interpretation and to research a play she was writing on the life of Gertrude Jekyll, the influential Edwardian landscape designer who lived to the age of ninety. Cara was such a joy to be with, a huge personality in a petite 4 foot 11 inch frame, a hilarious sense of humour and a laugh like a drain. She embodied so much of what this book is about that I knew I wanted to see her again.

Cara and her husband Frank live in a quiet rural area of New York State in a house cleverly converted by Frank from an old warehouse. It is right on the edge of a creek and bounded by lovely woods. On this Sunday afternoon children and grandchildren arrived, and everyone helped to cook a great family lunch. The turbulence of Cara's transition can now be seen in its wider perspective - ructions have healed, the family has survived, her marriage is enriched - but pursuing her passion for the theatre has not been easy. It has required a determination, some might even say a ruthlessness, which is seen as being at odds with the image of wife and mother.

Cara Caldwell was a young actress from Nashville, Tennessee, who landed her first part in a Broadway play at the age of twenty-two. When she met and married West Point graduate Frank Watson, she somehow imagined that she would have a couple of babies and get back to the theatre but she reckoned without Frank's decision to go to theological college and become a Presbyterian minister. Thus she landed her longest-running role - that of reluctant minister's

wife. It was to be nearly thirty years before she trod the
boards again.

Cara even tried to bring her dramatic skills into the
community by starting a theatre company called Channel
Stage at the White Plains Presbyterian Church. 'The concept
was to create a channel of communication between the
community and the church, revitalizing both, encouraging
role play which can be very effective in curing social ills. But
I had to battle against a lot of convention,' said Cara. 'It never
came from Frank but from looking in the mirror of the eyes
of other people – the congregation. They couldn't really cope
with me. We had too many children, our cars were too old,
our dogs were too loud, we did too many things, we didn't
conform to the norm. I think I was the most unorthodox
minister's wife ever.'

She had two more children and adopted a fifth. She played
the part but all the while she was starving. 'I constantly sought
to fill up the empty space in the centre of my being with
children and home-making, with Southern hospitality – always
taking on too much. The hardest part about raising a family
was that my *hunger* was not being assuaged. My single desire
was to have a life in the theatre. I came from a line of strong
women and I always felt I was kind of a non-person when
I was not bringing in an income through my own independent
efforts. I knew that I had a responsibility to the world for the
gifts I had been given. I tormented myself with questions: Is
this my destiny? What am I? A cook and a laundress? Even
when I was pregnant, even when I was feeding tiny babies,
I was waiting. Waiting to get back to my real work.'

'I knew I had to stick it for a number of years,' said Cara,
'but as soon as I had those children in a secure spot, I split!
Gradually, one at a time, I had a sense that they didn't really
need me any more and that was *sweet*, so sweet.'

On her youngest child's eighteenth birthday, which falls on
4th July, Cara gave a big party and made an announcement.
'I said, "Everybody, this is Independence Day! I'm off!" It
didn't lessen my love for them. Quite the contrary, but it made

them very angry with me. Angry that I had deserted the nest and gone off to do my thing. Angry that I'd rather be working than at home taking care of them. A mother is supposed to be there. They had a long way to come before they could accept it and forgive me. Frank, on the other hand, was wonderful. He said "I know you have to do this. Come back to me when you're ready. I'll be here." He helped me to find an apartment in New York. It was in such bad shape that nobody else wanted it but it was cheap and he fixed it up. He did that for me. I've been able to do what I want because Frank gave his blessing and his permission. He's been a pretty exceptional husband to be able to encompass these huge needs in me.'

New York must have more struggling actors than anywhere. They work for nothing in awful little warehouses and draughty church halls. Ninety-seven per cent of the theatrical profession are out of work at any given moment. At one production I went to by a little uptown repertory company there were more people on the stage than in the audience.

Undaunted, Cara reactivated her union membership, found an agent, started auditioning. 'No, I wasn't scared,' she said in answer to my question. 'I was perfectly at home. I felt like I was back where I was supposed to be, doing what I always meant to do. My confidence was essentially undamaged but the fact that I was in my fifties limited me so much in the way of roles. I found that it's tough out there for older women. Look at any play. How many parts are there for women over fifty? They are always small roles and at least ninth on the list of Cast of Characters!'

Cara managed to get extra work in films for a few years and earned enough to pay her dues, keep her clothes nice and her hair done. 'But I never really got any further,' she admitted. 'Being out of the business for so long meant I didn't have the contacts. Let's face it, people hire their friends! I found I was longing to be more active - wanting to make things happen. I disliked standing and waiting for someone to tell me what to do so I began applying for directing jobs in regional theatre.'

Finally Cara landed a summer season in North Carolina directing a production of *On Golden Pond*. It got great reviews and she has never looked back. Since that time she has been travelling the country as a guest director as well as working with her own little company at home in Croton Falls.

'My kind of show is one that reflects hidden qualities in our own lives,' said Cara. 'One that takes the choices we have and shows them in a purer light. *On Golden Pond* was the perfect play to do. The theme is growing older. People ask me what happens in the play. Nothing happens. Nothing and everything. It's about the on-goingness of life. So much of what goes on in the play happens beneath the surface. There is a great sense of things left unsaid. I love the play and I hope it left the audience thinking, "Are there things I need to say to somebody I love that I haven't said?"'

Age is the subject we talked about most and the fact that in American society older women are marginalized to death. 'The invisibility is the worst thing. It's terrible!' said Cara. 'But you have to fight back! Fight back when you get bad service or get seated in the corner in a restaurant. I am given to outrageous behaviour in public now just to keep from being invisible.

'I thought getting old was going to be so frightening. I thought life was like a wheel getting slower and slower but it isn't. Getting older in itself is no threat. You just get better, richer, more varied, more faceted. Life has fed you enough vital material that you feel full all the time. It is society's attitude that we need to change. It's almost as if there's a slight bad odour if you're an older woman!' She warmed to her theme. 'Being old is not some kind of illness but a position of pride and respect that you have earned. People should *want* to be old. They should look forward to it.

'Life is like a garden; after you've blossomed in the spring and dropped your seeds in the summer, you remain for a while in the autumn and your colours are richer at that period of your flowering than at any other time. Being old brings so many advantages. It gives you a certain freedom to be eccentric. You are not going to be misunderstood by being friendly in a grocery line. You are not going to be pursued or harassed. You are accepted at face value. I talk to people very easily - total strangers - and they enjoy it.'

Luckily, one of Cara's productions was playing that week so I was able to see it. The play, *Who's Happy Now?* by Oliver Hailey, for which Frank had built all the sets, was a bleak, sad little tale of a small town violent, abusive marriage and the collusion which allows it to continue. It was very well done and the rapport between actors and director unmistakable. I asked her what special qualities she felt she could bring to the job, as an older woman.

'A much greater trust in other people's experience and instinct,' she answered. 'What I have become is a very gentle dictator - coaxing, midwifing, guiding - I'm more assistive than directorial. I watch people change in this benevolent setting. I see them becoming richer, warmer and less afraid and, oh, that feeds me well! It's much more important than the money, the time, the status. There is something about an actor laying down his life to try and take up the life of another human being that moves me so! If I can assist that process, there is nothing in the world more satisfying. I think I bring something of my long years of nurturing to the job. A tendency to allow things to happen instead of making them happen.

'Every play I do adds to my stock of wisdom and experience. I am learning all the time. Each play challenges me with a different set of issues and I find a connection with something that needs correcting in my own life. It is a constant enrichment. In this current play, *Who's Happy Now?*, the wisdom I am drawing is that what you see on the outside about other people's lives is never the whole story. People present whatever front they need to but it's only ever a partial truth. People make the choices they do for reasons that go back to their genes, their bones, their training, their fears, their dreams. Those are the things that make a person an individual. You meddle with devils if you try to form another person's life decisions for them, you kill off the growing roots of the human being.'

She spoke with passion. Cara, in her work and in her life, is not prepared to settle for anything less than the truth. 'I never saw that as brave,' she said, 'only as utterly necessary. I'd have died if I'd done otherwise.'

On my last day in New York I met Cara at the Museum Café on Columbus Avenue. We had a raucous lunch together - Cara's wonderful smile and infectious laugh radiating out from our table, turning heads. She looks like Cinderella's fairy godmother, cuddly and kindly. Looks which bely her tremendous determination and strength of character. At last the yearning and the hunger are satisfied. She is doing what she loves best. When she first left home to live in New York Frank had said, 'Go for it! Be everything you are.' And she did. 'It was lucky that I married a man with enough colours in his personality, enough flexibility to be with someone who lives in the present and I do live in the present all of the time.' She raised her glass. 'They said the prime of Miss Jean Brodie was forty-two. Nonsense! The prime of my life is now.'

CHAPTER TWO

Daughters of Slavery

Touching the surface and the depth of things,
. . . Tasting the sweets of being, fearing no stings,
Sensing the subtle spell of changing forms
Like a strong tree against a thousand storms.

CLAUDE McKAY, 'Like a Strong Tree',
from *Caribbean Voices*

Style was the word on the flight to Kingston. Everyone was decked out in amazing home-coming outfits covered in glitter and sequins, spangles and gold, ruffles and heels and skin-tight leopard print. There was so much hand luggage that passengers could hardly fit down the aisle. People even wore two or three hats at once, while the little children were got up like ice cream sundaes in lacy socks, embroidered designer denims, bejewelled hair ornaments plaits and curls. The flight attendants were going bananas. It was an exuberant way to come back to the Caribbean.

There is a hypnotic quality to the lilting dialect and the jumpy jump reggae rhythms, there's a thrilling diversity of skin tones and facial features, there's a wonderful economy and wit in the folk wisdom ('No put yuself in barrel when matchbox can hol' yu!').

But my *joie de vivre* wasn't to last. There followed several frustrating days of getting off to a flying standstill, with my one sure-fire contact never at home when I rang and the other having gone away for a couple of weeks. I recognized the need to relinquish control, to trust that the right person would materialize if I made myself receptive, but it was hard - time was limited, money even more so. My Western conditioned desire to get things moving always has to be painfully unlearned.

I had chosen to come to Jamaica not for its white sand beaches and blue seas on the north coast where most of the tourists disembarked but because I loved the idea of the Memory Bank which had been set up at the University of the West Indies with the objective of recording the oral history of elderly Jamaicans before it was too late. 'An old man dies, a book is lost' is their motto. But apparently the letter confirming the date of my visit had never arrived and the director, when I finally got through to her, was just about to leave the island on a lecture tour. She couldn't possibly see me, she said, but then relented and promised to squeeze me in later in the week.

I was trying not to be too disappointed. Somewhere on the island, I was sure, would be the Grandmother Jamaica of my fantasies - an old woman with skin like oiled teak, hearty, earthy, self-assured. An Everywoman steeped in traditional wisdom, dispensing herbal remedies, gossip, stories. A woman verbally imaginative, humorous, uninhibited who embodied all the unique flavours and traits of this country. Where was she?

The weather was perfect. Cooling trade winds, called Doctor Breeze by the Jamaicans, blew in from the sea to fan the daytime hours. People live long lives here. Artist/historian Howard Pyle wrote over 100 years ago:

> 'The air . . . is very healthy. I have known blacks 120 years of age and 100 years old is very common amongst temperate livers.'

I went to the Bureau of Women's Affairs to see if I could get a lead there and talked for a while with a nice woman whose main concern was getting legislation passed to assist the elderly living below the poverty line. Everything is changing, she said. There is a real problem with teenage pregnancies and consequently family structures have altered drastically. A girl of fifteen has a child who, in turn, gets pregnant at thirteen, making her mother a grandmother while still in her twenties. They don't live together or stay close. Often there is no father to speak of.

Successive waves of emigration have left many old people alone. The rise in 'new' diseases, she said, such as Alzheimer's and other forms of senility, may not be unrelated to the fact that many old people feel confused, uprooted and abandoned. If there is no family for them to have a useful role within, they have to be cared for in old people's homes where they do not thrive.

The Bureau of Women's Affairs was more geared to problems than wisdom, however, and I was directed to the National Council for the Aged. They gave me the name of an old woman called Aunt Dee, a livewire who lives out at Red Hills. She sounded lovely on the phone and invited me to visit her that very day. ('Come chil', you be welcome.') A lead at last!

Transport was another difficulty. Rental cars were astronomically expensive, buses erratic and overcrowded, taxis dangerous unless you knew the driver, and everybody warned me not to walk around on my own. I hadn't realized what a violent city Kingston had become. Horror stories abounded – a woman tourist had her arm cut off to get her jewellery, another had her throat slit in broad daylight for her gold chain. They don't just mug you, they kill you.

Up in the expensive real estate in the hills around the town there are plenty of newly built luxury homes which sell for around £200,000, so there is no shortage of wealth (rumoured to come from the marijuana trade) but it doesn't filter down to the poor who are really suffering. The slums of downtown Kingston are appalling. Inflation is galloping, banks won't lend money, there is no unemployment benefit or social security. Terrible stodgy flour-and-water dumplings with hot pepper sauce and zero nutritional value are often the only things to eat. Violent crime is soaring and a white woman carrying a bag is an obvious target.

I found a 'safe' driver (which may have referred to him but certainly not his driving), and his noisy, dilapidated yellow cab farted its way up into Red Hills, a little village high above Kingston and the home of eighty-year-old Mrs Daphne Betton. 'Past the gas station and the first house below the square' was the only address I had. Eventually I found her. Aunt Dee, as she is affectionately known, is a Rock of Gibraltar. She is President of the local Golden Age Club, she runs the Band of Mercy, she takes care of other people's children while they are at work and she looks after her own elderly, infirm husband. She nursed her aged aunt at home until the day she died. She is modest and unspectacular, seeking no praise, coping with very little money and muddling along with practically no help.

'You dress up fine today,' said her old husband, looking at her adoringly. She tutted and brushed him off. 'This isn't fine! Just a plain old dress,' but she looked pleased.

'It's a very pretty dress,' he went on and she patted his leg.

'He's in a good mood today,' she said, 'but sometimes he goes away and Mr Alzheimer comes in his place.'

She made us some tea 'to drink in fellowship' and the three of us sat round a table in their little kitchen. Mr Betton drank his own tea and then wanted hers. He kept trying to pour more water out of the empty thermos and he stirred about eight spoonfuls of sugar into his empty cup. 'A ninety-one-year-old spoilt baby,' she said indulgently and he laughed his head off and tried to kiss her. He told me a riddle, 'Me don' have life but me walking. What am I?' Answer: a shadow.

Aunt Dee teaches the local children how to bake and how to make artificial flowers out of old plastic bags. She has organized a first aid clinic where people can come for an aspirin or a plaster and she greatly laments the passing of folk medicine. Her own grandmother, she said, used to make wonderful remedies or send to old Mother So and So for a bottle of special tonic. But when these old ladies died, their secrets died with them. As a youngster she wasn't interested and now it's too late.

Her late aunt, she said, was the wisest person she ever knew. She instilled in her a sense of service and was the most important influence in her childhood. Devoted to helping people, she ran what they called a 'partner', a sort of savings club and mutual benefit society for times of need, whereby local village people put in a bit each week and could borrow when they had to meet an unexpected expense such as a funeral. More often than not, people couldn't afford to pay back and Auntie was always having to dip into her own pocket to bail them out.

Aunt Dee has been president of the Red Hills branch of the Golden Age Club for ten years. She is longing for the time when someone else will volunteer for the job but, as yet, no one has. It is an ecumenical, nationwide organization embracing all the various churches – at least fifteen different ones are represented in their membership alone. They run a soup kitchen for poor children from Aunt Dee's house and deploy the Band of Mercy children to carry food to 'shut ins' – the disabled and elderly folk who live in shacks up in the hills. They organize outings and occasional talks by visiting speakers.

The elderly folk, mostly women, who come to the Golden Age Club look forward to the fortnightly meetings as a real highlight in their lives. Come hell or high water they make the effort to come. They have no state funding at all. Some equipment has been donated by HelpAge International with the idea that this will enable members to generate their own cash but what they can make is so little and their needs so great that it's a pretty dispiriting task. Their most pressing need is for a recreation centre and properly equipped kitchen. Mrs Betton has already donated a small piece of her own land next to her house for this purpose and a relative who is a draughtsman has drawn up some plans.

For the present everyone crowds into her house where they cook and sing and sew. The old ladies enjoy needlework and are currently working on an elaborate and beautiful quilt. One of their members was highly commended for her embroidery and Mrs Betton was awarded the Meritorious

Order in 1990 for her services. A framed photograph of her
receiving her certificate hangs above the little treadle organ
in her parlour.

The Band of Mercy children arrived while I was there,
adorable smiling schoolgirls with old-fashioned island
manners. They began their meeting with a couple of rousing
hymns ('to cheer Mr B.'), Aunt Dee pedalling away furiously
at the keyboard. When she sings, 'What a friend we have in
Jesus', it comes straight from the heart. Each child in turn then
told of some helpful thing they had done, and before they
dispersed to carry food to the 'shut ins' – many a good hour's
walk away – Aunt Dee told them an Anansi story. Anansi is
the famous trickster folk hero, a spider who outsmarts all
the other animals. The stories were always told in dialect. The
children were spellbound.

If it turns out that the fantasy Jamaican Granny is a figment
of my imagination, much more typical is Aunt Dee, stoical,
patient, kind, the backbone of her community. Meeting her
reinforced my intuition that the women in Jamaica are so
much more impressive than the men. I can't imagine why they
aren't running the country. As one elderly Jamaican woman
said to me, 'Our history is one where the women had to hold
the family together against the most terrible odds. In the days
of slavery, the men most likely to survive were the ones
who became detached from their pain. They learnt to
avoid responsibility or commitment. Is it any wonder? The
women, on the other hand, had their children to look after
and developed incredible strength, endurance, patience and
resourcefulness.'

Whenever I read anything about slavery or see those terrible
illustrations of human beings packed like sardines in slave
ships I am shocked anew at the sheer enormity of the crime
and feel completely overcome with rage and sadness. It is the
same with the witch burnings the Middle Ages, the
decimation of tribal peoples or the Holocaust of our own
times – a despair at what human beings are capable of, and
the terrible, lasting legacy of violence and hatred. This may

not be a very original thought but sometimes we get so anaesthetized that we forget. Now that women are beginning to find their voices again, can we make it different?

I was lost in this reverie as I went to visit another great old lady - Miss Lillian. I followed up her invitation and took a bus to her house the next day. Miss Lillian lives in a small, down-at-heel concrete house at the end of a dusty drive in a large compound with mango trees in the garden. A skinny dog and six puppies lay in the shade of the porch. Miss Lillian was sitting in her rocking chair wearing a T-shirt with 'Lady Soul' emblazoned across her shapely bosom and, her pretty hair, still as black as a young girls, pinned on top of her head. At seventy she is an extremely attractive woman.

First she wanted me to see all the family photos of herself when young and her five children. Bit by bit I pieced together her story. The father of her eldest daughter ran off; the father of her eldest son she threw out because he had 'too much women'. She married the father of the next three sons but he died, leaving her to manage on her own. All her kids got scholarships and have done her proud. I met the two younger sons who still live with her - a reggae bass guitarist and a school-teacher. She has also brought up one of her grand-daughters, now twelve, whose young mother (a girlfriend of one of the sons) couldn't cope and left her in the long grass outside Miss Lillian's front door.

Times were hard when the children were little. They never knew where the money for food was going to come from and she had to rely on help from relatives who were good to her. She never knew her own mother who died giving birth to her and her twin who also died. She never knew her grandmothers either and didn't have a happy childhood, as her father gave her to another woman to bring up. All her mothering skills she had to learn by instinct. It is amazing how very loving and warm a person she is in spite of all the hardships but she doesn't have a very high opinion of men.

'Pssshhh,' she said dismissively. 'They only comin' to grab. I don't need no man molesting me now. No man go stay in my bed! What the children say? Men! They just use you *up.*'

She has one old suitor who fancies his chances and cruises by every so often. 'He never came once when I was ill a while back but now I'm on my foot again, him comin' roun'. These men today running after young girls. Too much germs! You don' know where they been. I don' need that in my life. No man going to care about my children like I do. I can survive on my own. Always have, always will.' Her kids now look after her. They pay her rent and her phone bill, they send clothes from America. Her little pension from the job she used to have in the post room of a big company pays for extras like going to the hairdresser.

Miss Lillian is the product of an exotic racial mix – one grandfather a Portuguese Jew, one an Indian, one very black negro grandmother. Her youngest son is marrying a French-speaking girl from Guadeloupe. Another son is an archaeologist and speaks fluent Russian and French. Her pharmacist daughter married a white Irish-American and sent her a plane ticket to come to the wedding. Her family embody the Jamaican motto 'Out of many, one people'. She talked with wonder about travelling on a Greyhound Bus in America where everyone was lovely to her and 'a white man carried my bags'. So sad to think that that should be a cause for amazement.

Miss Lillian showed me round her little house, the small bathroom, the bed she shares with her grand-daughter, the rooms where her sons sleep. 'You have to make the children welcome, and their friends, else where they goin'? Get in bad company, that's where.' She cheerfully tolerates the decibels of the musician son's practice sessions and the teacher son's power drill on the porch (he was making a bedside cabinet). They all patently adore her and come by all the time to make sure she is OK.

'Love is the only thing that counts and the only wisdom I want to pass on,' she said, holding me by the shoulders and looking into my eyes. 'What you give is what you get.' She repeated that three times. 'What you give is what you get.'

She walked with me all the way to the bus stop and made sure I got on the right bus.

I felt very moved as I watched her little receding figure waving by the roadside. Once again, not a dramatic or charismatic presence, not a magical storyteller steeped in Jamaican folklore, but an ordinary woman who has held her family together single-handed, loved them well and come through. Her contentment shows. 'I have everything I need,' she told me. 'I give thanks and I am grateful.'

Next day at three o'clock a cab dropped me at the Memory Bank director's house and drove off. The gate was locked and nobody came when I rattled the chain. I climbed over the fence and called through the letter box. No answer. I walked around to the back and suddenly four serious-looking, large dogs materialized, barking ferociously and snapping at my ankles. I visualized myself being torn to pieces by slavering hounds, with no one to hear my cries. I hollered through the window and finally a sleepy voice answered. Dr Lewin appeared and let me in.

I got a pretty frosty reception. She greeted me with 'I have to go out soon,' and made it clear that I was going to have to earn the entrée I sought. What had seemed an innocent request for an introduction or two was apparently not going to be such a simple matter. I was informed that film crews and anthropologists were forever crashing their way insensitively into people's lives, taking what they wanted and vanishing without so much as a thank you. There was even an incident where photographs had appeared in an American journal without permission and the person concerned had felt really violated. Dr Lewin felt very protective towards her countributors and didn't want them exploited.

I suppose I was naive to imagine that it would be otherwise. Conservative societies are always suspicious of outsiders (with good reason), and cultures that grew out of slavery even more so. They had nothing to gain from being open and everything from being secretive. Even though she has now officially retired, all my enquiries through the correct channels kept leading back to Olive Lewin. I had made so many phone calls and visits trying to find my wise old woman through the Memory Bank but nobody seemed to want to tell me anything without her approval. I was learning at first hand what a guarded and impenetrable society this can be. However she softened a little as I tried to explain that I was neither an academic nor a media rapist, that I didn't want to 'study' anybody or exploit them but merely to share stories and build bridges.

My impression of Jamaica was of a rather formal society – parochial, Protestant, church-going and correct. Everyone addresses each other as Mrs So and So, standing on their dignity, setting great store by correct etiquette. From the grapevine I gathered that there had been some differences of opinion at the Memory Bank as to the best way to go about recording the old people's stories. Olive Lewin wasn't happy with the approach taken by the younger, brasher newcomers; she didn't think they understood the immense responsibilities and commitment that go with such a job.

More than a collector of hidden treasures of memory and history, Olive Lewin also fulfils a caring role in the lives of the elderly people who come within her orbit. The new approach is to offer payment and be much more academic and sociological in research method. Counter-productive, says Dr Lewin. People have to like you before they will tell you anything and news of one betrayal or slight or insult will travel all round the island in no time and you will never be trusted again.

Anyway, we parted on friendlier terms, with her issuing an invitation to join her choir for an evening's practice and promising that she would tell the field director that I was OK.

According to the *Guinness Book of Records* there are more churches per capita in Jamaica than anywhere else on earth and you can certainly believe it on a Sunday morning. Everyone is on their way to church. The bright morning sunlight shines down on old men in dark, double-breasted suits with baggy trousers, clutching Bibles. Little girls with frilly frocks and white socks and ribbons sin their hair hold hands with small brothers in bow ties. Big women with huge behinds and tiny veiled pill-box hats pick their way along the pot-holed roads in high, white stilettos. It is the social event of the week. Every denomination you could imagine and then some.

I confess, though, to being a little puzzled by this devout Christianity when I thought about the bloody slaughter it was founded on. After Columbus and the arrival of the pious, the Spaniards set about wiping out every other religion and massacring its adherents in the name of God. I wondered what those native peoples had been like and tried to read up everything I could on them.

The Arawaks, a peaceful, inventive, farming people who were the original inhabitants of this land and the later Caribs, if they managed to survive at all, were enslaved and worked to death. Nothing is left of the Arawaks except a few artifacts and the few words they bequeathed to the English language: barbecue, hurricane, hammock, tobacco, canoe, and Jamaica (Xaymaca) itself.

Then there were the blacks, captured from West Africa during the 200 or so years of the dolorous slave trade, who brought with them their own blend of animistic spirituality. Yet, somehow, the faith of the colonizing tyrants was so pervasive that it endured long after the conquerors had gone their ways.

However, since about 1860, there has been a big Revival movement in Jamaica - the Pukkumina (also called Pocomania or Kumina), Zion and Myal cults - a rich blend of African-flavoured worship and Christianity. The members of these cults have found straightforward Christianity too restrictive and have invented a dramatic hybrid faith of trances, drumming, candles, incense and speaking in tongues. A rollicking, swinging combination which cheerfully grafts the whole pantheon of African spirits onto the Christian scriptures and seems to have done no serious harm to either. The orthodox Christian churches, however, have a hard time

coming to terms with these Revivalist cults, and I generally
met with stony disapproval when I asked about them.

I was lucky all this time to be staying with a lovely friend,
Annabel, who is actually a Trinidadian but currently living in
Jamaica. I don't know what I would have done without her.
She fed me and phoned everyone she knew for contacts.
Through her efforts I got to meet Miss Martha and Miss Hall.

Miss Martha lives in a poor little village in the hills not 2
miles from the affluent homes in Smokey Vale with their
swimming pools and servants but it seemed like another
world - a tumble of tiny, ramshackle dwellings with rubbish
in the yards. Miss Martha came out of her front door to greet
me as I walked up the winding road to her house. She is nearly
blind, with just a little vision in one eye. I took her hands and
put them on my face so that she could feel what I looked like.
She was surprised. 'You don' scorn me?' she asked. I was
horrified at her question and the conditioning that could have
produced such an idea. 'Of course not,' I said and she kissed
me. She is eighty-two and the only surviving sibling of twelve.
She never had children of her own but adopted several and
she lives with one of them now - Audrey who has four little
ones of her own.

Audrey, a plump sexy woman wearing a faded old red dress
and an orange plastic shower cap covering her hair rollers,
showed me her photo album which consisted mainly of
pictures of herself in very cheeky clothes lying on a bed or
posing bending over in artfully slashed mini shorts or a pair
of knickers with 'KISS' written across the bottom. She might
be a hooker but she didn't say as much.

Old Miss Martha reminisced about times gone by when
she had many fruit trees in her yard and a penny could
buy you an egg. She was born right there in the village
and has never travelled further than Kingston. All her
breadfruit trees blew down in the recent hurricane, making
for even more hardship, and everything costs too much
nowadays but, as she said, 'There's plenty people worse off
than me.' She, like every other person I met in Jamaica, was

uncomplaining. Enough was as good as a feast.

I walked back down the hill and got a lift to the convent where I had a rendezvous with Sister Maureen Claire. She had invited me to come with her on a drive out to Old Harbour past Spanish Town - about an hour away along the coast to the west - to visit her aunt, Miss Hall, who is 102 years old. The oldest person I have ever met.

I had first seen her in a BBC television programme about the Caribbean and been captivated by her lucidity and the fact that she still teaches school every day! 'I'm so delighted to meet you,' she said when we arrived and insisted she wasn't tired so we talked for over an hour. In her yard is the tiny schoolhouse she built nearly seventy years ago, in which she sowed the seeds of a love of learning and a feel for the value of education in the hearts of three generations of local children. Many of the most prominent people in Jamaica today, including her nephew, the writer Stuart Hall, passed through her hands. 'I did my best to enthuse them with my love of English literature, Shakespeare in particular,' she remembered, adding with a wicked grin, 'I still beat the children if they don't concentrate!' I don't know how she catches them. She can hardly see and can't walk much.

Another teacher now comes in daily but Miss Hall still sits there on her porch every day and a few children at a time come across to her for lessons. She seemed very sweet-natured, although I am sure she could be quite a fierce taskmistress.

'Isn't it time you thought about retirement, Aunt Gerry?' asked Sister Maureen Claire in a teasing voice.

'No man!' she snapped back, quick as a flash. 'I'm never going to retire. I like to earn my own money!' It was wonderful to see someone of her age so alert, so valued and respected in her own right, as she always has been, and still with something useful to do. In spite of her extreme frailty she retains a sense of independence and dignity.

Miss Hall never married and doesn't think much of men on the whole, though she had plenty of boyfriends in her time.

'They all used to fall in love with me but I pushed them off!'
she cackled, making a shooing motion. She now lives with
a niece and a few helpers who look after her. As a devout
Catholic her great sadness is that these days she is unable to
attend Mass. Sister Maureen Claire had brought the
sacrament from the convent to give her Holy Communion
and she received it hungrily and joyfully. It was as if she was
illuminated from within and she repeated several times, 'Jesus
is my strength and my salvation.' She blessed me and kissed
me goodbye. Holding her little bird hands in mine, I was
conscious of reaching back in time for more than a century
to touch the year 1889 when she was born.

Thank heavens for ear plugs. Hordes of dogs let loose by
property owners to deter burglars howled and barked
incessantly every night and a gaggle of geese outside my
window (that actually turned out to be a large lizard) added
to the din. The ear plugs deadened the sound sufficiently for
me to doze a bit but then, at about 4 am, an eerie wind would
whoosh through the shutters making me think about what it
must have been like here when Hurricane Gilbert came.
Everyone has a story about Gilbert. One elderly lady, Mrs Ettie
Sharp, from the desirable suburb of Mountain Spring Drive,
described to me how their roof had been torn off, the entire
garden trellis had sailed through the air and landed on the
car, and the plate glass window had been blown to
smithereens. The family had lain on the floor of an inside
bedroom with all their dogs for forty-eight hours until the
worst was over. The devastation was unbelievable.

It was very interesting to meet Mrs Sharp, not the granny
of my dreams but another piece of the jigsaw. With her pale
skin and her genteel lifestyle, she exemplifies the wealthy
Jamaican middle-class preoccupation with light skin colour.
Wealth, privilege and status in Jamaica still seem to be
minutely tied to shades of white which seems so extraordinary
in this era of black pride and power.

Mrs Sharp was ninety years old, with eleven grandchildren

and eleven great-grandchildren who call her GiGi. We sat on her terrace drinking freshly squeezed mango juice brought by a servant, looking out over the spectacular view. Bougainvillea blooms drifted onto the immaculate lawn. As her daughter-in-law had told me, she doesn't have a lot of visitors and was glad of the company. She came from a generation and a class where the girls were not allowed to work. She had lived a sheltered life in the country and married a prosperous farmer. When he died seventeen years ago she came here to live with her son.

She felt saddened and confused by the changing times, emigration, the break up of families, and migration to the towns where there were no longer grandmothers to look after the children while the parents went to work. Instead, she told me, the kids run wild or frequently get locked in the house on their own. Just in recent weeks there had been several horrific incidents of locked-in children being burnt to death alone in the house.

Although I had been having interesting conversations with many women, I was halfway through my time in Jamaica before things really began to move. I finally managed to get an appointment with Hazel McClune, the new Field Director of the Memory Bank, and I went to meet her at her office in the African-Caribbean Institute of Jamaica. I liked her straight away – a big, friendly, humorous woman who got straight on the phone trying to fix things up for me. The Memory Bank is such an important concept, trying to save for posterity the rich oral history of Jamaica. There is such a wealth of stories, information, skills and memories carried only in the minds of a generation of senior citizens who are fast dying out.

Memory Bank has trained co-ordinators in each parish, to identify and interview these senior citizens. In a nation descended largely from a people whose original culture was brutally suppressed, things have traditionally been passed on by word of mouth and never written down. Everyone agrees that it is vitally important that nothing more is lost and that this rich inheritance be preserved for future generations. The problem, of course, is insufficient funding. While I was there, one of the co-ordinators phoned in from the province of Westmoreland to say she'd located an old gentleman of 104 who had stories to tell but their tape recorder had broken down and they couldn't exactly wait forever until a new one arrived. 'You see what problems we have?' said Hazel with a resigned shrug.

The archetypal, strong Jamaican woman of my fantasy definitely exists, she told me. She exists everywhere – holding families together, performing miracles in order to feed and care for her children and finally becoming the stoical grandmother who is left to look after the grandchildren when the parents have to go abroad to seek work. She is the one who tries, against enormous odds, to keep the traditions and the culture alive. The women run the businesses, manage the money, get things done. 'Why on earth they don't run the country, I don't know,' she laughed, echoing my own thoughts. 'Caribbean women generally are a force to be reckoned with but Jamaican women have no equal.'

The three women she suggested I meet were: Queenie, a Kumina priestess; Mrs Francella Russell, a candy-maker; and Mrs Muriel Whynn, a Maroon grandmother and storyteller.

Nothing can happen in the Maroon community without the prior approval of Colonel Harris, their leader, so the first thing we did was dispatch a telegram to Mooretown, high in the mountains, requesting an audience and permission to visit a few days hence.

I was a bit puzzled by the 'candy-making'. It was always said with a sort of nudge and a wink so I imagined it was probably a euphemism.

The next morning, after a surprisingly delicious breakfast of ackee and salt fish, Jamaica's national dish, I went off with Hazel McClune in her car to visit the candy-making lady, Mrs Francella Russell. She is also a spiritualist and Water Mother in the Church of Zion. She has the gift of tongues and is guided, she says, by the spirit of Jesus to help her find herbal cures for people's illnesses. In addition, she is a nana - a midwife - and just the day before had delivered one of her own great-grandchildren. Granny Russell was sitting in her yard with the newborn baby on her lap when we arrived.

As well as a birth in the family, that night they'd also had a death. One of her grandsons had died after a long sickness. He had been improving but suddenly took a turn for the worse and fell down in the yard. They carried him in but he didn't recover. His body was still in the house. 'Demon power,' said Granny. She set her face and hissed, 'Bad 'ooman [woman]', but she wouldn't elaborate. He was a youngish man in his early forties and, as a builder, one of the few wage-earners in the family.

Inside we could hear the pitiful sound of his mother, Granny's daughter, wailing loudly over his body. The second of her seven children, he had been a good boy and helped his family, everyone said. They asked me to take his photograph. His mother shone a dim bulb hanging from a frayed flex onto the corpse and turned back the sheet. He was as thin as a stick, with lumps all over his body. His dreadlocks lay like a nest of snakes about his head. His body was naked below the waist, wearing only a torn vest and a bandage to keep his jaw closed. Children came and went. Neighbours called in to pay their respects. Death was no stranger.

Old Mrs Francella Russell, aged ninety, lives with her daughers (in their seventies), her grand-daughters, her great- and great-great-grandchildren in appalling poverty, squatting, as they have done for thirty-five years, in a disused warehouse by the railway track on the outskirts of Spanish Town. Men seem to be marginal in their lives and only come round to plant their seed and make more babies. The women, like the scrawny hens pecking along the railway line, scratch a bare living from selling ackee fruit by the roadside or from making candy.

Granny Russell is the acknowledged mistress of this art and she has taught it to two of her grand-daughters, Patsy and

Poonsie. On account of looking after the sick man and his eventual death, no candy had been made recently but they were anxious for me to see how it was done and so long as I could contribute a little something towards the cost of the sugar I could come back the next day for a demonstration.

Granny Russell was born and brought up on a big sugar estate and remembers *her* grandmother telling her about the day they finally abolished slavery and all the rejoicing and celebrations that went on all the way to Kingston. Well they're free now but you'd hardly know it. Free to suffer and starve. But Granny wasn't complaining. She sat on an old truck tyre in her yard under the shade of a soursop tree, rocking the day-old baby in her arms. She's worked hard all her life, she told me, first as a cane-cutter – a back-breaking job where your hands and legs get lacerated by the razor-sharp cane – then employed by the railways to weed the tracks and burn off the verges.

Through all this, with no help from anyone, she managed to feed her kids, keep them clean and send them to school. More than one lazy, good-for-nothing grandson, she says, comes scrounging her old age pension when she gets it, which isn't very regularly. She still delivers babies, baptizes souls in her capacity as Water Mother for the Church of Zion and helps out with the few dollars she gets from the candy-making.

Granny Russell also has the gift of 'seeing' and many people come to her for advice and divination. She says she has a spirit helper who goes everywhere with her. If she wanted she could have her own church but she's happy the way she is. Her gifts only began to manifest about twenty years ago. 'You have to be old because you have to have lived life,' she said. 'The younger ones just don't know enough yet. Their turn will come.'

I don't know how the family manages to live and it made me feel so useless and guilty – so heartbroken. I gave Mrs Russell $100 (about £4) 'to help with the funeral expenses' and another 'to buy sugar'. It's what I would spend on a taxi fare to get to Smokey Vale from New Kingston and it probably fed the whole family for a week. There must have been at least twenty people living in their squat. Granny, with her little white pigtails sticking out, wearing an old pair of woolly socks and a worn-out pinny, broke into a little dance saying how lucky she was - wealth was pouring in and somebody had just given her a mattress. The Lord was providing just like she knew He always would!

I love the Memory Bank's commitment to recognizing people's unique beauty and worth - by honouring their knowledge and their skills. Hazel McClune was wonderful with Granny Russell's family. Affectionate and warm, she treated everyone with respect and courtesy, constantly mindful of their fragile dignity and pride, never condescending or patronizing for a second, asking them about their lives and their needs. She came away feeling, as she so often does, choked with the hopelessness of it all. How little one can do. How huge the problems.

By the time we came back the following day, the dead body had been removed and the house cleaned. In spite of everything, they keep the place as neat and tidy as possible, with threadbare cloths spread over the mattresses and even one or two plaster dogs placed here and there as ornaments.

They had erected an awning made from a tattered piece of blue polythene for shade and set out some rickety benches and chairs to accommodate the stream of visitors who came to sit and talk about the dead man and bring comfort to the mourners. I was afraid the presence of a stranger would be an imposition at such a time but they seemed to welcome the diversion and the candy-making commenced.

First Granny lit a fire on the back porch and boiled some water in an old kerosene tin. She added 6 lb of sugar, the juice of a lime and a nob of butter. When the sugar was melted she poured off the syrup into a 'dutchee' or cooking pot and boiled it ferociously for about half an hour until it reached the 'crack' stage. Then it was poured onto a big flat stone. In the meantime, a nearby telephone pole with a metal spike hammered into it was washed down and buttered. When the slab of toffee could be lifted it was hung on the spike and pulled, folded and flogged repeatedly against the telephone pole until it became white and shiny. Some drops of peppermint essence and colouring were added, then it was stretched and twisted some more by Granny who cut off lengths with a pair of scissors and formed them into cane and ring shapes.

That was it. The old 'taffy' of my American childhood. A very basic, unsophisticated candy that most of us learned how to make in the Girl Guides but here it is surrounded by tremendous mystique and only Candy-Makers are empowered to pass on this skill.

Candy-making, as I had found out, is not a euphemism at all but exactly what it says it is! All the *sotto voce* and knowing looks stem from a long history of secrecy surrounding what was probably a forbidden and extremely risky activity on the sugar estates when slaves could turn small amounts of stolen sugar into profit.

The umpteen children had a marvellous time and settled like flies on all the cooking pots, adding water to the dregs and drinking the sweet 'candy water'. In a hand-to-mouth existence, sweets of any kind are always a luxury. Candy-making was a big event and selling it a good way to earn a bit of cash. They sell each piece for about 10 cents, though with the price of sugar what it is today, profits are so minimal as to be hardly worth the effort. Anyway, nowadays cheap sweets of every description are widely available and the rare treat of buying a pennyworth of the candy-maker's art has sadly lost its magic. Also it is hot, smoky, hard and long-winded work, so naturally most young people aren't particularly interested in carrying it on.

So much of Granny Russell's pride and self-respect is tied up with her traditional knowledge. When one of the tiny children was trying to give me a running commentary on what she was doing she cuffed him round the ear. 'Shut you mout' now! You know my bidniss?' she said furiously.

Of the various children who live in the compound, not all

are theirs. Orphans, foundlings and abandoned babies are taken in. Granny's grand-daughter, Poonsie, was feeding a bowl of cornmeal porridge to a filthy wee girl sitting in a pile of coal dust (making and selling charcoal is another way they get a few dollars). The baby's mother, herself only sixteen, had dumped the child and gone off to the bright lights. Family planning seems a lost cause. The men won't use condoms because it dulls the pleasure and the women are suspicious of the pill because they believe it will make them barren.

So they endure, stoically and as cheerfully as is humanly possible. 'God provides,' says Granny. The fact that I had turned up out of the blue and offered a contribution towards the funeral expenses meant they could eat today. This was proof, said Granny, of providence and grace. 'I eat each day's bread with praise,' she said. 'Some people want the whole world and them don' want Jesus. Me, you can keep everything else, just give me my blessed Jesus. He is my strength and my salvation.'

Sitting there with her great-great-grandchild in her lap, Mrs Francella Russell embodied all that was simultaneously most fragile and most indestructible about a woman. No man has ever helped her, she said, and she only wears a wedding ring to keep them at bay. 'Dey tink me marry, dem leave me alone!' She shook her head and laughed a great toothless cackle. 'I don' want no trouble wid no man no way! Dey all bad! Bwooy! I'm tellin' you. Lawd have mercy!' She wiped her eyes and pulled a funny face.

If I lived like they do I would curse God and rail against my fate. They are content if only they can afford a little sugar. God knows, they don't ask for much. Only a little encouragement and the wherewithal to be self-sufficient. Does their faith keep them poor and passive or is it a blessed ray of hope in lives of impossible hardship?

Queenie, the Kumina Queen, lives in an area called Waterloo on the Sligoville Road in the province of St Catherine. There was no way to let her know we were coming so we got there early in case she was going out. She was there and welcomed us into her compound where she conducts her Kumina rituals. Her little wooden house painted sky blue stands in the middle of a wonderfully picturesque yard of swept earth filled with jungly plants and trees, carved wooden African-looking figures and a large cage of birds, mainly doves, which are used in the rituals.

Kumina centres on possession by and communication with ancestral spirits, and a great many aspects of the Kumina tradition - such as the ritual language, the music, drumming and dance through which contact with the ancestors is established and maintained - are said to come from the Congo. When somebody requires a healing or wants a ceremony for something they request Queenie's services as priestess and she holds a 'duty' in her yard.

She is often asked for help. Sometimes the spirit tells her to hold a 'duty' and for this she also provides food to feed the participants. Her brother and another man help out with the drumming and one of her grandsons who lives with her assists with whatever she needs. We sat around the little table in her house and I said I had heard of her gifts and hoped she might tell me how she first came to know she had been chosen for this work.

She was seven years old, she said, when she felt very peculiar one day - as if summoned by a great power. She fell into a trance and couldn't move or speak or eat or drink for twenty-one days. She lay where she fell in some long grass under a tree and even though she could hear her mother calling for her and crying, she couldn't answer.

Eventually an uncle was sent for who knew the ways of the spirit and he understood at once what was going on. He found her and by this time she had received the gift of tongues - a knowledge of 'the ancient African language'. She was drawn to the drums by the unseen motivating power and given some of the songs and dances. These are still being shown to her even today as the spirits never leave her. She sees and hears them constantly.

Queenie wasn't feeling too good that day. She is getting on for eighty and suffers from shortness of breath and arthritis. I offered to give her some healing which surprised and pleased her and she accepted. As I laid my hands on her chest and painful joints, channelling healing into her tired old body, she closed her eyes and began to sing a praise song in a sweet, soft voice. It was a lovely feeling to be joined with her in a common bond of trust that stretched across all the centuries of pain and misunderstanding that have divided us. She sang me three songs in the 'African language' and they did, indeed, sound remarkably African although I couldn't identify from which country. She never learnt any of this in school – it has all come to her in trance, she says, through the spirits of her ancestors.

Young people do not seem to want to learn the Kumina traditions the hard way, said Queenie. They are enticed for the wrong reasons by the states of ecstasy and the African drumming and dancing, but unfortunately they tend to meddle in the magic and get in out of their depth. When someone becomes possessed by the spirits you have to know what to do to make sure they come to no harm and how to get them out of it afterwards. It is a great responsibility and not to be taken lightly or used disrespectfully. I told her that the same thing happens in my country where many young, disaffected people are drawn to the trappings of spiritualism and witchcraft without the wisdom or experience that must go hand in hand with occult powers.

Queenie takes her duties very seriously and sees herself only as a humble servant. In recent years her fame has spread. She has been honoured with a medal for distinguished services to Jamaican culture by ex-Prime Minister Edward Seaga, who was, himself, very knowledgeable about cults and spiritualism. She is often asked to perform in cultural festivals and has travelled abroad. Her photograph, arrayed in her wonderful robes and jewelled hat, adorns the living-room.

'Come, meet my boy,' said Queenie, and yelled 'Ian!' at the top of her voice. A ragged, mentally handicapped child came in from the yard where he had been playing in the dust. He can hear but is dumb. He was brought to Queenie as a baby suffering from an evil spell, she said. He was dying and no doctors could cure him. She drummed and chanted for him, put olive oil on him and massaged him until he vomited up masses of green leaves.

He started to get better but his parents had disappeared and never came back to fetch him. Queenie would rather not have been lumbered with looking after him but does it because nobody else is prepared to. He has to be watched constantly or he wanders off and the other kids tease him. He eats her out of house and home and doesn't know enough to let her rest. When he wants something he comes and pulls her sleeve even if she is asleep, so caring for him is very exhausting.

She shook her head and smiled ruefully as if to say, 'What have I done to deserve this?' He smiled up at her adoringly, put his arms around her and butted his head gently into her soft, warm body, and she stroked his little face. I was moved by this juxtaposition of high priestess, powerful conjuror of spirits, and woman as ordinary, selfless care-giver. How much of our spirituality as women is bound up with these daily, unremarkable acts of love?

The drumming and dancing, singing and possession by ancestral spirits that the slaves brought with them from Africa must have been seen not only as a wretched heathen practice but also as a dangerous cohesive influence. It would have coordinated people and given them a focus so, of course, the authorities made its practice punishable by death. But something of such vitality never disappears entirely. It bided its time and surfaced during the Great Revival which swept Jamaica about 130 years ago.

One of the safe havens where this had flourished was away in the Blue Mountains with the Maroons - and this is where I journeyed with Hazel a few days later. The Maroons - whose name derives from the Spanish *cimarron*, meaning 'wild' or 'untamed' - were the runaway slaves who had taken to the forest and made their homes in the uncharted, inhospitable

Cockpit Country – a treacherous limestone tundra pitted with huge sink-holes and threaded with innumerable cave systems where a person on the run could hole up. Fearless, organized and armed, they would prove a thorn in the side of the British for 150 years, harrying them with murderous raids, and eventually winning a remarkable measure of self-government.

Mooretown, their present-day headquarters in the province of Portland high in the mountains, is reached via the coast road to Port Antonio. It is in a pretty remote spot which must have been virtually inaccessible before the road was built – such as it is! It took us over three and a half hours, travelling through spectacular mountain scenery, to get there, travelling along a dreadful, pot-holed, winding switchback littered with stones from the recent rain and nearly washed away in places.

Even today, fugitives and criminals who want to disappear for a while know they won't be followed up here to the Cockpit Country. It is an extraordinary landscape, rarely visited by tourists. Nearly 3000 varieties of flowering plants grow here, including 800 species found nowhere else in the world. There are 200 types of wild orchids alone and more than 500 ferns. Huge 3-foot-long pods, which are stewed and eaten by the Maroons, hang from giant 'Jack in the Beanstalk' vines.

Even though we had sent our telegram to Colonel Harris a week before, informing him of our intended visit, he had only received it that morning. Nevertheless this splendid-looking, elderly, white-haired autocrat very hospitably invited us in. Colonel Harris is the lifetime elected leader of the Maroons and nothing happens without a decree from him. I made a bit of a gaffe when stating the purpose of my visit by saying I was hoping to have the opportunity of talking with some older Maroon women. 'You mean there are things I can't tell you?' he said, lifting his eyebrows in surprise. I hastily back-pedalled and said no, of course not. I was only worried about taking up his valuable time. He snapped his fingers for someone to go and fetch a suitable person and then launched into a long monologue about the incredible feats of the famous Maroon heroine, Nanny.

Nanny is a sort of cross between Joan of Arc and Boadicea. Half legend, half historical figure, she was the brave and ferocious chieftainess of the Windward Maroons during their bloodiest battles with the British – a cunning strategist and superhuman adversary. She is said to have once caught a volley of bullets in her bare buttocks and fired them straight back at the British! She devised guerrilla tactics, with followers disguised as trees and camouflaged with leaves and branches, which are still re-enacted in Maroon dances today.

Queen Nanny, although referred to as an 'obeah woman' or sorceress by the British, is remembered by the Maroons as an ordinary woman, small in stature but possessed of extraordinary powers. She was their leader at the time of their greatest glory and their first town was named Nanny Town after her. Today, Nanny is honoured as the only woman amongst Jamaica's eight national heroes.

The courageous and daring Maroons were never defeated and in the end a peace treaty was negotiated. They were granted land rights in perpetuity for which they still pay no taxes and enjoy special privileges. Nanny's exploits are told and retold, and every Maroon woman is proud of this ancestry. They have a reputation for always having been emancipated, equal, respected and given to fighting alongside their menfolk; and in their African-derived religion, known as Myalism, women have always played an equal part.

There is one significant blot on the Maroons' historical copybook; part of the deal, after the signing of the treaty, was that they would cease to harbour escaped slaves and, indeed, would help to track them down and turn them in to the British. How they could have agreed to this when they, themselves, were descended from freed or fugitive slaves is hard to understand. But then people often stoop to terrible deeds to save their own skins. After all, there were Jewish overseers in the concentration camps.

When Colonel Harris had finished holding forth, I got a chance to talk to his cousin Mrs Lou who had come in

response to his summons. A mother of fifteen children, eleven
of whom are still living, she had lived in Britain for a while
and worked as a nurse. She was very proud to be a descendant
of Nanny.

Mrs Lou told me how, in the last days of each of her
pregnancies, she had dreamed a prophetic dream showing
which one of her ancestors was going to be reincarnated as
the new baby. It was as if they needed to introduce themselves
to her before they arrived and tell her what to name them.
In every case she felt that her children's gifts, as drummers,
dancers, singers, storytellers, healers, herbalists, seers, were
inborn talents which only needed to be encouraged and
developed through study and practice. Not so much a formal
training, but an opportunity to use the skills they had
inherited.

I loved that idea – honouring the things that a child brings
into this life and gently allowing them to flower. I thought
of Wordsworth's profound words from 'Intimations of
Immortality':

> Our birth is but a sleep and a forgetting:
> The soul that rises with us, our life's star,
>   Hath had elsewhere its setting,
>   And cometh from afar:
>   Not in entire forgetfulness,
>   And not in utter nakedness,
> But trailing clouds of glory do we come
>   From God who is our home.

Each time I have held one of my own newborn grandchildren
in my arms, and looked into their old faces, those words have
come to mind.

And as for prophetic dreams, said Mrs Lou, old women get
better and better at having and interpreting them, the longer
they live. Maroon elders, she said, were always looked up to
and their superior wisdom respected. Because they continued
to live with their families in a tight-knit community, their role

was clearly defined and they stayed healthier and mentally active much longer.

The other Maroon woman elder I was lucky enough to meet was a personal friend of Hazel's. Hazel thinks the world of her and often seeks her wise counsel. She is quite choosy about who she speaks to, so I was honoured when she agreed to meet me. Mrs Muriel Whynn, grandmother and storyteller, works as a humble office cleaner but what an interesting and beautiful old woman she turned out to be. The moment I set eyes on her I knew she was the one - the Jamaican grandmother of my dreams - and I thanked my guardian spirits for bringing me to her door.

A direct descendant of Nanny, Granny Whynn has a wonderful way with words and a deep sense of pride in the fierce, indomitable spirit which is the Maroon inheritance. They were a haughty, ferocious, stubborn lot, she said (all the things which made a bad slave), and they had risked everything for their freedom - from perishing in the hostile Cockpit Country, if they made it that far, to unspeakable punishments if they were caught.

Those who survived lived and still live in communities which have continued to follow African practices and customs entrenched in the forest and its spirits. They have kept alive the concept of the earth as a vital, universal, nourishing mother. The banned African religions were a binding force amongst the rebels and fugitives isolated up in the mountains. It gave them an identity, and Myalism is still a potent force among the Maroons today.

Mrs Whynn, a fine-looking, dignified woman, spoke with quiet assurance in a voice both comforting and uncompromising. She spoke of fate and nature, of history and hurricanes, of life and death.

Up here, she said, far from the impersonal labour wards of modern hospitals, a woman is helped to give birth in the time-honoured way. Her breasts and belly and vulva are gently massaged by other women with special oils infused with herbs 'until she feels melted and soft'. She made the whole thing sound really erotic, the birth almost like an orgasm. The mother squats facing a wall so she can press against it with her arms and somebody supports her from behind. As the newborn baby is delivered into the waiting hands of the midwife, it is immediately bathed in special herbs to protect it from evil spirits and the mother is pampered, steamed, wrapped and anointed. She is not left alone for a minute for the first nine days and nights and no one but she and the midwife may handle the baby. When visitors are finally allowed in they give a token gift of money before they hold the baby and everyone brings food to the mother.

It sounded so beautiful, so natural. Women's business and nothing to do with stainless steel or epidurals or episiotomies.

Granny Whynn also told me what happens when a person dies. There are no undertakers who don't know the deceased. Rather, it is family members and particularly the old women acquainted with herbs and plants who lay out the body. They make a balm of pimento leaves and salt. People stay with the bereaved for nine days and nights. As with the coming in, so with the going out; you are never alone. People sleep with you, talk, reminisce, sing, feed you. You are held in the warmth of ritual and tradition until the first shock of loss has passed.

I listened, enchanted, as she sang a special song for grandmothers. She told me how her own mother, the fabled Momee Rennock, had passed on her knowledge of plants and herbs to her only daughter, having, in turn, learned the secrets from her grandmother.

Spirit voices come to her in the night when she needs to know what remedy to make for a certain illness. She can become quite possessed by the 'Myal' which then leads her to the right plant. Ignorant people are afraid of the Myal, she says, because it is magical and inexplicable. They confuse it with 'obeah' which is the greatly feared sorcery used to gain power over others. But, in fact, Myal is just a way of attuning oneself to the natural forces and harnessing them. Very little divides Granny Whynn from an English village witch such as

Paddy Slade. They are both grandmothers, humble and wise and deeply connected to the strength and beauty which is their inheritance. They have kept the flame alight.

Alas, Mrs Whynn's own daughter is not particularly interested in these traditions, as is the case with many of her generation. They want to be part of mainstream Jamaican culture and so the distinctive Maroon customs are in danger of dying out. Mrs Whynn is hoping that one of her grandchildren will choose to carry the baton.

As we are talking it started to rain - a real tropical downpour hammering on the tin roof with a deafening din and turning the yard and the road beyond into a sea of mud. It would have been crazy to attempt the drive back to Kingston so we waited another three hours until it eased up. One of the women in Colonel Harris's household brought us each a whole young green coconut with the top sliced off. We drank the delicious coconut water inside and scooped out the soft jelly.

I loved it there in the secret hills with the descendants of those who would rather have died than be slaves and I felt so grateful that I had been granted a glimpse of a Jamaica most people never see. My one sadness was that I never had a dip in the Caribbean.

CHAPTER THREE

Feathers and Bones

My people are few. They resemble the scattering trees of a storm-swept plain. There was a time when our people covered the land as waves of a wind-ruffled sea cover its shell-paved floor, but that time long since passed away with the greatness of tribes that are now but a mournful memory.

CHIEF SEATTLE

It was 4.30 in the morning when I took a cab to the airport bus terminal on Park Avenue – still dark in the skyscraper canyons. Even in the city that never sleeps this is the deadest hour of all. The streets were deserted, with only wisps of eerie steam rising from the manholes.

The 5.30 bus was already parked under a streetlight, around the corner from Grand Central Station – no other passengers on board. The taxi dropped me and my suitcase and drove off. I suddenly felt that prickle of fear as I realized how vulnerable I was. When I was a child my mother used to invent headlines to encapsulate real or imagined dramatic events in our lives ('London Girl Wins Piano Competition', 'Rebellious Teenager Found Dead', 'Brave Dog Saves Family'). In my mind's eye I saw 'Twickenham Housewife Mugged in Manhattan'. Then a man stepped out of the shadows and asked me for the fare. Obedient, unsuspecting, English, I got my purse out. 'Give me $20, I've got change,' he said in an urgent voice, eyes swivelling about, and before I really registered what was happening, he snatched my purse out of my hand and took off.

I stood there stunned. The real driver, who'd been having a snooze inside, appeared and gave chase briefly but didn't want to leave either his bus or me standing by the roadside. 'I thought he was one of those homeless guys who are always standing around asking for a dollar for a cup of coffee,' he said, quite shaken by the incident and the speed with which it had all taken place. He was even more upset than I was and swore he'd get that kid next time he saw him. With the whole bus to myself, I sat up front and he regaled me all the way to Newark airport with other, worse stories of muggings and rip-offs he had known. Although I could ill afford to lose the money, I wasn't hurt and I had taken the precaution of hiding $20 in my money belt so I could still pay the $7 fare, but I felt depressed. 'Welcome to New York,' said the driver, shaking his head. 'I hate this goddam city.'

Well, fortunately, I was leaving it, not arriving. In fact I couldn't get away fast enough. I like to think of myself as a city sophisticate but I am no match for New York.

It was great to see my cousin Peter's smiling face waiting for me in Tucson. On a long journey away from home, any fleeting experience of belonging is disproportionately wonderful. Peter has two delicious babies so I could get my granny fix. I was like some pathetic addict craving for that indescribable sweet-smelling tenderness, burying my nose in the backs of their necks, breathing them in.

Leaving home was so much harder than I thought it would be. My whole centre of gravity was altered. Everything was turned inside out. I was consciously trying to let go of what felt safe, comfortable and sure, in order to allow new possibilities to unfold. But the physical isolation and the pain of separation were proving very hard to cope with.

Old myths and legends are full of men setting forth on spiritual quests, seeking the Holy Grail, testing themselves against the unknown but there aren't that many instances of women doing the same. We are always the ones sitting at home knitting until the hero returns. In fact we *are* the homes that men leave. If we leave, what will become of the home? Women's spirituality seems to be inextricably bound up with the task of creating a home rather than leaving it. On the other hand, some force as irresistible as birth contractions was pushing me on. Comfortable as the womb had been it was time to leave it, time to confront the Crone and prepare myself for the next stage.

One of the names I had been given by an anthropologist before I left England was that of an old Navajo woman, Annie Kahn, reputed to be a knowledgeable healer up at Lukachukai in northern Arizona. I had always imagined, somehow, that the Navajo or the Hopi people, with their reputation for wonderful art, fine spiritual traditions and peaceful farming, would be the least difficult to make contact with. I had written to Annie Kahn but never received an answer. Now I managed to reach her on the phone and stated my purpose – that I was hoping to share life stories and learn from the wisdom of older women in different cultures.

At first she agreed to talk to me if I paid a fee of $25 an hour but then she had second thoughts. She was very unhappy, she said, about outsiders making assumptions and drawing conclusions about her life on the basis of a short acquaintance. She had learned the hard way from her experience with another author who had, in her opinion, taken advantage of her hospitality and friendship, and violated her trust. It had made her very angry. She refuted the idea of any one person being singled out as a spokesperson or star. 'Nobody can see things through my eyes except me,' she said. She didn't appreciate the fact that I'd been given her phone number in the first place. 'I'm not a telephone exchange and I don't represent the Navajo people.'

I know how easy it can be for a writer to leave an impression of vandalism and manipulation. My constant nightmare is that anyone I have talked to will feel used or misrepresented. It is a very serious occupational hazard and requires the greatest of care and self-monitoring.

But are there to be no more innocent, friendly meetings? Instead of the pleasure of mutual discovery, is it all about duplicity and commerce? 'The American Indians have been betrayed and ripped off by white people so often,' said a school-teacher I met in Tucson, 'they don't trust anyone any more. They don't care whether we understand their culture or not. They just want to be left alone.' Annie Kahn is a busy, working grandmother and not about to give a total stranger the time of day. Fair enough. But the whole conversation made me feel quite disheartened. It's horrible to be rejected before you've had a chance to present yourself face to face. My assumption that people would be willing to sit around and talk, sharing grandmotherly wisdom, was turning out to be quite naive. Either they're too busy or too private or they want to make money out of it. Struck out, as the Americans say. But when one door closes another usually opens - often through chance meetings.

One of the employees in my cousin Peter's pottery factory, a mechanic named Hank, had fixed a car belonging to a man who did research on American Indians at the Historical Society. Hank offered to arrange an introduction. I went gladly, but felt woefully ignorant. However Jay was kind and patient and filled me in on some basic details such as the fact that there are no such things as 'Indians' or even 'Apaches'. They have always been mostly small family groups who form into larger bands. They don't really like the word 'tribe'.

I walked around the Historical Society museum after our talk had finished and got chatting with the ladies who ran the gift shop. One of them gave me the name of a friend of hers, a Papago basket-maker called Juanita Manuel who lives on a reservation near the Mexican border. In fact they hate the name 'Papago' which was given to them by the Spaniards and means 'Bean-Eaters'. They prefer to be known by their beautiful original name which is gradually being reinstated - Tohono O'odham or 'People of the Desert'.

Ever since I can remember I have been drawn to the

sustaining, inspiring spirituality and wisdom of the American Indians. Coming here to the South-west was the fulfilment of a long-held dream. This desert landscape of rocks and sand, canyons and cactus formed the imaginary background to so many of my childhood games.

When 'playing cowboys and Indians' I always wanted to be an Indian. Knowing how to walk silently through a forest without the giveaway crack of a twig, knowing how to track animals, make arrowheads, ride bareback – these were skills indeed. My best friend at school was one-eighth Cherokee and I longed to be her. (She longed to be Jewish like me and thought matzos were the most delicious food in the world!)

All around the edges of Tucson you can see 'Indian neighbourhoods'. They look pretty broken-hearted places. As Jay said, the level of good relationships to the anglo/white community is in inverse proportion to proximity and class. Local working-class people see the Indians as drunks, work-shy and trashy. They are jealous of the government handouts and special privileges they get. The further removed they are, the more they are romanticized as 'noble' and 'spiritual'. There doesn't seem to be an ordinary middle way where people are just people. There is also the foreign misconception that there is any kind of unified, shared endeavour on the part of 'Native Americans' to improve their lot. They are as varied and uncoordinated as any other bunch of people trying to find a place in the sun. There is no homogenous 'Indian culture'.

I phoned Juanita Manuel and she agreed to see me so I organized a rented car. I went to pick it up and was delighted to find that I could get Mexican music on the radio – rumpty-tumpty cheerful Speedy Gonzalez mariachi tunes alternating with beautiful, mournful serenades sung in close harmony with liquid guitar accompaniments that sound like love-sick coyotes baying at the moon. I set off for the Tohono O'odham reservation, about one hour's drive west of Tucson, for my appointment with Juanita Manuel.

As you get out of town the landscape becomes more and

more arid. The turn-off up to the reservation is only a dirt road. I don't know what I expected but it wasn't the cluster of bleak concrete box houses and the white adobe mission church I found. Apart from a lone Indian on horseback, the place appeared deserted. I finally saw some smoke coming from a chimney and knocked on the door. A woman directed me to Mrs Manuel's house but there was no one there. A dog slept under a table in the yard and a book, *Power and Wisdom*, lay open on a chair. I waited for an hour but no one came. Being stood up is a fairly regular *leitmotif* on the wisdom trail. I never get used to it, though, and it always hurts. Struck out again. Remember, whatever happens is the story, I told myself.

My last chance was another suggestion of Jay's - an approachable man named Ernest Victor, one of the administrators at the Apache Tribal Office at San Carlos - so I decided to head up north to the reservation in case I could get an appointment to see him. Everything in Arizona is a long way off. The reservations themselves are bigger than some states. Out of Tucson I took the Oracle Road that goes northeast through the desert, on and on through the Coronado National Forest, over the El Capitano Pass where Kit Carson took his troops through the mountains, through more forest and more desert to the town of Globe.

I had been feeling rather pleased with myself, bombing along through the desert without another car in sight. I'd filled up with petrol and brought a gallon of drinking water with me as advised. The road was straight as an arrow. Yodelling along to the Mexican music, and feeling a bit cramped by the 55 mph limit, I let my speed creep up. One minute my rear view mirror showed nothing but desert road to infinity and then, from nowhere, a squad car was behind me flashing his lights. I still don't know how he got there. He must have come up through a trap door in the sand. Practically scared me to death.

I acted divvy and English and got let off with a warning. Everywhere around me stood the imposing saguaro cacti sending their semaphore to each other. They seemed to be laughing at me, their arms thrown up, the little holes made by the cactus wrens like round mouths, ho-hoing with mirth. Maybe it was them that ratted on me.

Globe seemed as good a place as any to stop for the night. A sleepy little town that was once the heart of the copper-mining industry. Now it dozes in the sun and life has passed it by. I chose the Willow Motel from a few straggled along the highway. They all looked like the Bates Motel from *Psycho* and I found myself checking the lock on the shower door and looking to see if there were any peepholes in the wall. The room was sleazy and smelled of stale cigarette smoke but it was clean enough and cheap. I took it and went out to eat at the Blue Ribbon Café where I was the only customer, apart from two drunk guys who came in asking for Mexican food. The waitress explained, courteously, that they didn't serve it, whereupon they both keeled over and fell off their chairs. Nobody seemed in the least perturbed. After a while a police officer arrived but by then they'd picked themselves up and swayed off into the night.

The next day was exciting and full - just as I'd hoped - although I was in a state of quite high tension. As I drove alone through vast stretches of Indian reservation I was thinking all the time: 'Will something go wrong with the car?', 'Will those two men in the truck try to force me off the road?', 'Will I get to my destination by nightfall?', 'What if there's a flash flood?' Too many movies in my head.

The day started prosaically enough in a little breakfast diner. Enormous people with bellies set like shopping baskets on their laps shovelled in mountains of eggs, fries, burritos, beans, chilli and cornbread. Working men, with cowboy hats, exaggerated, high-heeled, pointy boots and western drawls, discussed local politics. They must have had jobs that required a large vehicle to transport them. No horses could have done the job.

It didn't take long to drive to the Apache Reservation at San Carlos. Again, it was a very unpicturesque place and I couldn't help feeling that morale would be better if the surroundings were more aesthetically pleasing – more like the old-style wickiup village. But there were the dilapidated motor homes, the concrete box houses, the down-at-heel general store, the chain-link fencing, the rusting broken-down cars.

San Carlos is quite large and the reservation itself covers more than 1½ million acres of some of Arizona's most spectacular scenery. I went to the Apache Tribal Office feeling rather intimidated by my lack of knowledge about Apache tribal culture. I knew minus nothing, I'd barely spoken to an Indian person and never met an Apache.

One of my favourite films as a child was *Taza, Son of Cochise* – starring a white actor, of course, but at least it showed the Indians in a dignified, heroic light. So different from most of the stuff we saw at the drive-in – films featuring savage redskins, renegades and murderous raiders.

I was both curious and slightly apprehensive about meeting them because of their largely negative reputation. Everybody loves the artistic Navajo and the spiritual Hopi – the peaceful pueblo-dwellers, pottery-makers and blanket-weavers but the fierce Apaches aren't sentimentalized in the same way.

I had made an appointment with Jay's friend Ernie Victor and he showed me into his office. Ernie is a striking-looking man with wide, high cheekbones, shoulder-length black hair parted in the middle and a red bandana tied around his head. In his office were posters urging 'Apache Pride' and advertising Alcoholics Anonymous meetings. Apache pride was pretty non-existent, admitted Ernie, but even so, after 500 years of continual oppression, they were miraculously still here. Their language, which was forbidden, still exists and their oral history is still remembered. 'Forget your food, forget your stories,' they were told at school. 'Forget the names of the mountains and the rivers. And above all, forget your language. Just speak English.' The Apaches fought longest and hardest against the 'White Eyes' who usurped their homelands, broke the treaties and tricked and massacred their people. It is a dolorous tale.

Ernie was perfectly friendly but doubted if any of the old

ladies would want to talk. He felt they would probably be too timid but, nevertheless, he took me across to the seniors' centre where a woman named Elizabeth Classay runs a nutrition programme, providing a hot lunch for the elderly people of the reservation and bussing them in from their homes every day so that, whatever their circumstances, they always eat at least one decent meal.

'What a pity you're not going to be here in two weeks,' said Elizabeth, and told me about the Sunrise Dance which was going to be taking place. This is the most famous of all Apache ceremonies – a young girl's puberty initiation. The godmother who guides her through it is an older woman chosen by the girl's parents as the person they most want her to be like when she grows up. Elizabeth was to be the godmother. I was so excited by this bit of amazing good luck that I instantly decided to alter my plans and come back for the ceremony. It was too good an opportunity to miss.

In the meantime it was lunch hour and suddenly the place started to fill up with old people. Wizened old ladies with faces like polished walnuts came waddling in, swathed in the attractive long cotton skirts and high-necked smocks that constitute traditional Indian dress for older women (the young wear the ubiquitous jeans, of course). They collected their trays and sat at the tables. Ernie introduced me to one tableful – a doll-maker, a bead-worker and a talkative old cattle rancher named Frances Cutter.

'Sure, sit down,' said Frances and that was the beginning of our friendship. Frances selected herself as my informant and didn't let anyone else get a word in edgeways so they gradually drifted off. Finally it was just the two of us in the canteen as they were sweeping up and putting the chairs on the tables.

Frances, aged seventy-two, was one of five daughters and because there were no sons her father taught her to be a cowgirl. She could ride like a man, mend fences, lassoo, brand and castrate (she called it 'castrasize') calves. 'My dad never said, "Little girls don't do that".' Her father, like many Apache men, had been a cattle rancher. Their expert horsemanship and rugged, nomadic nature has ironically turned them into the modern equivalent of their former adversaries. In fact, no other tribe has changed as radically as the Apache.

When her father died, Frances took over the running of the place. She, herself, had four sons and two daughters. When they were old enough, she gave them each five head of cattle to be responsible for. But things have changed. The children were all educated and most have now married out and moved away. One married a white girl, one a black, one a Hawaiian ('She cooks *fish*,' said Frances in disgust. 'I can't stand the smell. The only time an Apache would eat fish is if she's a pregnant woman!').

Frances has twenty-seven grandchildren but none of them live on the reservation. She would move to be near them but her husband is an invalid suffering from diabetes (many Indians have it). He doesn't want to move and she can't leave him. She pines for her long gone children constantly. 'I remember the sound of their little voices asking me things. I remember how cute they looked going off to school with their books under their arms. I remember hugging them and loving them and now they're all gone. It's terrible.' She shook her head. One of her sons, who returned safely from Vietnam, died from diabetes. She cries for him every night.

Frances is an excellent linguist. She speaks fluent Spanish, English, Apache, Navajo and Yavapai and is often asked to be an interpreter. For a while she taught at the school in San Carlos but she found it disheartening. Most of the teachers were white and the children were actually forbidden to speak their native tongue. Today, she said, so many of the young people are just not interested in carrying on with traditional ways. The colleges are away in the cities where they meet kids from the big world outside and often, like her own, they never come back.

It is a source of great pride to Frances that none of her children have succumbed to the dreaded plague of alcoholism which stalks the Indians more mercilessly than the US Cavalry ever did. Their constitutions seem unable to process the booze and they are poisoned and incapacitated by it in a truly horrifying way. Liquor has finally decimated the Indians more surely than any massacres.

Frances is fiercely independent. Her cattle business is still a going concern. She is the only woman member of the Cattle Association and says the men listen to her. Apache women have always been respected in their own sphere of influence. She doesn't wait for the transport to bring her to town, she drives her own pick-up. She prides herself on being strong and healthy and likes to go off into the hills looking for peridots (one of only three places in the world where they are found). The hills here are radiant with gemstones and crystals of every type. Arizona has immense mineral wealth.

Frances's short-term memory has become a little vague since her son died. She tends to repeat herself and keep going over his death again and again, but when I asked about her earliest memories she talked as if they had happened yesterday.

She lived with her grandmother when she was little, way out on the land where the Coolidge Dam now is - land abundant with quail, wild turkey, pinon nuts and palo verde trees. The lake was formed when the dam was built and many homes and the little village school were drowned in the rising waters - her own childhood home amongst them. No more wickiups, no more silent pastures. The people were moved to San Carlos, and although they're grateful for the electricity which has made life a bit easier, the old ways have gone forever.

Frances can't remember a time when she couldn't ride a horse. She rode from the earliest age, learning to be absolutely silent and wait alone minding the horses in the canyons while her grandmother went upriver collecting berries and acorns. She knew she must not show fear or cry out if she heard anyone coming or saw a bear or a mountain lion. A large mountain lion once walked right past where she was hiding but it was fat from a recent kill and only wanted to get to the river to drink. Frances's face shone as she recalled the old days. 'People cared about each other then,' she said, 'and everybody knew how to make things: baskets, buckskins, beaded moccasins.'

Frances's next-door neighbour is a renowned basket-maker so she offered to take me to meet her. I followed her truck a little way out of town and she knocked on Sannie Russell's door. Sannie is a beautiful pure-blood eighty-year-old Apache woman with classic high cheekbones and straight coarse long grey hair. She was pleased to see us as she lives alone and brought out a couple of her baskets to show me. They are rare 'burden baskets' only made nowadays by a few skilled craftswomen.

Originally used by the nomadic Apaches for transporting all their belongings and carried by a head strap, these cone-shaped burden baskets are mostly kept for ceremonial purposes these days or sold to tourists. They come in several sizes and are characterized by long dangling strips of buckskin, each one with a little metal cone attached to the end. The beautiful, soft muted colours of the straw come from reeds and grasses found along the river bank which Sannie collects herself. Unfortunately the local deer like to eat some of the rarer ones so they're not always easy to find. A lot of work goes into making a burden basket and this is reflected in the price, but they are snapped up just as soon as Sannie makes them. In fact people come specially to seek her out. 'I ain't much good talking words,' said Sannie. 'I put my feelings in my baskets. That's my language.'

I did not need another basket but this was a rare opportunity to buy one from the artist herself. I love basket-weaving very much and I am often struck by the distinction that seems to be made between art (usually done by men) and craft (much cheaper, less status, usually done by women). Anyway I shelled out $60 and when I saw how poor and bare her house was, I was glad all the money would go to Sannie and not to one of the smart gallery owners who make a big profit selling them in New York.

Sannie's story was very sad. Her husband, a violent

alcoholic, finally left her ('Good riddance', she said). She immediately divorced him and reverted to her maiden name. Her eldest son was killed in Vietnam and his body is buried in Texas. She would like it returned to his ancestral lands but his widow, who lives in Fort Bliss, won't give her consent. Her other son is in jail for alcohol-related crime. Both Sannie and Frances agreed that the whole alcoholism problem and the incidence of violent crime became much worse when the young men returned from Vietnam. They had been trained to become killers, they had seen and done terrible things and then, if they came home at all, they found themselves unemployed.

One of Sannie's daughters is also an alcoholic and has had her three children taken into care. One of her grand-daughters had a baby at thirteen. Because she lives alone, with no man to protect her, young drunks constantly break into her house – a bare, concrete shoebox – to steal anything they can sell for drink. She showed us where her front door had been kicked in repeatedly. She has had to put a steel bolt on the inside. Sannie has grabbed at Christianity because there's nothing much to hold onto and she reckons she's 'saved' but I saw a can of Budweiser under her bed so I suspect oblivion beckons from time to time.

The contrast between the grim reality of Sannie's life and her exquisite baskets was unbearably poignant. All those dreams, all that beauty and tradition that she weaves from the depths of her soul, while her children self-destruct or die in White Eyes' wars.

I went home with Frances to meet her husband John. A neatly dressed old man with a red bandana around his neck, he used to work in the copper mines near Globe until ill-health forced early retirement. He now gets a disability pension and makes jewellery. When John heard I was interested in rocks and crystals and that one of my sons was a jeweller he got out all his stuff to show me. He is completely self-taught and his work had a lovely rough-hewn quality.

John had me try on a little silver and turquoise ring which

he then altered to fit me. When I asked the price he said, 'You can have it for a souvenir.' He loaded me up with rocks from all the buckets in his workroom - chunks of fire agate, amethyst, peridot, tiger's eye that he had found while digging about in the hills. I felt bad about not buying anything but giving gifts is a sacred part of the Apache culture, he said, and put a lovely little necklace of opal, turquoise and tiny rattlesnake bones around my neck. I realized how difficult it is for us to accept anything without feeling beholden.

We sat outside on some rusty old chairs in the yard looking over the nice little garden they've created, with mulberry trees for shade, some green grass and even some rose bushes. It's good land, they said, anything will grow here. Five pretty puppies played round our feet and a dozen chickens pecked happily. 'It's good to keep chickens,' said John. 'Whenever they see a snake they get to hollerin' like anything. We get rattlesnakes come right in the yard.'

He talked a bit about his time as an infantry soldier in the Pacific in 1944. It was an indelible trauma and he still speaks of it with horror. He saw things which he says are still burned on his eyeballs: a baby trying to suck on its mother who had been dead for two days; his best friend, Little Beaver, another Apache, shot to pieces in front of him; a pilot falling from a shot down plane. (They preferred to jump without their parachutes, he said. It was a cleaner death. If they drifted down slowly the Japanese used them for target practice.) John was shot in the spine and mercifully invalided out after eighteen months. Doctors said he would never walk again but he was determined. 'Chief' he was called but he was only twenty-seven years old.

Frances cooked some supper and invited me to stay the night. She wanted to get an early start in the morning to take me way out to the Apache reservation wilderness area about 70 miles across country towards the White Mountains to a place called Point of Pines and Ash Creek. It is near where she grew up and where her father used to keep his cattle. We took binoculars and her old polaroid and a gallon of water.

'Look at this land. Isn't that beautiful?' said Frances whistling under her breath. 'Gol-*ly*! Boy, God sure thought of everything! You name it!'

She talked about going out with her father when she was young to catch wild horses. He was brilliant at trapping them with a special kind of rope noose that he would fix up near their watering hole at night. Then they'd get out their little bed rolls and he'd say, 'Come over here and I'll make a tamale out of you', and she'd lie on the blanket and he'd roll her up like a sausage, put a flat stone under her head for a pillow and she'd go to sleep straight away, tired from a day in the saddle.

In the morning they invariably had a horse caught in the trap. He'd be rearing and whinnying, wild-eyed with fear. Her job was to sit nearby just talking to the horse and making soothing noises until he quietened down. 'You just have to treat 'em kind and gentle,' she said. 'They is just like a human. You get a bit nearer until you can put a canvas over them. You put your knee by their neck, keep talking and let the horse sweat it out. In about half a day they're OK.'

Frances said they would often meet a bear or a mountain lion. 'If you meet a wild animal, freeze!' she said, and demonstrated by turning to stone. 'You just stare at each other, then you turn to the left and they turn to their left and you go on about your business. They know where they are going just as well as you do and they won't bother you none so long as you don't scare 'em.'

She told me which bush her grandma used to collect leaves from to dry and pound into a powder for use as a poultice dressing for wounds and boils. Sometimes when her own grandchildren come to stay she takes them climbing in the hills and does a real Geronimo-style war cry when she gets to the top. 'Well, I'm an Indian, ain't I?' she said, grinning. 'I was raised on the land, raised to be a cowgirl and I'm happiest when I'm outdoors doing something physical.'

After we'd eaten our picnic lunch Frances took me over to the hills around the town of Peridot where the gemstones are found. Poor folk from San Carlos come and spend all day pick-axing the rocks and sifting through the debris trying to earn a few dollars. It was hot as hell out there with no shade and everybody throws their trash all over the place. Whole families squat all day in the dust and ghetto-blasters pound the air. At 3 o'clock a white man with a truck and a pair of scales arrives and pays people for their day's find.

We tried our luck and I found a small handful of gravel-sized chips, worth about 40 cents, in an hour of looking. Frances had much sharper eyes than me and picked up a few sizeable ones. John has found some beauties in his time which he makes into jewellery but it's a tough way to try to make a living.

The surrounding meadows were a glorious carpet of orange poppies and purple spiky flowers like bluebells with the noble saguaros standing guard. 'Oh boy, will you look at that!' said Frances, visibly moved. 'Ain't that pretty?' We took photos of each other sitting in the poppies, then drove on to the Coolidge Dam – the scene of a recent tragedy. Only a few days before, a young Apache policeman, on a drunken blinder after his wife had left him and his children had been taken from him, climbed out onto one of the huge cement eagles which grace the massive structure and threw himself into the thundering cataract below. Frances had taught him at school and was very shocked by his death. We looked over the edge and shuddered. It put her in mind of her son's death again and it made her sad to survey her flooded homeland. The mood had changed and it was time to go home.

At seventy-two years old, Frances had been driving all day with no sign of flagging while I was struggling to keep my eyes open. I managed to stay awake long enough to make us a tuna salad for supper and then we all fell into bed by 9 pm.

The next day I decided to travel on and see something of Arizona until it was time to come back for the Sunrise Dance. Inviting me to stay with them again on my return, Frances hugged me and wished me luck. It is humbling that it is so often the people with very little who are the most generous.

By the time I left San Carlos it was getting late and I wanted to try and make Show Low, 80 miles away, before dark. A huge wind got up and it started raining heavily as I set off on the lonely road north through the high country. It became quite cold as the road climbed into the mountains. 'Watch Out for Animals for the next 77 Miles' said a sign but all I saw was a squashed coyote and a flattened jack rabbit. I knew the forest was full of bears, mountain lions and elk (bears come snuffling round Sannie's trash can all the time) but they sensibly stayed out of the driving rain.

I stayed in the Deuce of Clubs Motel in the town named after a card game and it was so cold in the night I had to put my socks on. I shivered under two blankets and had terrible dreams about big muddy tidal waves whooshing up and washing out roads, people being sucked under, and me watching from behind a plate glass window as they struggled to swim.

I read this in Larry Cheek's book *Arizona*:

> No ethnic tribe on the planet has bounced so far and so often from utter vilification to romantic glorification as have the Apaches . . . they were 'blood-drunk and beast-hot . . . fetid-breathed and shrieking . . . lecherous and without honour or mercy . . . the Apaches hate life and they are the enemy of all mankind.' (All this from the 1950s novels of James Warner Bellah) Or alternatively, from another novel of the time: 'There is no private hoarding, no cheating. Whatever they have is divided equally . . . there's no caste system, and no aristocrats and no commoners . . . I wonder by what standards we have arrogated to ourselves the right to call Indians savages?'

In the morning I was longing for a walk so I decided to do the Mogollon Rim loop. I was the only person there – my little Dodge parked all alone in the Apache-Sitgreaves National Forest car park. From the sublime escarpment of the rim overlook there are trees as far as the eye can see. Huge stands of tall ponderosa pines, pinon pines, alligator pines and juniper trees. Quite surprising when the popular image of Arizona is a desert. This is Arizona's least-known high country scenery and there's not one town along the 87-mile Route 666.

Of course, it wasn't really a wilderness - too tamed for that - but for a townie like me it felt pretty wild. Most of the male quest journeys I have read about involve some sort of search for their connection to the sacred. Mine doesn't feel quite like that. The sacred seems to be already within and around me. It is my body and the trees and the land. I needed to leave home for other things - to learn to trust myself, to learn to be open to whatever comes next.

I thought about the tango I have danced with cancer and how grateful I am, in retrospect, for the way it brought my options into sharp focus. Procrastination was no longer one of them. 'Change or die!' said my inner voice. I was forced to face the truth that it wasn't just cancer of the breast, it was cancer of me, of the whole multiplicity of things which make up my life. The challenge presented by a confrontation with death is about living fully in the present moment. Leaving the seductive cocoon of home and going into the pit of the unknown is my initiation. Maybe you can't learn anything without giving something up.

We are healed by what we turn towards, not what we turn from. I lay face down on a carpet of sweet, pungent pine needles and embraced the earth.

Heading north, the forest suddenly gives way to scrubby, stony flatland, with red earth and tumbleweed. Snow-topped hills far to the east and a straight ribbon of road stretching ahead of me to infinity. I was making for the town of Klagetoh to try to meet Annie Wauneka - a woman I had written to six months before but also never had an answer from. Known as 'the legendary mother of the Navajo people and the embodiment of Changing Woman', Dr Wauneka was a tireless political and health activist who had single-handedly and successfully combated the scourge of tuberculosis on the reservations.

After getting the bum's rush from Annie Kahn at Lukachukai I was more than a little nervous but determined at least to try. The Klagetoh Trading Post was very closed, as was the gas station, and the scruffy town gave me a sinking feeling so I chickened out and drove on to Ganado where I got talking to a young Navajo Indian woman park ranger in a Smokey the Bear hat. I asked her if by any chance she knew Annie Wauneka. 'Oh yes, everybody knows her,' she said. But when I mentioned that I was hoping to meet her she clammed up and said she would surely be too busy and anyway she had recently been ill. I said I had promised to convey greetings from a friend in person so she finally relented and drew me a map of how to get to her house in Klagetoh.

There were no motels in the immediate vicinity but the ranger told me it was sometimes possible to rent one of the guest cottages at the nearby hospital. Luckily there was one vacant. I put my stuff inside and was just about to take my courage in my hands and drive back to Klagetoh when an old white-haired doctor walked by and said good evening. We exchanged pleasantries and he asked me where I was going. When I told him he said. 'Oh dear, you didn't know then?'

'Know what?' said I.

'She is in the sanatorium at Toyei, 30 miles from here, and she probably won't be coming out.' He went on to tell me that Dr Wauneka, now in her eighties, was, until recently, very alert and active but she had rapidly deteriorated and was now suffering from Alzheimer's Disease and very paranoid. 'You could try visiting her but I can't say what sort of mood you'll find her in.'

I thought I'd better wait and see how I felt in the morning and, meanwhile, went up the road to the only grocery store in town – a depressing place with a wall-sized fridge full of beer and soda pop, packets of soft white bread, packets of angel food white cake mix, crisps, candy and frozen ready-made pizzas. As Frances had said, 'Look how fat our people get! Not healthy big but huge rolls of fat hanging down. No wonder we get heart problems, diabetes, high blood pressure.'

Of course there are plenty of health-conscious, successful Native Americans but I think it's true to say that substance abuse, including junk food, is rife. They have had and are still having a hard time bringing themselves back from the brink.

In the morning I decided to risk the 60-mile round trip to pay my respects to Annie Wauneka. The staff at the nursing home would tell me if it wasn't appropriate. It was a clear, cloudless day and a pale haze of sage green vegetation washed the desert floor after all the recent rain.

The nursing home was an undistinguished bungalow standing next to the Navajo Police Training School and I was shown into the canteen where elderly Navajo men and women were sitting round a table making Easter decorations out of polystyrene plates and cut-out cardboard rabbits. All round the room were others in varying degrees of distress or senility, howling, drooling and repeating compulsive gestures. A radio was blaring an up-tempo version of 'You Are My Sunshine'. It was a vision of hell. I would rather be left on a hillside to be picked clean by vultures than end my days thus.

Dr Wauneka, 'legendary mother of the Navajo people', was sitting by herself, a fine-looking woman with a determined mouth and eyes like raisins that must once have been piercing but now had a faraway look. She looked beautiful in a high-necked brown blouse that set off the exquisite silver and turquoise brooches she was wearing. I introduced myself and she took my hand in both hers. 'I don't want to stay here,' she said. 'I want to go home now. Can you get me out of here?'

I tried to have a conversation but nothing seemed to register. All her mental energy was directed towards her only preoccupation. She repeated, 'Shall we go now? Shall I put my coat on?' Her eyes overflowed. I asked about her family. 'They never come and visit me,' she said and the tears ran down her face. Stricken with dismay, I didn't know what to do. I put my arms around her and we just rocked for a while. When she said again that she didn't like it here I said

I didn't blame her. I'd want to go home too.

I went to have a word with the matron, a sympathetic, friendly woman. 'Her daughter comes every week,' she said, 'but Annie doesn't remember. She gets taken out quite frequently and sometimes overnight but she doesn't remember anything.' I said it was terrible to see her so unhappy - a woman so revered, a woman whose life was devoted to pursuing ideals of better health for her people. 'I'll call her daughter,' she promised, patting my arm.

Annie Wauneka, meanwhile, had gone into her room and came out wearing her coat and a little scarf tied under her chin. She was waiting for me by the door. 'Which one's your car?' she whispered conspiratorially. 'Will this thing fit in?' She waved her walking frame. I felt a coward and a traitor. I wanted to rescue her but what would I do with a kidnapped octagenarian? I said I wished I could take her away but it just wasn't possible. 'Do I have to stay then?' she asked, crestfallen, and I nodded. I left her sitting alone in a corner of the common room. That awful Austrian marching song 'I Love to go a-Wandering' was playing through the loudspeakers: 'Fal Da Ree, Fal Da Ra . . .'. 'When will you come back?' asked Annie Wauneka as I stroked her soft wrinkled old cheek and wished her goodbye and God bless, but of course I never will.

I cried all the way back down to the junction with Highway 264. The contrast between her fierce reputation and the dreadful powerless reality of being old and infirm was so terrible. I shouted to the desert. 'Is this what will happen to me? is this the pay-off?' 'Changing Woman', she was known as - the archetypal Navajo Goddess/Healer/Crone. No one said she would change into this and end her days in loneliness and bedlam.

There is a Mayan dawn prayer quoted by Paula Gunn Allen in her book, *Grandmothers of the Light:*

Look at us! Hear us!
Heart of Heaven, Heart of Earth.
Give us our descendants, our succession,

As long as the sun shall move!
May the people have peace
May the people be happy!
Give us good life, Grandmother of the Sun,
Grandmother of the Light, let there be dawn,
Let the light come!

After I left Toyei I carried on to the little town of Chinle which
is at the mouth of the beautiful Canyon de Chelly - one of
the loveliest natural wonders in a state filled with them. It
is forbidden to enter the canyon without a Navajo guide. It
is their land and many people live in there, have farms and
grazing land and ceremonial summer camping grounds so I
asked one of the waiting hopefuls to take me on an all-day
horseback expedition.

We rode between the steep, sheer, 1000 foot high sandstone
walls which look like slabs of Norwegian caramel cheese cut
with a wire. We rode through the soft sand and shallow water
for 30 miles to visit the ruined cliff dwellings of the Navajo,
the Hopi and the Anasazi people - the earliest Indians, known
as the Ancient Ones. Human beings have lived in the canyon
for 2000 years and left over 400 ruins throughout the
centuries. Handprints and paintings of antelopes, horsemen,
snakes, suns and moons adorn the rockface where overhangs
protect it from the rain.

The canyon, like so many of the mute witnesses to the
atrocities of the past, has a melancholy history. One branch
of it, the Canyon des Muertos, testifies to the terrible
massacre in 1805 of more than 100 Navajos - mostly women
and children - by a Spanish expedition seeking gold. They
refused to believe that there was really no gold hidden there
and slaughtered everyone in their path.

My guide wasn't exactly taciturn but he was not very
talkative either. 'The old people told us to take care of the
land,' he said. '"Take care of it and it will take care of you,"
they said. Land still here, Navajo still here, Spaniards gone.'
He rode with his hat pulled down over his eyes. I, foolishly,

didn't have one and in addition to my saddle sores I got a frightful headache from the blinding dazzle of the sun. I felt parched and desiccated, my nose and throat prickled, my eyes stung but I was glad I had come.

Chinle, the little town where I stayed the night, perfectly encapsulated the paradoxes of modern Indian life and only served to strengthen my feelings of frustration and alienation. Everyone in the town of 3360 people is a Navajo but I had no way of knowing to what extent they still feel connected to the old Navajo ways which have been eroded as inexorably as the sandstone rock formations which dominates the Great Basin Desert.

The values and influences of white culture have seeped across the reservation borders to eat away at the traditional customs. Videos, pop music and liquor, fast food and push-button living make the hard life of their foremothers unattractive to modern kids who just want out as fast as possible. There was a big supermarket in Chinle where I stopped to buy some fruit. There, pushing their trolleys and loading up with washing powder and microwave dinners, were nut-brown, crinkly-faced old ladies laden with turquoise and carrying hand-woven bags in brilliant colours.

I longed to stop one and say, 'Please tell me something about your beautiful traditions and ceremonies. How can I learn to be a wise old woman? What can you teach me?' But I was too shy. Anyhow, from what I had already gathered, writers and seekers like me are seen as just the latest manifestation of the genus 'Colonialist' – a line that descends from soldiers and missionaries, through settlers and traders to anthropologists and folklorists – who sweep through, help themselves to the riches and leave the Indians somehow the poorer. They have stolen the land and the crops, they have murdered the buffalo, they have looted the very bones of the ancestors and now they are after the spiritual and aesthetic treasures.

I can understand the suspicion but I think it is a great shame. Spiritual treasures are not diminished when shared, they are multiplied. The Tibetans know this. After centuries of being sealed in their Himalayan kingdom they are now scattered in exile. But the time has come for the world to hear their teachings and our ears are ready. Their pain is the planet's gain. It is the same with the wisdom of the Native Americans. We need each other and ultimately we must trust each other.

In the morning I carried on up to the Utah border where Monument Valley straddles the two states. It is still Navajo land although designated a national park. I decided to walk the trail on foot as I was aching and stiff from so much driving and riding. Again, visitors were supposed to be accompanied by a guide but it wasn't worth anyone's while to go with just one person, they said, so I could go on my own as long as I stayed on the dirt road.

But I didn't. Once out of sight, no one would know where I went. I walked around in the desert all day carrying a rucksack with water and suncream. Everywhere were tracks saying 'Private, Keep Out' and pick-up trucks full of Indians would roar past on their way to distant farms dotted about the valley. I felt as cut off from them and their secrets and their culture as they probably would if they visited an English stately home. It felt like being in an enchanted nursery where the toys only come alive after dark. I was sure that once the visitors left they would drop their impassive gazes and spring to life, putting on their feathered bonnets, filling their hogans with wonderful chanting, dancing and stories.

By one of the most picturesque spots, I came upon a woman selling jewellery. It was dreadful old tourist tat although what she, herself, was wearing was gorgeous - old silver and enormous chunks of turquoise glowing with the patina of age. 'How's business?' I asked and she shrugged. 'Not much. Still early in the season.'

Just then a tour jeep drove up. Several men in baseball caps got out. 'This is Suzy,' said the tour guide.

'Well hello Suzy,' boomed a very fat man with lots of photographic equipment dangling in front of him. 'Can I take your picture?'

'Sure,' said Suzy. 'One dollar.'

'Oh boy! This is what I've been wanting to get ever since I got here,' said the man and he took his photo of a real Indian in Monument Valley. As soon as they'd driven off Suzy went and sat back in her pick-up and closed her eyes.

Monument Valley certainly reinforced any feelings of insignificance I might have had. It is a bizarre, haunting landscape – the Navajo Badlands – a jagged, forbidding country with a geology like nowhere else. Massive monoliths, mesas, buttes, cliffs and spires tower into the relentless, burning skies like cathedrals or aircraft carriers but hundreds of times bigger.

I believe the valley was formed by erosion, though it is hard to imagine that this once was a flat plateau the height of the tops of the mesas. The strongest impression is of being at the bottom of a vast ocean, 1000 feet deep, from which all the water has been drained. It stretches as far as the eye can see in every direction with snowy mountains on the distant northern horizon.

It was a rare gift being able to hike there alone all day. I kept rounding bends in the trail and gasping, 'Oh my God!' This time I saw a live jack rabbit who ran like the wind, his perfectly evolved, huge, sensitive ears translucent in the sun. I shared the vastness with a solitary hawk. I saw a tiny lizard and lots of rattlesnakes which turned out to be pieces of bleached desert driftwood. I also saw beer cans and condoms but I'll erase them from my memory.

The local Navajo residents whizzed along the road going about their business and I understood how important it was for them to keep us at arm's length. Our culture is so dominant, our reputation so tarnished, our tongues so forked that they're better off behind their 'Keep Out' signs. Much as I hate to admit it, I guess I'm no different from the guy with the camera, wanting to find my real Indian too.

'I'm not like the others!' I wanted to shout. 'I'll honour and respect your culture. Just let me get a bit closer, let me in.' I want to fit in everywhere, anywhere, to be a chameleon, to

be a bridge, to speak the language, to be one of the charmed
inner circle, knowledgeable, trusted. Why aren't I content just
to be a member of my own group, whatever that is? Maybe
becoming wise isn't about finding out how everybody else
does it but about discovering your own inner authority. I'm
sure no Navajo crone feels the need to be accepted by me.

The following day I saw the Grand Canyon. What must the
first humans who set eyes on it have thought? How did anyone
ever find their way across it or even down into it? As you drive
the 160 miles from Kayenta the land looks innocent enough.
Nothing prepares you for it except a few ominous cracks in
the ground that begin to appear around the Little Colorado
River. It is dinosaur country - primitive, arid, prehistoric-
looking - with a few fissures and crevasses in the flat,
featureless sandy scrub. Then you round the last corner and
there it is! Aaaaaargh! Yikes!

The trouble with trying to describe the Grand Canyon is
that the brain has no precedent for processing visual
information on this scale. All human endeavour is dwarfed
by comparison except, perhaps, Bach's or Mozart's.

You can trek to the bottom of the Bright Angel Trail or ride
on a mule. You can raft the waters. You can fly over it in a
plane or a helicopter. What would be 10 miles across to the
other side if you were an eagle is 215 if you go round by the
only road. It gets the adrenalin racing to walk along even the
tamest of trails. I bought a hat this time and scared myself
silly by hiking along the precipice for about four hours. My
whole body twitched and lurched with a mixture of vertigo
and emotion. At least the person who named the various
peaks and buttes understood that this was the landscape of
the gods. They are called Isis's Temple, Jupiter's Temple,
Osiris, Shiva, Brahma, Venus, Vishnu, Solomon . . .

I had slept in the car so as to be there at dawn. In the perfect
stillness of that moment when the sun rose I wanted to fly.
I wanted to cry. I wanted to sing and shout praises. Instead
I sat on a rock and watched the panorama of changing
colours, marvelling at my good fortune in being here, in being

alive, in being a child of Mother Earth. I wrote in my journal:

> All my life I will remember that beautiful day. Thank you Great Spirit.

On my way south again I stopped to have a cup of coffee at the Tuba City Truck Stop on the edge of the Hopi reservation. A Hopi woman, Marilyn, with her chubby baby and her elderly mother, came and sat next to me and we got talking. The old lady didn't speak English but her daughter was sophisticated and chatty. Although she lives in another town Marilyn brings the baby to stay several days at a time with Grandma so that the little girl will grow up knowing her language and her heritage.

God help her, was all I could think. All around me, every day, I saw Indian people looking all but defeated by the ravages of too much grief, too much shame, too much helpless inexpressible fury. The figures for child and teenage suicides here are truly shocking. I had been reading *Spider Woman's Grand-daughters* – a collection of writings by Native American women edited by Paula Gunn Allen, Professor of Native American Studies at Berkeley. The miracle is that so much creativity and beauty has survived the chronicle of horrors.

Children, until only about ten or fifteen years ago, were still beaten at school for speaking their own language. It had happened to her, said Marilyn. Their religious practices had been forbidden. In a famous case where the parents of Hotevilla on the Hopi reservation refused to send their kids to school (knowing only too well what an insidious form of conquest 'education' could be), the men were all arrested and the children forcibly sent away to boarding school. The women and babies were left alone in Hotevilla to fend for themselves.

As for me, coming directly from Jamaica where the humiliations of slavery have left such a terrible legacy to here where the systematic genocide of the Indians has created a grief from which one wonders if they will ever recover, I found myself feeling, 'Thank God I'm Jewish and a woman and can identify at least some of the time with those who have been sinned against.'

CHAPTER FOUR

The Sunrise Dance Ceremony

Their eyes mid many wrinkles, their eyes,
Their ancient, glittering eyes, are gay.

W.B. YEATS, 'Lapis Lazuli'

The sound was thrilling, primal, electrifying. It seemed to reach right back to our most ancient connection with the sacred. Somehow we have all known this - the fire, the night, the stories, the drums. I didn't feel I was eavesdropping on something exotic and alien, rather that I was remembering something I had always known. I marvelled to think that all this had *survived* in spite of the prohibitions, forced exile, brainwashing, beating. Here in 1992 another generation of young Apaches were singing their hearts out in their ancient language, bringing tears to their grandmothers' eyes.

As advised, I had purchased some suitable offerings - tobacco, a case of Coke, a large tin of coffee, a few pounds of biscuits and some bags of tortilla chips. It was nightfall by the time I got back to San Carlos and Elizabeth Classay was already out at the Beaver Springs Camp Ground making preparations. Someone drew me a map of how to get there - off the highway, under a bridge, over the railway tracks, a couple of miles down a dirt road to a grove of cottonwood trees. I'd know it was her by the maroon and grey truck.

It was pitch dark and everything on the reservation looked different. I had felt quite nervous heading off alone into the night with only my headlights and the eerie sound of distant Apache drums to guide me. I got myself horribly lost going down at least three wrong dirt roads and nearly stuck in a soft, sandy river bed but finally I made it to the right place. Now *this* was more like it. This was the place I had imagined. A place of aesthetic beauty, communal endeavour, Apache pride.

Elizabeth Classay came forward to greet me. She had changed into her traditional camp dress with feathers in her hair and looked wonderful. Although she made me park next to her truck as a precaution against drunken revellers who have been known to break into cars to steal money for booze, I didn't see anyone who looked unruly. In the middle of their camp ground a fire was blazing and my gift joined the mountain of food they had been collecting. Many guests would be coming and everyone had to be fed.

Elizabeth, her sisters and several of her women friends had been cooking up great vats of stew and fixing tortillas all day. The men had been building the wickiup - a beautiful, fragrant-smelling structure of leaves and branches - in which the godparents would sleep for the whole week. People had set up tents, motor homes and brush lean-tos. Way across on the other side of the enormous clearing was the girl's family making their own preparations.

About a dozen men sat in the middle of the enclosure, drumming and singing the ancient chants. Elizabeth explained that the words were blessings, prayers for peace and prayers of thanksgiving. 'The words are so beautiful I get quite emotional every time I listen to them,' she said. 'So much wisdom and poetry. So much deep meaning.'

Then she laughed, 'Come on, let's dance,' and showed me what to do. A group of women link arms and stamp rhythmically from foot to foot - six steps forward, six steps back - while travelling in a clockwise circle. The structure is very informal. People join in and leave as the spirit moves them, dancing for as long or as short a time as they like. The whole spontaneous choreography was so peaceful, graceful and harmonious - each dancer unique and yet part of the whole, in step with the rhythm of the universe and the music of the spheres. It was everything that the wretched reservation towns are not. The sense of belonging and sisterhood with women from such a different culture was so comfortable. I fell into a hypnotic, meditative reverie and hardly noticed the two hours go by.

The ceremony itself was scheduled to begin at sunrise the following morning and I hardly slept because I didn't want to miss anything. Frances and I got up just as the sky was lightening in the east and raced over to the camp ground by 5 am. It was spotless and beautifully organized. Everyone helped. The men were building the fires, splitting logs, carrying heavy, cast-iron pans. The women were peeling, chopping, frying chicken, making tortillas. A big breakfast of fried bread, fried potatoes, bacon, eggs and coffee was dished up to the workers.

As the sun rose, the godmother's party walked across to the girl's camp to dress her in her symbolic accoutrements. Frances had lent me one of her camp dresses so I could join in. Reynelda Cassadore, the young girl, was waiting demurely in her wickiup arrayed in a lustrous purple and gold camp dress and beautiful beaded moccasins and necklace. Planted in the ground outside her doorway was a staff with eagle feathers and ribbon streamers tied on.

Elizabeth circled around the staff and entered the wickiup. She then tied a thong with an abalone shell disc on Reynelda's forehead. By this she is identified as White Shell Woman or Changing Woman. Another strip of rawhide with a drinking tube and a scratching stick hanging on it was fastened round her neck. During the four days she must only drink through the tube and scratch herself with the stick.

A white eagle feather - the colour her hair will be when she is old - is fastened to the back of her head to symbolize long life and the eagle down feathers on her shoulders will enable her to walk and run as lightly as a feather. The staff is placed in her hand, reminding her of the cane she will need

in old age and thereby symbolizing the many years she will
live as a wise old woman. Elizabeth, her godmother, has been
specially chosen as the older woman of ideal character whom
the parents most want their daughter to emulate.

The Medicine Man then made a long speech in Apache,
translated for me by Elizabeth. He told us that this four-day
ceremony called 'The Gift of Changing Woman' or 'The
Sunrise Ceremony' is the single most important event in an
Apache girl's life. Each time the ceremony is held, the Apache
world is created anew – nothing is more meaningful in the
Apache world view.

In their language the ritual is known simply as 'Nai'ez' or
'It is Happening'. Changing Woman was the first woman on
earth (created before man). Longing for children, she made
love with the sun and gave birth to twins. The twins grew up
to clear the world of evil and make it good for humankind.
During the Changing Woman ceremony, Reynelda will
become the embodiment of the deity's spirit and be prepared
for her role as an Apache mother and life-giver. The ceremony
also ensures that she will have strength, an even
temperament, prosperity and longevity – all qualities
associated with Changing Woman. It is a re-enactment of the
creation of the world and the coming of the Apache people.
It is a celebration of life.

The Medicine Man then called on the assembled company
henceforth to respect the young girl as a fully fledged woman.
Then we all departed and returned to our cooking. Mid-
morning the great gift exchange began. All the vast cauldrons
of food – stews, cakes, roast meat, salads, punch – were to
be taken over to the other camp and they would do the same.
This symbolizes the willingness to give away everything you
have and the special bond of friendship which now unites the
two families.

First a modest quantity was taken across the camp ground
to the men's sweat lodge on the banks of the river. Men had
been going over there on and off all night long to purify
themselves and there were still several men inside chanting

and praying. They needed fortifying.

The drummers in our camp began the beat and all the women in their colourful dresses started to dance. Men, in their finest embroidered shirts and white stetsons, linked arms with us and joined in. After about five songs we could hear a terrific cacophony as the food-bringing procession from the other camp, led by Reynelda and her parents, arrived dancing and drumming, singing and beeping their truck horns. We ignored them and carried on dancing to our own rhythm while they circled around us and set all their offerings out on a long table.

Then they joined our circle and we all danced together. After a while they returned to their camp again and we formed into a procession of our own led by Elizabeth and her husband. Someone put a cake in my arms to dance across with and off we went - heavy cauldrons in the trucks, lighter things carried by the women, men chanting and drumming.

It was exhilarating to be in the middle of it. The heat, the swirling dust from everybody's feet, the blowing, drifting seeds from the cottonwood trees creating a dreamlike silvery haze. It was hard to believe I was really there: Twickenham Housewife Dances With Apaches! Colours whirling, moccasins stamping, people laughing, tiny children joining in, fat old women reliving their youth. This was real Apache pride.

We set our food down on their table in the same way while they pretended nothing was happening. Then we synchronized our footsteps with theirs and all danced together again. By this time everyone was famished. We returned to our camp, tucked into the feast - everyone piling my plate with things I had to try: acorn soup, roast corn, Indian tacos, squash and lima bean stew - and then relaxed in the shade for a siesta during the heat of the afternoon.

I asked a young girl of seventeen how it had felt when she had been the focus of all the attention. She said it was both wonderful and embarrassing, 'Like, everyone's looking at you and knows you've just got your period - but you feel so proud to be a woman.'

Apache society is matrilineal. This was the first time I had ever been in a culture where it actually felt more important to be a woman, a culture where the whole tribe celebrated the onset of the life-giving menstrual blood. An occasion for joy, not a 'curse'.

The men, though, have suffered terribly. As someone said to me, 'Women always have their role as mothers and nurterers whatever happens to them but the warriors, defenders and hunters of the conquered, defeated society have nothing. Only their shame.' It's true and it was wonderful on this day to hear the powerful, virile sound of the men's singing and drumming, reclaiming their manhood and their dignity.

There were quite a few jokes at my expense – 'Aren't you afraid to be here with us wild Indians?', 'Hasn't anyone told you that we scalp people?' – but after the initial banter the mood became more serious. 'Don't let anyone tell you we were a bloodthirsty people,' said one man. 'We're all so tired of hearing that. It just wasn't true. It was US Army propaganda to paint us as subhuman.'

'We had a reputation as fierce raiders,' said another, 'but the terrible bloodletting never really happened until the white invaders threatened our homelands.' Personally, I cannot imagine that any culture with such a poetic and female-based creation myth could have been as cruel and savage as they were portrayed.

They called themselves simply 'The People' but to nearly everyone else they were known as 'The Enemy', perhaps because few people have ever fought harder to preserve their territory and their way of life. A very ancient people, they were one of the last to be defeated. Their famous vitality and tenacity have served them well, even though they finally lost their struggle against the usurpers of their land and were confined on reservations. Their spiritual view, which treats each day as a sacred path to be walked with concern for all created things, has new life breathed into it with every ceremony such as this.

Frances never gave her own daughters a Sunrise Dance because these rituals were illegal forty years ago and people were still mightily crushed by missionary efforts to change their religious beliefs. They have only recently begun to reclaim their history and salvage their identity. It is a terrible story.

By evening a huge bonfire had been lit in the middle of the central clearing. Drummers from both camps were drumming and strings of dancers were stamping about. Tradition demands that sixteen songs are played (each one can last up to twenty minutes). Reynelda, accompanied by her godmother Elizabeth, must dance from beginning to end to display her stamina. This session was mostly a social dance with much whooping and hollering and snogging in cars and over-excited children running around chasing each other in the dust. It all looked exciting in the firelight and felt like a very ancient heartbeat. Frances and I lasted till about 10.30, then snuck off to bed.

The next day was another dawn start so we returned to the camp ground by 5.30, helping to make the tortillas for breakfast. Six or seven old women, each with their own cooking fire, sat around companionably slapping and stretching the balls of dough to the right thinness. Nothing has ever tasted more delicious than those tortillas freshly baked on bits of old sheet metal bent over little piles of hot embers!

Just after first light, both camps formed into one huge circle in the big clearing. Down the middle had been laid a line of crates of oranges, cases of Coke and burden baskets filled with sweets. Facing the east stood the drummers in full voice with a pile of blankets and buckskins in front of them.

While the rest of us kept time with our feet, Reynelda knelt on the buckskins with her hands raised in the air and her eyes closed. She began to sway from side to side, her beautiful little face illuminated by the rays of the rising sun. Elizabeth, as her sponsor and godmother, stayed beside throughout, giving instruction and moral support, wiping her face and giving her drinks through the tube. By re-enacting the posture in which Changing Woman underwent her first menstrual period the initiate opens herself to the spirit of the deity which now enters her body. She did, indeed, look quite possessed.

All the time this was going on, little raiding parties of three or four ladies would detach themselves from the circle and dance over to capture a man from the other side and dance him back over to their side. The old grandmothers were tireless. Two of them linked arms with me and off we went, stomping our way across. 'Come on, let's go and get *him* before somebody else does,' they cackled. Although the underlying theme of the dance was serious, it was tremendous fun and everyone was laughing and joking. Very young girls captured old men, children danced with each other and with their fathers. At the end of each set, the men would return, only to get grabbed again by the next chain of marauding ladies.

The next part of the ceremony required the girl to lie face down on the buckskin and to be massaged all over quite roughly by the godmother. This is to symbolically mould her into a woman - to give her straightness, beauty and strength. The staff with the feathers is set out in four positions, each a little further away, signifying the four stages of childhood and adolescence, maturity and old age that she will pass through. She then has to run, while everyone chases her, to the four directions, showing that, like Changing Woman, she can run swiftly and never get tired.

A man stood holding a basket of sacred yellow cat-tail pollen and we all lined up to file past Reynelda, taking a pinch of it to sprinkle on her. Another basket filled with candy, corn kernels and coins was poured over her by the Medicine Man, the crates of oranges and Coke were flung in the air and everyone scrambled to take something. By now all the food had become blessed and holy so the people were assured of abundance.

Reynelda's last action of the day was to throw the buckskin to the east and the blankets to each of the other three directions. This ensured that there would always be deer meat, plenty of blankets and good hunting for everyone in her camp.

By this time there had been over four hours of continuous dancing in the hot sun and everyone was wilting. We went back to our separate camps for the great lunch-cooking marathon. More tortillas flap-flapped in deft hands and cooked over hot coals on pieces of bent tin, more lumps of dough fried in hot oil. Corn and acorn soup, beans and bacon, big bones with meat on, pig's trotters and salad . . . It was all wolfed down and people sat around in the shade talking.

'I'm glad you've come to see the truth for yourself,' said one old lady. 'A lot of white people believe the terrible things that have been said about us for so long.' I was feeling quite overwhelmed by what I'd seen – by the beauty and importance of a ceremony which gives a young woman on the threshold of adulthood such a wonderful sense of self-worth and a role which will continue right through into old age. It is the miracle of a woman's life-giving womb which is being celebrated, bringing happiness and plenty to the whole tribe. It links the present to the ancient past, giving a sense of continuity and cultural richness.

I also learned some more about the Western Apache creation myth: Changing Woman never became old. When she got to a certain age she went walking to the East and saw herself walking towards her. When she came together, she was only one – the young one. So Changing Woman has the power of perpetual renewal.

At dusk another enormous bonfire was lit in the central clearing. Reynelda and four young female companions, stood together, all dressed in the most gorgeous, fringed, buckskin, beaded dresses and moccasins. The rest of us formed a giant circle around them. Suddenly, in a great hullaballoo of stamping and bells and the ghostly moan of a bull-roarer, into the firelight leapt the Crown Dancers who impersonate the Mountain Spirits – four benevolent ones and a trickster/clown who represents the whirlwind, the mischief-maker, the unpredictable aspect of nature. They had come to bless the new incarnation of Changing Woman and to ensure her well-being through life.

The musicians drummed and chanted and the Mountain Spirits, with their painted bodies, elaborate head-dresses and carved wands, danced in the firelight casting grotesque shadows. It was a spectacular sight and it really felt as if a magical transformation was taking place. The spirits led Reynelda and her companions in a dance, weaving in and out of the circle and finally ending up around an open-sided wigwam made out of four saplings with the musicians inside. Again they danced wildly to the four directions, yelping and hollering - clouds of dust almost obscuring them from view. Little Reynelda bore it all with great dignity and fortitude.

On the last day the Mountain Spirits came again. They arrived at sunrise as the girl stood waiting under the four saplings facing east. While we linked arms and danced on the spot, they painted her all over with a preparation of white clay until she was transformed into White Painted Lady with the power to bestow blessings, which she did by dancing round the circle flicking the clay on all of us. Finally everyone followed her and the Mountain Spirits as they danced four times through the saplings to the four directions, honouring the unifying qualities that reside there. And that was it.

There would be another feast, a time for the old men to tell again the teaching stories and myths; then, in the evening, a final gift exchange. All the remaining food, some blankets, camp dresses, turquoise jewellery would be danced across to the other side. Nothing is hoarded, everything given away. What a tragedy that we didn't learn all this while we had the chance. Maybe it's not too late.

Elizabeth handed me some of the sacred yellow cat-tail pollen to keep and take with me on my journey as a blessing. Frances gave me a bag of oranges. I also took away with me an indelible vision of renewal - of older women handing on their wisdom and experience to the next generation. After so much suffering the gift of Changing Woman is vital to the continued life of the Apache people.

An invitation from some friends to spend four days at the Feathered Pipe Ranch, hidden among the pine-forested mountains of Colorado Gulch in Montana, offered a welcome opportunity to rest after all the excitement of the Sunrise Dance ceremony. I flew to Billings where I had made a very informal arrangement with the 'Rent-a-Wreck' car hire company. ('It's the blue Buick Skylark parked by the fence.' said the guy. 'The keys will be under the floor mat.') This time there was Country and Western music on the radio and a sticker in my windscreen which read 'If You Love Me I'm Yours'. I just hoped people would know it meant the car, not me.

During the summer my friends run residential personal development courses at their ranch which is in the most beautiful setting imaginable in the foothills of the Rockies. In April the season was not yet under way so I could stay in one of their log cabins in the woods.

Although at first it did not seem to have much to do with my search for wise old women I had one magical experience on my final day in Montana which can't be left out of the chronicle.

All that night the full moon shone in through the curtainless windows of my room. I could hear the land breathing, the trees breathing, the animals breathing. All was transfigured in the silver-blue light and I could hardly wait for the dawn to answer the siren call that beckoned me out. I knew that I must brave hiking up in the mountains by myself.

I have always been very afraid of being lost and I had never been into real wilderness forest alone before. I knew there were bears, moose, mountain lions and porcupines in there but I was armed with two valuable bits of information given to me by Tom, a local wildlife photographer:
1. If you are always aware of the *drainage* pattern of the mountains you can't get lost. Notice which valley your

mountain drains down into and then wherever you end up
you can get back down to where you started.

2. You could spend your whole life trying to get mauled
by a mountain lion and you'd probably die, disappointed,
of old age.

I took a penknife, an orange and a waterproof jacket (no
point in taking a compass as I have never learned how to use
one). Another thing Tom said was, 'Never turn your back on
the weather up here.' It can start out fine and sunny and then,
out of nowhere, be snowing or hailing hailstones the size of
lemons right up into June.

I paid close attention to the track I was taking, here scuffing
the pine needles to mark a twist, there stacking a few stones
to mark a turn. I walked through dense Hansel and Gretel
pine forest with the sunlight streaming through in low,
slanting shafts. Breaking through the last patches of melting
snow were tiny wild cyclamen, shooting stars and crocuses.
When I stood still the loudest sound in the whole world
was my own heartbeat with the occasional call of a bird
way up high in the quiet branches. No wind, no water,
perfect silence.

In a clearing I came upon a group of about sixteen deer.
They all stood absolutely motionless, staring at me with
their big ears tuned like satellite dishes. I remembered
what Frances had said about meeting wild animals and
froze and stared back. After a couple of minutes I turned
left and walked off and they lowered their heads and
began grazing again.

When I reached the top of the mountain about an hour later
it opened out into a high meadow grassland with a few rocky
outcrops and I could see forever. (This is where it's important
to remember where you came out of the woods or you can
get your drainages confused. Then you are really lost.) I
walked along the ridge for a while, conscious of how much
I normally rely on Richard to know where we are on the map.
This time I didn't even have a map.

I found a lovely flat rock and sat down cross-legged facing

east, with the sun in my face. It was a beautiful spot to meditate and I lost track of time, thinking about the conversation Tom and I had had the day before on the vexed question of being alone. Up here it suddenly seemed very clear that we are alone all our lives but can't bear to accept that truth. We imagine that somehow another person will *complete* us and we search for a mirror to see our own loveableness reflected back. It's a hopelessly addictive drug and, by its very nature, eternally unfulfilling. No sooner do you find it than you want more. You want guarantees forever, eternity . . .

A large part of my wisdom quest and the challenge of ageing, I think, is to learn to be at peace with aloneness - to find inner contentment when I am on my own and not need to fill up the space with people or constantly justify my existence in terms of some kind of relationship. I love my partner, my friends, adore my children and grandchildren. What they have given me is there, whether I'm with them or not. Nothing can ever take it away. But who am I? Who lives in this ageing body sitting in the sun on a mountain top? Could I live here alone in a little cabin like Tom does?

I know he gets lonely but, then, living with someone doesn't stop you from being lonely. I have sometimes felt as if I would die of loneliness when Richard has seemed to be on the other side of a plate-glass divide which lets us see but not hear each other . . .

Just then, I heard a soft sound and opened my eyes without moving. There, in the meadow, not 10 yards from where I sat, stood a magnificent elk looking at me. I held my breath and felt my heart quicken. He had come to meet me and to stand alone before me - the embodiment of strength and stamina, an icon of grace and self-containment. He was the most beautiful creature I had ever seen. I was moved to tears and afraid to breathe. What a precious gift! What luck! 'Oh, thank you,' I wanted to say, 'for keeping this appointment.' I watched him until he moved away, then stayed on for a while in the enchanted space. Finally I slowly found my way back down the mountain.

The Indians believe that when you encounter certain animals either in nature or in your dreams they have come to teach you something. I read this in a book called *Medicine Cards* by Jamie Sams and David Carson:

> Elk medicine teaches that pacing yourself will increase your stamina . . . Elk has no other defence except his ability to go the distance . . .
>
> Elk have a curious kind of warrior energy because, except at mating time, they honour the company of their own gender. They can call on the medicine of brotherhood or sisterhood. In discovering the strength which is gained from loving the gender that is your own, you will feel the comradeship that arises from similarity of experience . . . Elk could also be telling you to look at how you are holding up physically to the stresses in your life and to pace yourself so that you maintain an equilibrium of energy over the distance you plan to cover . . . allow some personal quiet time for replenishment.
>
> Elk is telling you to look at how you choose to create your present pathway, and how you intend to perpetuate it to reach your goal. Your best weapon is the same as Elk's: to stop when you need to, persist when you need to, and to allow room for change and exchange of energies.

I knew I would have to get up at 3.30 am in order to drive to Billings in time to catch my flight so I woke every hour throughout the night in anticipation. The wind had whipped up, and fast, dark clouds were flying through the sky as I drove away in the moonlight. I was fine for the first two and a half hours, playing the radio loud and humming along to Crystal Gayle and Glen Campbell. I hardly passed another car. Then the fatigue and lack of sleep started getting to me, and it began to rain. Lights were glaring and making my eyes sting and a lot of big, heavy rigs doing 75 mph started appearing on the road. I realized I was in danger of falling asleep at the wheel.

'Stop when you need to stop,' said Elk, so I pulled off the road at a dingy truckers' café where guys in plaid shirts and peaked caps advertising brands of cement sat hunched over the steam from their coffee cups.

The place was cheerless and the waitress offhand. I had a strong black coffee and raced on towards my destination. The flight was due to take off at 8.30 and I still had to return my Rent-a-Wreck. I made it, with five minutes to spare, slumped in my seat and slept right through take-off and all the way to San Francisco.

I was shattered to discover that Cecelia, the woman with a PhD in Creative Ageing whom I had come all this way to see, was 'out of town for several days', according to the person who answered her phone. I couldn't believe it and didn't understand what had gone wrong with our communications. There was nothing to do but accept the situation so I went over to help my cousin's wife stuff mangetouts for an Easter lunch party. It felt quite bizarre to have flown 6000 miles and end up piping cream cheese into pea pods, but there I was. Life's little lessons in patience and acceptance come in strange packages. I decided to stop fretting and had a nice, silly day decorating Easter eggs and sitting around in a marvellous enclosed garden full of wisteria and lemon trees right in the heart of the city.

Everything changed the next day when I got a phone call from Cecelia who had muddled up her dates and was driving down from Santa Barbara for a few days holiday with her boyfriend ('The man in my life, my significant other,' she said. 'The man I love,' yelled a voice in the background). On the spur of the moment I offered to fly down and meet up with them. She was apologetic for the cock-up and impressed with my impetuosity. 'Come,' she said, 'and be our guest.' So I paid the airfare which was terribly expensive and hoped I wasn't making a big mistake.

When I arrived at Santa Barbara airport there was no one there to meet me. Terrible sinking feeling. What if they'd had

an accident? Anything could have happened and I had no way
of finding out. Cecelia is old enough to be my mother. I had
never met her before. What if she was totally mad and had
no intention of coming? What if she had slipped her trolley,
lost her cookies, was a couple of coupons short of a pop-up
toaster? I sat there for half an hour thinking 'Now what?'
when she rushed in. She looked wonderfully zany, wearing
white leggings, a rainbow-striped T-shirt and hot sherbet-
coloured lace-ups. She was apologizing profusely, with tall,
handsome Don at her side.

That was the start of a great friendship. We adored each
other on sight and talked for three days until we were hoarse.
We felt like long-lost sisters brought together by the hand of
destiny.

Cecelia Hurwich is an unbelievable seventy-two-year-old
dynamo. When we met she was wearing a straw hat and dark
glasses to cover the bruises where she'd bashed her face and
broken her nose white-water rafting down the Columbia River
a couple of weeks previously.

We checked into the luxurious Spanish mission-style
Montecito Hotel, founded by Charlie Chaplin back in the
1920s, and Cecelia insisted on taking care of my bill. I had
planned a proper recorded interview with her about her
degree course on Creative Ageing but it was all the off-the-
record talk, the impressions of vitality, openness, energy and
generosity that filled in the background and fleshed out the
voice. A phone interview just wouldn't have done. I was really
glad I had come.

Cecelia had brought up three children while married for
twenty years to an ambitious man who neglected his family
but left her well-off when they divorced. She then had twenty
years on her own as a successful interior designer. 'By my late
fifties,' she said, 'I knew I had a talent for fixing things and
making them beautiful on the outside but I was becoming
more concerned about what was going on inside.

'I hadn't been to school for forty years and I was worried
about whether I'd be able to keep up. Would I be the oldest

one? Would I even be accepted? Would I have the discipline to stick with a regular degree programme? Then I heard of a unique holistic studies programme at Antioch University West which offered an MA in psychology and was attracting people from all over the world. It included a lot of work on the physical level - meditation, Feldenkrais body work, jogging, encounter groups, biofeedback, anatomy - and was a simply wonderful way to begin my studies.

'For my thesis, I decided to find out about ageing from women who had aged well, women who were past seventy, who were admired by their friends and community, who seemed to be doing something meaningful and who had zest for life. I found that although there were many studies of men by men, there was very little published material on the positive aspects of ageing for women. I put out a call to the community for suggestions and got over 100 names.'

Cecelia narrowed the choice down to twenty-two, best defined by the word 'vital'. There were clues to a universal quality - a series of characteristics shared by each. 'They lived very much in the present but had plans for the future,' she said. 'They realized it was important to have friends of all ages because it is in the nature of things that one's contemporaries are going to start dying off. They were initiators and they were optimistic. They all had a feeling of self-worth and were their own educators in dealing with health problems.'

Contrary to expectations, Cecelia's informants were not necessarily in the best of physical shape. 'Not at all,' said Cecelia. 'They had the diseases of age - arthritis, hearing problems, loss of vision - but they didn't let that stop them. They focussed on what they could do, rather than on what they had lost. They had all lived through two world wars and were no strangers to grief but in spite of the upheavals and tragedies they'd say things like, "After my husband's death I learned to . . ." Hardships were a source of growth into richer and richer territory, not a defeat. It was so wonderful and encouraging.'

One woman, in particular, who had retired at sixty-five,

decided to take a degree in engineering and physics because
she wanted to understand the implications of atomic energy.
She wrote an influential paper entitled 'Split Atom, Split
World', became an expert on the subject, founded the
International League for Peace and Freedom, became a peace
activist during the Vietnam war and now, at nearly ninety, has
amassed a huge peace library and still provides information
for peace groups.

'Continuing involvement in the community is one
definition of vital old age,' said Cecelia. 'So is increased inward
reflection. These women were concerned about the world
and the environment and as they grew older they found
themselves becoming more spiritual – shifting the emphasis
from the ego to the soul.'

Cecelia began her study in 1980 and re-interviewed the
same women ten years later for her PhD thesis. In that decade,
some of their partners had died and they were having to face
the loss of sexuality in their lives. For some it was devastating,
for some a relief, but it wasn't all sad. One woman in her
eighties took a younger lover and said sex was better than it
had ever been with her two previous husbands. Another said,
'Well, put it like this, I've become almost a vegetarian but
every once in a while I enjoy a good piece of meat if I can
get it!' Everyone acknowledged the importance of some form
of physical contact which didn't, of course, just have to be
with a male. Women friends, grandchildren, young people –
it was imperative to have someone to touch, to hold, to be
affectionate with.

Cecelia has been living with her partner Don, who is
younger than she is, for seven years. They had known one
another way back when they were each married to someone
else and got together when they both found themselves alone
again. She talked with refreshing candour about their
relationship. 'When we were young we used to be very sexual,'
she said. 'Now we love cuddling, touching, hugging. We don't
feel the urge to have intercourse as often but when we do
it's very satisfying and contenting and sometimes very

exciting. The *love* and the intimacy are as strong, if not stronger than ever.'

It was lovely to see them together, walking with their arms around each other or holding hands. The two of them were outrageous, going into all the ice-cream parlours along the streets of Santa Barbara, asking for tastes of everything then leaving without buying any. All done with immense charm and gaiety. 'One of the best things about being old is not caring what anyone thinks,' said Cecelia. She suggested a nude swim at night in the hotel pool but Don and I weren't really up to it. In fact we were both rather trailing in her wake. Her vigour and *joie de vivre* were astonishing and delightful and certainly a great inspiration to me. I thought of how decrepit and defeated my poor mum was by the time she reached her late sixties. She died at seventy, a very old woman, whereas Cecelia at seventy-two is no older than I am.

Now she, herself, has reached the qualifying age for her own study and embodies all the qualities of vitality she looked for in her subjects. Her study formed the basis for the lectures and seminars she now gives all over the country on Creative Ageing. She has given papers for the past ten years at the annual conferences of the Gerontological Society of America and the American Society of Ageing.

'I can't believe I'm doing what I love and people are inspired by what I have to say. Before I started all this I really had fears about ageing,' she said. 'I was in my fifties, and seventy seemed old. I didn't know how I would cope. Now I'm in my seventies and I don't feel old at all. Because of my research, eighty doesn't seem so old either. I think it's like anything else – if you learn a foreign language it seems easy to you. If you learn about ageing you can become your own advocate. If you understand about preventative health you can keep well longer. Knowledge dispels fear.

'I've invented this role because there wasn't anyone doing this. I ask my students, "How many of you have an older role model? How many of you know a woman over seventy you really admire?" About one-third raise their hands. I say,

"Get out there and meet them. Make friends with an older person, they're going to give you something. Also, they're not a separate species - they're you in a few years time. Don't isolate them from your life, your job, your parties."

'I like myself so much better now than when I was younger. I'm more interested in others, less preoccupied with myself and my problems. I love being a grandmother. Mostly what my grandchildren want is for me to listen to them. They don't necessarily want my opinion, they want to talk things out. I've got much better at that.'

Like the subjects of her study, Cecelia says her main preoccupation is the challenge of staying mentally active. "How do you do it?" I asked one woman and she replied, "Well, I not only read books, I've started a book discussion group!" The worst thing is to give up the ghost. The ageing brain *can* be kept active with stimulation. Use strategies to aid memory and don't put yourself down for forgetting your glasses or losing your keys. Those aren't the important things any longer. If you keep saying, "Oh, my memory is terrible", "My mind's falling apart", "I forget everything", "I can't do it", "I'm stupid", you are creating a climate of negative conditioning. Very bad. Instead say, "I know I know that, just give me a few minutes." Take the time you need and you'll retrieve it because you have it. All that wisdom and experience is there. Don't panic.'

Cecelia comes from strong female stock. Her grandmother, with whom she lived when she was a child, was a real Jewish matriarch. Her mother, after being widowed in her late fifties, passed the Civil Service examinations and went on to take up a whole new career. From them she inherited her confidence and her curiosity. 'I feel I am learning all the time,' she said. 'I have just done a weekend course with a naturalist on spring wildflowers and ecology, how rocks are formed and how glaciers made those huge national parks of ours. Wonderful!'

She has also learned how to use a computer. 'That was one of the hardest things,' she said. 'A lot of older people are terrified of computers. They think they won't be able to understand anything technical. Negative conditioning again. I had to take the word processing course three times before it sunk in but the sense of satisfaction was terrific. I am well aware that there might come a time when I can't get out. Then I will be able to use a modem to link into the library, call the airlines, talk to people. It will be a boon.'

We rented a couple of bikes and rode along the well-maintained cycleways beside the glittering Pacific Ocean. We drove up the coast to the little Danish town of Solveng for lunch, we visited the beautiful old Santa Barbara Mission. Cecelia said that in her middle years she went through what I have been feeling lately. 'There came a time when I realized that when I walked into a room, nobody turned round any more,' she said. 'Everywhere I went I was one of the older people, I could no longer trade on my looks. By seventy all that evaporates and you've learned to live with the loss of youth. What replaces it can be the very best time of your life, providing you claim it for what it is. On this wildflower weekend I was the oldest by twenty years but felt absolutely an equal.'

Friendships, being out in the wilderness and travelling are the passions of her life. She feels close to God when she is close to nature and draws her inspiration and nourishment from the countryside. Peace, tranquillity and physical contact with the earth in her garden renew and revitalize her. At least three times a week she gets out into the hills to walk and several times a year she goes on really long treks. She has climbed Kilimanjaro and trekked to Everest Base Camp. I loved her rare zest for life and her genuine interest in the world around her.

It was hard to tear myself away and fly back to San Francisco. We vowed to keep in touch and, good as her word, the next time I saw Cecelia was when she and Don stopped off for a few days in London after three and a half months hiking to Hunza, a remote region in the Himalayas whose inhabitants are famous for their health and longevity. Cecelia had organized a small group to travel there, meeting and talking with some of the older people in the rural communities.

She looked fabulous, festooned with dangling Indian jewellery and wearing a pair of fashionable Parisian boots. She was alive with enthusiasm and laden with photographs of their campsite up above the clouds and the avalanche that nearly wiped them out. They'd made so many good friends. They'd felt such a connection to the culture. They'd revelled in the sunsets, the smells, the colour of the sky, the look of the people . . .

Not everyone has the means to travel abroad and live life to the hilt as Cecelia does but money is only a small part of the story. A lot of people with the means don't know how to live at all. Knowing her has made me determined never to take my health for granted. Looking after yourself is essential in order to enjoy an active and independent old age. Understanding your body - making informed choices about food, exercise, preventative medicine, mental health, spiritual growth and continued learning - is the way forward for those of us in the West who are having to start from scratch, reclaiming our identity, inventing a role for ourselves, getting out of the limbo into which we have fallen.

'Each moment is important,' said Cecelia, reinforcing the great lesson of my cancer. (Make life right now what it always ought to have been. There is no dress rehearsal. This is it.) She held both my hands. 'As older women we are a considerable force once we own our strength. We can use it by becoming teachers. Acknowledge that you have a sense of destiny, that you know who you are and have something to say. *Say* it! You may be a film-maker or a writer. You may want to stand on a box and shout about it, you may make a basket or weave a rug. At whatever level, be a teacher - an exemplar. Say, "I have done something worthwhile with my life and I count." '

CHAPTER FIVE

The Goddess of the Volcano

Civilization exists by geological consent
subject to change without notice.

WILL DURANT

By the time I reached Hawaii it felt as if the worst of my
withdrawal symptoms were over. I was feeling more
comfortable with the journey as a metaphor for the change
of life and less inclined to yearn for the warmth and
reassurance of what I know. The Buddhists teach that the
nature of life is impermanence and that all our suffering
comes from our stubborn refusal to accept this irrefutable
fact. Impermanence is our greatest fear, yet change is the only
thing we can be sure of; and the most sensible attitude
towards something inevitable is recognition and acceptance.
Everything is constantly changing or dying - nothing stays the
same and we can't pin anything down. Anguish and
disappointment are bound to follow when we fall into the trap
of believing things to be permanent and solid. In those
moments when I trust enough to be able to let go,
paradoxically there is no separation - just freedom and even,
dare I say it, enlightenment or at least a sort of clarity.

I get glimpses of this truth from time to time but old habits
die hard and the instinct to cling on is hard to break. Loving
your children well is about giving them warmly to the world.
Growing old well is about letting go of youth and accepting

whatever comes next. THE NATURE OF LIFE IS CHANGE. The nature of growth is change.

I had reserved a room in the home of Kapua, an eighty-year-old Hawaiian woman who does bed and breakfast accommodation. She had written back in wavery script in answer to my letter: 'There are a few of us old-timers left and I guess I could introduce you to some.' She was out when I got there and I found a note on her door telling me to come in and make myself at home. Kapua's house is one of the oldest in Hilo. Few were left standing after the last tidal wave. It is a lovely old wooden place with a shady porch and a big garden going down to the ocean. Frangipani blooms had drifted onto the lawn and sprays of wild orchids hung from every tree. Oranges and bananas, hibiscus and lilies jostled with the lush green foliage plants and little chubby bantams with feathery trousers on strutted about as if they owned the place.

Hawaii instantly overwhelms the senses. 'It was a dream, a rapture, this maze of colour and form, this entangled luxuriance, this bewildering beauty . . .' wrote Isabella Bird in *The Hawaiian Archipelago: Six Months in the Sandwich Islands* (the original name Captain Cook gave to the islands). I was so thankful that fate had brought me to the Big Island of Hawaii which is also the least visited by tourists - my brief encounter with the horrors of Honolulu just made me want to run away.

Quite by chance I arrived in Hilo on the first day of the annual three-day inter-island hula festival. This is where you see the very best dancing and it is all dedicated to Pele, the fiery Goddess of the volcano, who dominates this land of flames and blooms, the most seismically active region on earth. Pele is both adored and feared - ancient emotions still pulsate under the prevailing veneer of Christianity and American cultural influence.

For the most part, Pele lives quietly, high up in the mountainous interior of the island. When she wishes to bathe, she rises from her home in the Kilauea crater and rushes headlong into the cool waters of the sea, consuming everything in her path in a tide of molten stone and liquid fire. The miracle of boiling rocks gradually being transformed into fertile land is continually enacted on Pele's island, for she has the ability to create the earth - and to destroy it. When she stamps her foot the ground shakes and splits apart. She calls forth the lava, the lifeblood of the mountain and rides on its wave. In her fire form she devours everything. Pele is a living presence. Most locals have a story to tell about her. She is often seen before a big eruption as either a strange, beautiful woman with a white dog or as an old crone asking for help along the wayside. Many times photographers have inadvertently captured her image in the lava flow.

The other couple staying in Kapua's house told me it was impossible to get tickets for the hula festival. They sell out six months in advance but you can sometimes get one from a tout outside. I thought I might as well take a chance. I walked up to the gate saying ruefully that I didn't have a ticket and luck was on my side. The ticket guy just happened to have one somebody had returned. He sold it to me at face value. Three bucks, and I was in! I found a little corner with good visibility next to four old sisters (all grandmothers) who could explain to me what was going on. Real aficionados, they leave their husbands and come together every year from their island of Maui to indulge their passion.

This was the night of the solo Miss Hula contest. Before coming here I had no idea of the deep spiritual and patriotic significance of the hula. It represents the mystical union between (wo)man and the universe. It is about harmony, beauty and transcendence. It suffered a lot from the missionaries who clothed it and tried to rid it of its subtle sexual innuendo and from tourism which saw it merely as a spectacle and made no attempt to understand the profounder aspects. The hula chants and dances are the medium through which the oral history is encoded and passed on.

Traditionally, the temple priests, the *kahuna*, controlled and taught the hula. When the old Hawaiian religion was wiped out by the missionaries and the oral tradition was succeeded by literacy, there was no longer much of a role for hula. Temples were destroyed, the kahuna driven underground. All this was only about 170 years ago. Then a famous and beloved king - Kalakaua - ascended the throne and bestowed his patronage on hula as a symbol and expression of Hawaiian identity.

My four old ladies kept up a running commentary in my ear. It is also important, they said, to differentiate between those who just learn the dance steps and those who know the language and the culture for which the dances are *the* means of communication. Of one famous interpreter, an old woman who danced almost until the day she died, it was said: 'When Iolani dances you feel thousands of years of ancestors concentrated in this one body. She dances for her goddess and the goddess dances through her.'

Anyone can teach hula but only a *kumu hula* - a true master - can keep the real thing alive. The kahuna who have laid low for 100 years are at last able to come out and teach what they know. Some of them have been trained in secret since early childhood. They are selected by some mysterious intuitive process by old kahunas, and given elaborate tattoos as badges of office which are only completed when their training is finished. One man is tattooed right down his leg. He is an expert in earth magic and the tattoo symbolizes his groundedness and rootedness in the earth. Another with the gift of things to do with the heart is tattooed across his chest and another with the gift of inner vision is tattooed across his eyes and face in a wide band.

It was foretold that the grandchildren of the conquerors might have ears with which to hear the ancient voices and it would become safe slowly to reveal some of the sacred knowledge. Not just safe but vital for the survival of the world. And it has come to pass that people all over the world are now ready to listen and are seeking to piece together a workable, sustainable relationship with nature and a life of spiritual purpose which is not domineering or rapacious.

Our precious environment is fragile and we, in our

arrogance, have all but destroyed it. Many thinkers are turning to other cultures for alternative views and insights. It is no accident that, as this journey has unfolded, I have found myself brought into contact, time after time, with ancient primary cultures who once lived in harmony with nature. There is so much gentle wisdom still alive and well.

Kapua, when I finally met her, was determined that I shouldn't miss anything. She was hugely forceful, as only an old lady used to getting her own way can be, and there was nothing for it but to let myself be organized. She had been honoured by being chosen queen of the festival parade and was to ride at the front on a golden palomino. In her party there would be ten horses wearing two flower leis each. Each one required about 150 blossoms to be threaded on dental floss so we sat on the porch in the shade and threaded away. Her grand-daughter, a lovely young woman named Christie, had been into the forest that morning and gathered three enormous sackfuls of purple and white crown flowers.

Christie fortunately had a spare ticket for the second and third nights of the hula contest: the ancient hula group section with accompanying chants, and the modern formation hula with ukulele and guitar music. People kill to get tickets for this. It was like arriving in London and being given a centre court seat for the men's finals at Wimbledon. This was purists' hula not tourists' hula. It was quite an endurance test to sit there three nights running but the full experience was what I had come for so I took a pillow and a bottle of water and joined the throng.

Hawaiians are *crazy* about the hula. Each opening sway is greeted by gales of applause and whoops of appreciation. Watching the audience was the best thing of all - everybody dressed to celebrate being Hawaiian in the most beautiful flower leis and muumuus of every colour: 'Strengthening ourselves, making our history', as the Master of Ceremonies said. It is a very special culture and the atmosphere at the stadium was electric. The Royal Family were there each night, near enough for me to touch, and their entrance was thrilling.

The haunting sound of the conch shells heralds the arrival of their procession and a man with a beautiful voice walks in front singing a wonderful chant, followed by the Princess and her retinue. The monarchy has been defunct for some time but there is now a strong movement to reinstate it and claim sovereignty – all part of the newly awakened national pride. The Hawaiian language, once outlawed, is now widely spoken and taught in kindergartens.

Hula is the symbol for all that is most passionately felt. It is the key to the Hawaiian identity. Age and size are no barrier to being a hula dancer and some of the kumu hulas are truly enormous. It was lovely to see fat and thin, equally graceful, being confident and acceptable. There is no standard shape. Several of the competing groups had grandmothers and grandfathers in them. One old man of seventy-six in a virility dance thrusted away like Tom Jones and got a standing ovation from the crowd.

Kapua was up at 6 am on the morning of the parade, baking fresh corn bread, making coffee and omelettes for her lodgers and yelling at me to hurry up if I wanted a lift. I sat in the sun and watched all the island teams prepare to ride in the parade in their costumes of jewel-like hummingbird colours. Kapua was being made up by her grand-daughter and looked so sweet and vulnerable all of a sudden. 'Don't make me look like a floozy!' she said. 'Hush, Nana,' said Christie.

All her grand-daughters were riding beside her on this important day and there was a palpable feeling of family love and unity. To mount the huge palomino, Kapua had to climb on a wall and jump on his back. She looked great and it was quite an inspiration to see the old matriarch surrounded by her beautiful grand-daughters and a couple of handsome sons dressed in white at the head of the parade. Later she told me she had felt the presence of her late husband around all day. 'He was just *there*,' she said, dabbing at her eyes, 'and I felt so proud.'

'That's why I put waterproof mascara on you, Nana,' said Christie.

I watched the parade go by and walked home. I was exhausted and dying to lie down but before long Kapua arrived back. 'Come on! I need a vodka and I don't like to drink alone!', she said, dragging me out to a party. The woman is eighty years old and has more energy than many people half her age. She started the bed and breakfast business about a year after becoming a widow. She loved her husband very much and losing him when she was seventy-two, after more than fifty years of marriage, was a terrible blow. A lot of women would have given up and gone downhill pretty quickly. Instead Kapua chose to enjoy her children and her grandchildren and now a whole crop of adorable great-grandchildren, and to be independent.

She was still up at midnight, and because there were extra guests in the house on account of the festival, she insisted that I sleep in her bed while she slept on the couch. Being around her made being fifty-one seem like being barely out of my teens.

'When you get old, I don't think you can go on living unless you feel you are not alone,' said Kapua one day when she sat still long enough to be reflective. 'God is with you, and so are the spirits of those who loved you but have gone on.' She was draping her husband's photograph with the lei she had worn in the parade. 'God is where you find Him, where you feel Him, in your heart, under a coconut tree, anywhere. You certainly don't have to be sitting in a pew. Once on a mountain, my horse fell through some undergrowth. It was my father who saved me. I heard his voice telling me what to do.' She looked out to sea. 'I feel my husband is right out there in the bay where we scattered his ashes. I always throw him the flower petals that I sweep off the lawn. I talk to him and to my parents all the time. They always seem to be around me. People you love who die don't go anywhere. They've just closed the door and you can't come in.

'I'm giving things away. Why hang onto them? As I get older I want to divest myself of material possessions. Let my grandchildren enjoy them like I did. The most important thing

I want to pass on to them is to remember what it is to be Hawaiian and to carry on the traditions. We are a generous, welcoming, friendly people. In fact our warm-hearted, giving nature was probably our downfall. Taking someone in and making them your own was a Hawaiian concept long before we'd ever heard of adoption.' Kapua has, in addition to her own children, a beloved adopted son in his fifties who comes by for breakfast every day.

Hula, she said, is just about all they have left. It is a metaphysical as well as a physical form. A student doesn't have to understand everything. Only what the kumu hula wants them to know. The more they do it the clearer the subtle aspects become. 'It encodes our history and also conveys messages about the present. It is the passion, the genealogy, the mythology, the love of the land, the mystery.' It is like a spell. If it is not done well - precisely, exactly - it will not work. Doing it right is the key to perpetuating Hawaiian culture. A hula dancer is in a state of oneness with nature. 'You can't pass on something that you don't feel,' she said. 'I keep in touch with the old folk - the *kupuna* - who feel the way I do; people who are in touch with who they are.'

The next day was bleak and wet. Low clouds hung over Hilo. Not a day to visit the volcanoes as I'd planned. Instead Kapua took me down to 'talk story' with the old timers at the club where they meet every day. Here is where I met the remarkable Eleanor Ahuna who used to be a craft teacher but suffered a stroke two years ago and is now paralysed down one side of her body and restricted to a wheelchair. However, as she says, 'I can talk, I can think, I can write and I'm still here.' Over the course of the next few days we talked a lot and she lent me the big old leather-bound ledgers in which she writes her thoughts.

The club, a government-backed initiative was the best I'd ever seen. All the older people who come participate directly in the decision-making process. It's a place for the people by the people, with a co-ordinator who listens to what they want. The average age is seventy-five, they come from a fairly small catchment area and have been friends and neighbours for most of their lives. A lot of them were strong, articulate community leaders in their time (like Eleanor) and retain all their old fire even though their bodies are frailer. They have weekly 'sharings' where everyone sits in a circle saying what's on their mind. They share their skills and teach each other what they know. They have monthly 'recognition days' when they honour anyone who has a birthday, play ukelele and dance for each other. These are deeply felt and serious offerings received with pleasure and given with love. They get emotional if they feel like it and kiss each other a lot. The money they receive from the government goes to buy craft materials and there is an interesting and varied programme of events, outings and interaction with schools.

Joining with them, being taught, by Auntie Annie, how to make exquisite flower leis, I found myself becoming deeply involved. You have to make them from the heart - the energy of love contributes immeasurably to their beauty. We used ti-leaves, split and dried, as the base and then wound on ferns, flowers and leaves with a piece of raffia. It was such an ancient and comfortable feeling to sit with the crones, weaving and spinning webs of beauty, companionship and mutual support.

After an initial reticence, the more we sat together the more people opened up and talked. I asked them what was the most important thing older women could do to pass on their knowledge and experience. 'Be a beacon of love,' said one, swaying her hips suggestively, 'and teach the young guys what it's all about!' They all laughed. 'Speak Hawaiian to the children,' answered another. 'The language is the key to our culture and our heritage.' In an oral tradition, if the language dies, it all dies. They tried to teach me a few words but as only twelve letters are used in the anglicized system of writing it - the five vowels and seven consonants, P, H, K, L, M, N and W - the different permutations all sounded the same to my ears. My attempts at saying the words caused a fair amount of merriment.

Auntie Helen (they all call each other Auntie), aged eighty-two, a very pretty old lady with a gardenia pinned in her piled-up white hair, came from the peaceful coastal village of Kalapana. It was completely wiped out by the 1990 lava flow. The home where she had lived her whole life was destroyed although there was enough warning to evacuate and no one was hurt. 'Man can never say what will happen.' She shrugged her shoulders philosophically. 'Only God knows. In Hawaii you learn that everything changes without warning. Living, as we do, so close to the unpredictable, we know that love and unity in the family are the only things that matter.'

Auntie Louise, aged eighty, a tiny delicate woman with Chinese features was crocheting an intricate tablecloth at the speed of light in spite of the painful rheumatoid arthritis that cripples her hands. She also conducts the kupuna choir and still makes hats. Louise gave birth to eight of her nine babies at home with just a midwife and her husband present. 'That's where family love starts,' she said. 'Having your babies at home. You feel the closeness of your husband and it makes a beautiful loving feeling. Hospitals are clinical and cold.

'I am a simple woman,' she smiled. 'My Hawaiian language and my family are the things that I love. I also like to be out in the sun planting things, working in the earth. I have to physically feel the soil, not wear gardening gloves, even though it makes my hands rough for crochet. Any Hawaiian knows that it is our place to care for nature – not just by work but by prayer. I *talk* to plants and I always ask before I pick anything or take anything, even a rock.'

Louise has twenty-eight grandchildren, twelve great-grandchildren and six great-great-grandchildren. 'All my children married *haole* [the Hawaiian word for outsider/white man/newcomer]. The Hawaiian blood has become very diluted. My grandchildren are of *now*.' She shrugged sadly. 'My greatest desire is for them to learn the Hawaiian language and to do the Lord's work upon this earth the best they know how. Love, respect and admiration are fundamental to the way we old Hawaiians view the world around us. *Aloha, 'aina,* we call it. "Love of the land." It is a way of life.'

The talk wasn't all serious. A raucous old kupuna with a yellow hibiscus flower behind her ear popped in for a few minutes. She was wearing jeans and a T-shirt bearing the legend 'Get some real excitement between your legs – ride a Harley Davidson'. When she learned I was writing about wise old women she said, 'Well don't ask me, I'm out of here. I'm only sweet seventy-six, the world is mine!' Everyone cackled. She used to be a counsellor for ex-offenders, she has twenty-one grandchildren and has been dating 'an old goat' since her husband died. She kissed everyone and left.

Auntie Rhea has had a brain operation and now her hands shake a little. She is cared for by her elderly husband. 'He is so kind and so wonderful,' she told me. 'I said to him, "I'm sorry, I'm good for nothing now," and he said, "You were plenty good before and I can wait!"' Rhea thinks the most important thing is teaching children to respect and love their parents as she was taught as a child. 'I find the children of today so selfish. If you ask them to wash the dishes, they wash only their own. They will fold their own clothes and leave the others on the washing line. We old Hawaiians always cared for each other and shared things. Now we are missing the real aloha. The kids learn the language but they're reciting it.' She banged her chest passionately. 'It's not coming from here. We need to return it to the heart.'

Aloha is an essential Hawaiian concept. It can mean 'hello', 'goodbye', 'welcome', 'until we meet again', 'soul', 'the love of God' and the 'spirit of place'.

Eleanor translated it is as *Alo* meaning 'to worship'; and *Ha*, meaning 'the breath of life'.

Many Hawaiian concepts are based on a belief in the interdependence of all things, the sentient nature of matter and the indwelling nature of spirit, so translations are often quite difficult. As Michael Kioni Dudley writes in his interesting book *Man Gods and Nature*:

> The effect of Descartes philosophy has been so pervasive that few Westerners today are willing to even entertain

the idea of a sentient cosmos . . . the ancient chants of the Hawaiians tell that we are related as family to all of the forms of nature from which we have descended. There is a kinship with nature which is not experienced by people who see a break between mankind and the species of nature which have preceded them in the evolutionary advance.

Eleanor offered me an example of the subtlety and complexity of the Hawaiian language and why it is so difficult to translate. It is not as specific as English but leaves much room for poetic interpretation.

This is her meditation on the concept *kapili*. 'The word itself says, "the closeness". The meaning of *ka* and *pili* is to meet together and to be firmly tight. Kapili is to hammer together at least two boards. It also means to fasten - it means to set up firmly as when building or putting up anything; to glue something to something else.

'But then reach out more. Let your mind tell you what else can be said about kapili - a contract, a promise, a covenant, something binding, your word. Your honour, integrity, honesty, truth. Kapili. Look further to the word *kohoia* which can mean either choice or no choice. Choice, that most wonderful, beautiful agency we daily enjoy as free spirits here on earth, as Americans, as God's children. Kapili follows every choice we make, good or bad. Kapili is consequence - the result of what has been chosen to be put together. It cannot be separated. Life is kohoia and kapili. For every step of our life there is a choice to be made. For every choice that we make there is a consequence - good or bad.

'Kohoia began before we came to earth followed by kapili - the sweet consequence of reaching out and upwards, a struggle of thoughts. Shall I or shall I not? The depths of kohoia is the enveloping darkness, the pain of decision, the difficulty of choice. Then kapili, the building, setting up, coming together, the closeness.

'Ah! The beauty of our language. Kapili - a lovely word. A

word to think about deeply. A parable by itself. A gift of wisdom.'

Coming from Eleanor, who acknowledges that her lifestyle more than likely contributed to her stroke, these words are brave and honest. She wrote poignantly in her journal:

> Time - how shall I use it? Life is for a lifetime but how long is a lifetime, *my* lifetime? . . . Use time wisely, it will not come your way again. Oh, thank Thee, Father. Now I know what your message is for me . . . to stay still. I never would have, I don't think, by myself, been so disciplined. How precious this great gift called 'time'. A time is given to us for all things - to be born, to grow, to learn, to know, to do, to not do, to come and to go, to live, to laugh, to cry, to die. That's how it is and I ask myself, what have I done with it? Have I given back enough love and sharing?
>
> I had sinned against my body and almost ate myself right out of life. Kohoia - I said 'Yes! I'll not eat sweets, fats, salt and all of those things causing higher pressure to life-giving blood' but I disobeyed. Kapili - I acknowledge and accept the consequences. So here I sit today and humbly obey. No ability to go on my own anywhere.'

Later she wrote:

> Bright light, though, sustains me always
> For thoughts flow down to me so
> There's no room in my temple for darkness
> I only need the energy to sit still
> and patiently colour these lines
> So others can view the heights
> and depths of God's light
> Kohoia and kapili . . .
>   Day and night, up and down, left and right,
> round and round, no way to run, the universe,

the stars, moon and earth . . . Life is an eternal
circle. Kapili follows kohoia as surely as night
follows day from Genesis to this minute . . .
Knowledge, great as it is, is not the ultimate gift
. . . wisdom is. So, our language, those melodious,
kind, mystical sounds speak volumes in one
word's connotations.

One of the perils of this research is getting bogged down in
personal recollections which really don't advance my quest
for wisdom and understanding. But, of course, I have no way
of knowing in advance and have to follow every lead just in
case. One morning was spent trapped with an amazingly
boring old lady who only wanted to boast about her son's
military career and how much money he now earns as a
property developer. I escaped when I decently could and went
back to spend more time with Eleanor. This time she talked
vividly about her mother who was a hula teacher and I felt
as if I could almost touch her. More than anything I am moved
by this continuity of ordinary, unpretentious, unremarkable
women passing down their skills, coping with all the everyday
demands of bringing up a family, distilling their love and their
wisdom into the practical actions of their daily lives.

'From my earliest memories I remember Mama teaching
hula,' Eleanor said. 'Making costumes, dyeing yards and yards
of cloth in boiling coloured water into rainbow hues for the
desired illusions. I am reminded of her when I hear certain
Hawaiian songs - the old hula tunes - and tears flow with
the memories, for I miss her. She loved her music and would
play slack-key guitar at night to lull us children to sleep. I think
of her working, happy, strong, sad, working, teaching, sharing,
sitting, thinking, worrying, walking, walking, walking,
working, caring, crying, coughing, working, caring, helping
. . . She used to cook on a little stove made out of a tin can,
burning guava wood, giving warmth to the home on a rainy
night. Dad was a stevedore and when he came home tired
and dirty Mama had a huge washtub ready for him.

'Mama cured her youngest baby's whooping cough by squeezing the juice of boiled sweet potato flowers into a spoon and feeding her. Gee whizz, I don't remember going to the doctor for any illness when I was a child. Mama did all of that, she knew her Hawaiian medicinal herbs - eucalyptus steam baths for a fever and so on.

'Mama taught me how to weave *lauhala* [pandanus leaves]. She knew how to make mats, bags, baskets, boxes, fans. She wove baby diaper bags and each summer we had a new sun hat. Talk about wall-to-wall carpeting! Mama wove the floor mats right up to the walls to fit the corners. She made our home warm and beautiful and comfortable. She made beautiful woven cushions - works of art - but she gave them away with love whenever anyone admired one. When I was seven or eight I made my first lauhala cushions. I was so proud of them but when someone came to visit and admired my little cushions, Mama gave them away. That was how you learned! Mama was a good teacher. She inspired me to do all I could.'

Since her stroke Eleanor has been teaching conversational Hawaiian at the Malia Puko O Kalani club to those who want to improve their language skills. 'I do my best to develop these lessons for all of us so we can learn together and recapture the essence, the pure essence of our culture and our heritage.' Eleanor Ahuna, a humble, thankful, spiritual person coping bravely with the limitations of her illness, writes every day, recording her memories, her poetry, her philosophy of life, trying to get up enough courage to go back to school and finish her degree. 'I am Hawaiian,' she says. 'A child of the land of Hawaii which has been and always will be a magical place. By our very make up and our very isolation in this great ocean we have kept close to our creator.' Ancient Hawaiians, she said, didn't have a system of land ownership, only custodianship which has made them easily abused and exploited. 'I have seen and continue to see so much of Hawaii lost to us native Hawaiians by those who come and express aloha for us but find our land so beautiful they must own it.'

'Aloha 'aina, a love of the land as well as the forces that created it, has been the Hawaiians' strength for more than 1500 years. The first Hawaiians worshipped nature. They saw its awesome forces manifested in a multiplicity of forms with divine powers. The storytellers chanted and the hula dancers danced these ancient tales, the exploits of the gods. This was the oral tradition - the creation myth, the genealogy, the history, their place in the universe. Forests, waterfalls, trees, springs, volcanoes - all had their indwelling spirits, ever-present and active. Behind all these beliefs was an innate sense of natural balance and order - positive/negative, yin/yang, life/death. A polarity of opposites.

It was a quiet, orderly society. When Cook first arrived in 1778 there were an estimated 300,000 native Hawaiians living in perfect harmony with their ecological surroundings. Within 100 years a scant 50,000 demoralized and dejected Hawaiians existed almost as wards of state. Today, although it has become more fashionable to claim to be Hawaiian, experts say that probably less than 1000 are pure blood. They were and still are a most loving, affectionate, welcoming people, which unfortunately, as Kapua says, probably contributed to their depletion. They enthusiastically cohabited with all visitors and were quickly decimated by the syphilis, gonorrhoea and other examples of Western civilization brought in by sailors.

When the great influx of festival visitors had gone home again and the island returned to normal, I was able to hire a little car for a few days. I was longing to visit the Volcanoes National Park after so much 'talk story' and sitting around but, again, it was black and stormy after a night of rain. I decided to chance it anyway and found to my delight that it was sunny up there, 3000 feet above sea level, with practically nobody else about. Hot steam vents made welcome little saunas in the cool, thin air. I felt very moved to be there on the steaming, hissing bluffs overlooking the rim of the crater - the home of Pele. I felt the warm breath of the Mother as she slept. How easy for her to shake us pesky fleas off! Last time she yawned and stretched, curtains of fire shot 2000 feet into the air and rivers of lava rolled down the mountain into the sea.

For the moment the violent eruptions had quietened down. All around, a roller-coaster of wrinkled lava was frozen in mid-flow, stopped in its tracks. Signs warned 'DANGER: TOXIC FUMES', and yet the cycle of regeneration and rebirth had already begun. In the unbelievably barren landscape tiny ferns had established themselves, grasses, a few delicate orchids. And everywhere the miraculous ohi'a tree with its fiery red flowers - Pele's own sacred tree, unique to Hawaii - is reclaiming the land after the wild and spectacular devastation of the last eruption. Death and renewal. Of all places on earth, this is one where you would develop a healthy respect and love for the goddess - for the powers of creation and destruction.

I drove down the Chain of Craters Road which drops to sea level again. It used to go all along the coast until two years ago when a massive 7-mile-wide flow poured down the cliffs and wiped out the road. So now the road stops dead, blocked by a fossilized liquorice cascade. I parked the car and talked to the Park Ranger in his little cabin. There was nobody else there. It would be about a two-hour hike across the lava, he said, to the site of Pele's temple which was left miraculously unharmed in the middle of the flow. There was no trail, just a few markers to keep you on course. The sun burned overhead and it was as hot as Hades. But I had to make my pilgrimage to Madame Pele's sacred site so I smothered myself in sunscreen and set off across the eerie wasteland.

A 7-mile-wide sea of lava surged in petrified waves, sometimes wrinkled like the skin of an old walrus, sometimes forged into chains or braided and coiled like the tarry ropes of an old sailing ship, sometimes streaming in wild strands like the wind-blown hair of a hula dancer.

Sticking up through the ocean of blackness, a skeleton of melted iron girders is all that is left of the town of Kalapana. Pele's little temple, which stood between the town and the sea, was in the path of this relentless river of destruction and yet when the molten lava reached the stone walls it parted, flowed around the sacred ground and joined up again on the other side, completing its path to the ocean. There it poured into the sea, boiling and steaming, to create several new acres of Hawaii as it cooled.

And here stood the temple - just a small fragile enclosure with a couple of palm trees and a prickly pear - a modern-day miracle every bit as awesome as the parting of the Red Sea. A few previous visitors had left flower leis or piled a few stones as offerings. I wished I had brought something. Instead, I self-consciously sang a couple of rather tuneless goddess chants, 'The Earth is our Mother, We Must Take Care of Her' and 'She Changes Everything She Touches and Everything She Touches Changes'.

The Park Ranger believes the lava will never enter the temple. Some people think it would be a good thing if it was destroyed because it was the site of the last human sacrifice to be performed on the island in 1820. But that was warlike man's misinterpretation of what the goddess wanted. Now she is demonstrating that tenderness and preservation can prevail. I saw a bee buzzing in the prickly pear tree. The triumph of life over death - that was the lesson.

It was a magical experience to be there all alone in the lengthening shadows of the late afternoon. I continued on to the newly created Black Sand Beach and stopped to walk through the uncanny Lava Tube - a perfectly formed tunnel made by an underground river of molten lava which subsided, leaving a tube big enough to drive a bus through. It is hidden in an enchanted rainforest of tree ferns and native Hawaiian birds right next to the blasted landscape of Devastation Trail. Everything depends on which way the wind blows and the lava flows.

A day of wonderment - to come face to face with the raw power of the forces of the natural world. 'The amount of lava thrown up by the eruption of '83 created enough material to pave an eight-lane highway twice round the world or equal in volume to 55,000 trucks of cement a day . . .' These are the sorts of statistics you read in the guidebooks but nothing prepares you for what you actually see on this frontier of life and death – islands appearing, mountains changing shape, seas boiling. The world being created.

I stayed the night on the other side of the island and decided to drive back the following day along the infamous Saddle Road. The car hire firms make you sign a waiver voiding your insurance if you drive along this road as it has a terrible reputation for accidents. In fact it was a perfectly good road and not dangerous at all. It cuts right across the middle of the island, high up, running between the peaks of Mauna Loa and Mauna Kea. New lava has flowed on top of old, giving the whole region an outer galaxy, pock-marked appearance with the cloud-shrouded tops of the twin volcanoes looming on either side. Sulphurous yellow dragon breath, smelling of rotten eggs, escapes from fissures in the rocks. The island rises from sea level to an incredibly dramatic 15,000 feet in half an hour. I didn't think I was nervous at all but when I got back to Hilo my knuckles were white and my neck and shoulders felt like concrete. No gas stations, no drinking water, no facilities. Who would put a gas station on the side of an active volcano anyway? In fact it is surprising that people calmly live here at all, poised as they are on the edge of existence. Kapua thinks it is only a matter of time before the mother of all lava flows heads directly for Hilo.

Who knows? In the meantime, is it not possible, as Michael Kioni Dudley asks, that the old Hawaiians and their world view have a great deal to offer the modern world? With their aloha 'aina – their love of the land and their worship of the breath of life – they found out a long time ago about fulfilment and a sense of belonging, concepts which still elude Westerners who think they can buy them.

CHAPTER SIX

A Dream of Eden

So instead of
getting to Heaven at last
I'm going all along

EMILY DICKINSON

When I sat down to breakfast on my last morning in Hawaii, Kapua had made me a farewell lei out of frangipani flowers and laid it across the back of my chair. How different from my arrival only a few weeks before. I had felt quite sad and alone that day when I didn't know a soul and everybody else seemed to be draped and festooned with welcoming garlands. But now that I was leaving I would proudly bear the outward sign that somebody cared about me and would miss me. I love the whole concept of leis - *aloha* made tangible. Making one for somebody is a gift of love, a gift of time. Having one placed around your neck by a smiling friend is one of the sweetest sensations of tenderness and belonging imaginable.

When my parents sailed back from Australia with me as a baby, their ship called in at several of the South Pacific islands. The tradition, said my mother as she retold the story many times during my childhood, was to toss your farewell lei over the railings into the ocean as the liner left port. If it floated back to shore the visitor was destined to return someday. Theirs did, and, although they never came back themselves, here I was over fifty years later fulfilling the old prophecy.

Alas the age of ocean liners has passed. No more the cabin trunks, the seventeen pieces of leather luggage, the crocodile travelling shoes, the mahogany deckchairs, the evocative whiff of salt corrosion and diesel . . . I joined the scrum at the check-in where my nostalgic reverie was interrupted by the sight of a bullet-headed lad wearing loud baggy shorts and a T-shirt which proclaimed 'I may not be Hawaiian but I still enjoy a good lei.' Nonetheless my head was full of the romance of it all as I changed planes in Honolulu and settled down across three empty seats for the flight to Rarotonga.

With leis still on my mind, I was rummaging idly through my seat pocket and came across an article in the Hawaiian Airlines in-flight magazine about the 1991 Lei Day Queen. Leis, she told the interviewer, had been woven into her life since early childhood when she used to help her grandmother pick blossoms in the yard. A lei is never thrown away, she said. She might crush the flowers after they have died and mix them with berries to make a hula skirt. She might take a fading lei to her grandmother's grave. 'Always I try to take a bloom and use it again in a different way,' she said. 'It's my way of passing the love on. The giving of a lei lasts only a few seconds, it's message of love is eternal.' Her grandmother had also taught her about preserving the ancient Hawaiian respect for the land. She gives thanks for everything she picks and collects only mature blossoms rather than cleaning an area out. 'Always ask for the flowers,' she says. 'Don't just take them.' These are the little capsules in which wisdom is preserved.

Looking beautiful, with a crown of orchids in her hair, Dorice was waiting to meet me in Rarotonga at the most enchanting airport I had ever seen – picnic tables with big straw umbrellas by the side of the runway, a chap playing the ukelele and singing a welcome song in the arrivals building. It was tantalizing to hear the surf and know the sea was there but not to be able to see anything in the moonless night.

Dorice is a hereditary chief, or *mataiapo*, of the Cook Islands and, although not yet old enough to qualify as a crone herself, she had offered, when I met her in London, to introduce me to some of the elders on the island and invited me to stay in her house which is right on the beach. It was an offer I couldn't refuse.

All through that first night I dreamed it was raining. I didn't want to open my eyes in the morning for fear it would be another disappointing day but the sounds I could hear were just the gentle rustlings of the coconut palms outside my window and when I peeked out, there was the washing-powder white surf breaking on the coral reef, the still, clear turquoise lagoon, the white sand and the sun shining. Could I really open the back door, saunter past a couple of hibiscus bushes and walk in to the crystal waters? No other footprints but mine? Yes! It wasn't a mirage. I was doing it. I was actually doing it. I had always believed that one day I would find a way to return to the South Pacific as an adult and here I was. 'This is me in the South Sea Islands!' I shouted to the immensity before me as I stood on the shore, surprised at how loud my voice sounded on the empty beach.

Rarotonga is the archetypal fantasy island. In the centre, the razorback emerald mountains covered in dense jungle, all around the edge the frilly reef like a lei. What will the world do for an image of the beatific life when there are no more 'unspoilt' islands left? The fantasy has nothing to do with reality, of course. Polynesians were and are good and bad like the rest of us and they sometimes ate each other in the not-too-distant past, but somewhere in the collective unconscious the illusion of an oceanic Eden, an island paradise, a garden of abundance and innocence shimmers like something once known and still remembered. As I looked out towards the horizon, the sensation of recognition flickered like a fish beneath the surface of my mind and I felt like this had once been home.

'The Cook Islands are overwhelmingly, enthusiastically Christian and at no time is this more apparent than at a Sunday morning CICC church service.' I had read this in my guidebook so, after my ecstatic swim, I was glad of the chance to accompany Dorice to her local church. She, like most of the other women, dressed in white and wore one of the lovely wide-brimmed hats that the islands are famous for, laboriously woven from the bleached and pounded spine of the coconut leaf. I made do with my one rather crumpled skirt and a borrowed ordinary straw hat. The service, in Maori, didn't sound particularly inspiring. The vicar droned on disappointingly, fuzzily amplified by a poor public address system. People fidgeted and fanned themselves but just as I was wondering what was so special, the congregation burst into song and the effect was electrifying. A spirit of pure joy filled the room and poured out through the open windows like honey from the comb.

One old woman, Mama Moe, stood up and in a strong confident soprano threw down the opening phrase like a gauntlet. Then everyone else joined in, lifting their voices to the rafters, weaving strands of melody into complex patterns of counterpoint, improvising gorgeous polyphonic cathedrals of sound. Everybody sang: the women soaring above in flying buttresses, the men shoring up the structure with rich *basso profundo* load-bearing columns. No sheet music, no hymn books, no conductor, just a spontaneous, superb natural musicality which must pre-date by a long way the coming of Europeans and Christianity. Apparently when the missionaries arrived they simply put Christian words to the existing songs. The rhythms, harmonies and basic contrapuntal structure are pure Maori. I was spellbound. I knew that I wanted to meet Mama Moe.

In the late afternoon I walked up the road, past the little church, past a pen of pigs, past a *taro* plantation (the dense fibrous root that is the staple food of the islands), past Dorice's family land with its sacred stone *marae* or temple, to the little house on the beach where Mama Moe lives.

All around, the breadfruit that brought Captain Bligh to the Pacific hangs not in the loaves of childhood imagination but in the shape of spiky green footballs. Sadly, the beautiful indigenous dwellings, the open-walled, airy, thatched houses that used to be scattered about the islands in the dappled shade of the coconut groves, are practically non-existent these days. Missionaries insisted on gathering the people into more condensed settlements within reach of the tolling Sunday bells and now everyone lives in cement boxes which keep the heat in and the ocean breeze out. Mama was sitting inside by her open door stitching a colourful appliquéd quilt – a skill introduced by the missionaries' wives and made their own by the local women. She invited me to come in and brought orange juice to drink.

Mama Moe epitomizes the traditional Maori grandmother. Pure Cook Islander, born on the island of Aitutaki, she lived for a while in New Zealand where all Cook Islanders have citizenship and residency rights. But she never really liked it and is very happy to be home again.

In New Zealand the islanders find themselves at the bottom of the social pile where they struggle against poverty, inferior education, prejudiced attitudes and the way the 'good life' shimmers, tantalizingly, just out of reach. Mama Moe has raised six children and now looks after two of her nine grandchildren. The eldest she took when he was only a week old. It is the grandmother's prerogative to claim the first grandchild to bring up and this is rarely disputed. 'It's nice,' she said simply. 'I love the babies, it helps the parents, it stops me being lonely.' She once took the child to Australia to visit his parents and left him there for a while but had to come back to collect him as she missed him so terribly.

Mama Moe has been a widow for four years. Her husband was a farmer, a good, loving man, she says, who helped her, did a lot of the cooking, never argued, never hit the children. It's hard with him gone but one of her sons who is a chef at a hotel gives her money and she doesn't want for anything.

Mama is well known and well respected by everyone for her singing and for her skills as a traditional cook, making an *umu* or underground oven, and burying the food with hot stones. Her husband taught her to fish when they were young. She used to be afraid of slimy octopus tentacles sucking hold of her arm and dragging her down but now catching them is her speciality and she can make $4 a kilo selling them to the tourist hotels. Popping them in the freezer, she says, does away with the tedious task of bashing them on a rock to tenderize them. Then you boil them up, add onions and coconut sauce, and you have one of the island specialities. She goes out on the reef fishing whenever she can - line fishing, net fishing, poking about in holes for octopus, gathering shellfish and edible seaweed. She promised to take me with her one day.

Mama says to her grandchildren, 'Learn what I'm telling you while I'm still alive. Look after your life, stay home, learn the ways of your grandfather - planting, fishing - it's a good life to stay here. Don't leave your land, there's a living in the earth if you're not lazy.' She lamented the fact that so many of the young folk go abroad, never to return. Over the past couple of decades, 23,000 Cook Islanders have gone to live in New Zealand while only 17,000 remain on the islands.

This is the way things fall apart. In Cook Island tradition, for example, when an elderly woman dies, her grandchildren are called in to help bury her in the front garden. The villagers bring food and sing her praises. Upon her death, she will be wrapped in a comfortable cloth to be kissed, sung to, cuddled, massaged. Death is no reason to shun a person. Her family would not leave her alone, cold in the earth in some faraway burial ground. They will ease her into death. They will sleep next to her tomb for as long as they feel she might need the comfort. As time passes, her grandchildren will come to play on her grave as if it were her lap, the continuity unbroken. But what if the world has changed? 'The young don't grow up with their grandparents any more,' said Mama Moe. 'Sometimes they don't even know them. The respect isn't there so when they get old they put them in the sanatorium and that's the end.' And the fragile thread of tradition breaks.

Antony Alpers, in his book *Legends of the South Sea*, makes a beautiful point about the difficulty outsiders have in understanding the Polynesian concept of time. For example, old Polynesian epics and narrations never seem to have endings. Stories stand outside time, as we believe we understand it. That makes us uneasy. We can't see the point. We want a conclusion. According to Alpers:

> We like tick tock rather than tick tick . . . We need years, decades, eras for the reassuring sense of order they provide. In Polynesian storytelling the seasons play no part. They had no word for 'years'. Life just 'goes on' . . . Polynesians had never heard of tick tock until Captain Cook arrived with his chronometers and the whole sad ending was begun.

Mama Moe had been shy about meeting me initially, claiming she didn't speak English well enough and, it's true, we couldn't exchange philosophical ideas as such, but the timeless heart language flowed. She showed me the fine *pandanus* mats she had woven out of the leaves sent by relatives from another island. She sang me the opening phrase with which she had initiated the singing in the church that morning. Mama had always loved to sing ever since she was a little girl. She stood close to the old women who led the singing in her church and learned all the hymns. Now it is she who chooses what is to be sung. 'If you sing with your heart, you know the Holy Spirit will lead you,' she says. 'Sometimes when my voice is hoarse or my throat is rough I ask, "Please help me, give me strength, make my voice beautiful to sing for you," and it always comes.'

Mama Moe is first cousin to Dorice's mother but called Mama or Tutu (grandmother) by many who aren't even in her family. She has the *mana* of age without holding any elevated position such as chief. Mana, as Dorice was later to explain to me, is a complex cluster of ideas which includes personal, spiritual and supernatural power. It is a mixture of karma, charisma and the life force itself which flows from a great universal source.

This sense of a higher power flowing through all living things, a force which could be harnessed, was the basic concept underlying all religious thought in pre-Christian

Polynesia. Prayer consisted of planting a seed of thought and nourishing it daily with the gift of mana. Sad how the missionaries often failed to see that the existing symbols and metaphors, such as sowing and reaping, were so extraordinarily similar to their own. Their literal minds were unable to see another finger pointing to the moon or conceive the possibility of merging another path to enlightenment with their own. Christian colonization was total but although Cook Islanders today vehemently disclaim their pagan past, the concept of mana is alive and well.

Perhaps mana is what I am looking for - a mysterious substance with which to nourish my little seed prayers for wisdom and spiritual growth. Perhaps this is why I have come to the South Seas. A Pacific poet, Vaine Rasmussen, wrote this:

> . . . When I grew old they gave me . . . a legend and a song. And a language to master a dying culture I had lost in my search. And I grew up at last . . .

Avarua is the biggest town on Rarotonga and therefore in the Cook Islands - comparatively untouched by the destructive aspects of modern tourism. The pace is languid and no building is legally permitted to be taller than a coconut palm. It is a main street with a few shops, bars, cafés, a bank where I picked up some colourful money depicting a bare-breasted goddess riding on a shark, and a police station where I collected a Cook Islands Driving Licence (an international one will not do here) so I could hire a scooter.

I had been feeling overdressed in my sensible Rohan travelling clothes ever since I had arrived. The local style is a piece of tie-dyed gauze called a *pareu* knotted about the chest and a flower behind one ear. As little as £3.50 bought me a lovely one. A bloom from a handy hibiscus bush and I was all set. Absolutely the coolest, most comfortable apparel and flattering to all ages and figures. I felt pretty and feminine and the carapace of Western guardedness began to flake away. I went to the University of the Cook Islands Bookshop and bought two little volumes of poetry and took out temporary membership of the library in order to make use of their excellent Pacific section.

I plucked up the courage to rent a little motorbike. I had never ridden one before so the man gave me a lesson. ('This one brmmm brmmm, this one brake. OK?') I more or less got the hang of it and careered off home in bare feet to practise a bit before launching myself on the open road. It may not have been a Harley Davidson but I felt like pretty hot stuff on my Yamaha 50cc.

I remember when I was about fourteen years old, feeling buffeted by the contradictory currents of adolescence which both held me in the childhood I didn't want to relinquish and propelled me towards the freedoms and adult responsibilities I longed for. Middle age has many similarities – a backwards pull to whooping it up and a simultaneous yearning for the higher ground of wisdom and serenity. On my motorbike, I rode the tightrope.

It only takes about an hour to drive right around Rarotonga but I took my time and stopped along the way to daydream. At Black Rock, a jagged outcrop facing the place where the sun sets, I scanned the horizon. It is from here that the souls of the dead are said to depart for the homeward journey to Avaiki – the source. 'Where is Avaiki?' I asked Dorice later. 'Aha!' she answered, 'The $64,000 question.' Perhaps on the island of Raiatea near Tahiti. Legend has it that this is the place from which the original Polynesians sailed forth to explore the Pacific. Once upon a time, against enormous odds, courageous sailors and their womenfolk came here in a couple of canoes with dogs, pigs and plants. Why? How? Was it chance or did they know where to come?

On a map of the South Seas the Cooks appear as a sprinkling of tiny stars. Fifteen little islands (with a combined land mass smaller than that of Luxembourg) spread out over 850,000 square miles of ocean, halfway between Tahiti and Samoa. Unity would seem to be hard to achieve but they have strong ties and the 'coconut wireless' spreads news and information at the speed of rumour. What connects them to other Polynesians is the generous and benevolent mother, Moana Roa - the Pacific Ocean - and the ancient plaited rope of history that takes them back to a common ancestry, common gods. I sat on the shore and read *Island Boy* by Tom Davis, the ex-Prime Minister of the Cook Islands. It is the story of Polynesian navigation, boat-building and seamanship told by a Polynesian, himself a world-class sailor, who feels passionately that the real truth has been suppressed.

European history books and European anthropologists with their Eurocentric myopia, he maintains, have always assumed that the original inhabitants arrived here accidentally after having drifted aimlessly about the South Pacific. Not so. He believes they knew exactly where they were going and had a good idea of how to get there. The people would have been very familiar with the sea, with the tides and currents and weather patterns. Fishing expeditions would have taken them on long offshore adventures and, like the nomads of the desert, these nomads of the wind would have developed great skill in traversing huge, featureless expanses of ocean.

The marathon journeys, probably taken in order to reduce population pressures, would have been meticulously planned and skilfully carried out in well-designed, fast, seaworthy craft. Men and women travelled together, their skills complementing one another's. They brought livestock, tools, fire and plant seedlings. They navigated by the sun and by the stars and had invented a kind of sextant. Their huge ocean-going doubled-hulled sailing canoes were as sophisticated and manoeuvrable as anything ever built by Europeans. But this didn't fit in with the Western view of Polynesians as primitive savages and heathen cannibals who had to be civilized, so the evidence was deliberately overlooked, and biased accounts geared towards imperial supremacy replaced the true story of their breathtaking achievements.

Tom Davis' view is that Polynesians were the greatest sailors and navigators of the ancient world. Before the birth of Christ and long before the Vikings crossed the Atlantic, Polynesians were sailing across the largest, emptiest stretch of water on the globe. Nowhere else has one people occupied so great an area. Along with the tools and the fire, they also brought their mythology. They came from the legendary homeland of Avaiki – the source, the world below, the south lands, a darker place of origin. Not necessarily an actual geographical place but somewhere other than the upper world, the world of light, the world of being. Like the Dreamtime of the Australian Aborigines, it is their creation myth. When you hear the blazing polyphony of their singing it doesn't matter what the words say. The music comes from the source.

I contemplated the reef. On a calm day it foams and hums gently in the background but its presence is what keeps this tiny dot of land from being entirely submerged by the crushing power of the sea. And when the wind gets up, as it began to that afternoon, and the noise of the surf becomes more and more thunderous, the sense of vulnerability and insignificance becomes acute. When a cyclone passes by anywhere within 1000 miles, the waters surge over the living coral barrier and the benevolent lagoon arrives in your living-room like a furious monster. When a hurricane strikes – as it did not long ago – the devastation is almost total.

By the evening the coconut palms were doubled over and the noise of the wind howled through the louvres of Dorice's house. I walked alone along the beach with my pareu and my hair whipping about dramatically as I thought about the fragility of existence. I am a mere speck of life, a vital spark incarnate, existing in the universe by only the most incredible fluke and yet somehow part of the whole with a place in the scheme of things and a feeling of destiny. I felt close to the mystery. Einstein once said, 'The most beautiful thing we can experience is the mystery.' I feel that more and more. The sense of wonder carries us forward as it did in childhood. We are healed by what we turn towards, not what we turn from. Dorice thought I was mad to go out.

That night I lay in bed with the roaring, crashing reef and the screaming wind pounding in my ears. Nobody else seemed in the least perturbed. There is an assumption that the reef always has and always will keep the Pacific Ocean at arm's length but I am very conscious of perching on the rim of the crater of a submerged volcano in the middle of a million square miles of water. A tiny dot of earth, if earth these fairy rings of foaming coral can be called.

Everywhere on this journey I have been confronting the gulf between fantasy and reality, between how I want things to be and how they are. Here in paradise it is no different. Terrible things went on in these islands. In the late nineteenth century Peruvian slave ships raided the outer islands and the London Missionary Society turned a blind eye to the true nature of their activities, accepting $5 a head for helping to organize 'volunteers' - the proceeds going towards building their church. Robert Dean Frisbie, an American trader on Puka Puka, wrote in 1928:

> Clothes, clothes, clothes! The missionaries are obsessed by the thought of clothes . . . longer skirts, longer sleeves, higher necks for the women's dresses. 'Cover up the sinful body' is the text of most of their sermons.

All this has left a legacy of confusion - almost schizophrenia - in the minds of the Cook Islanders. I want to hear somebody say, 'We had a rich culture before we were brainwashed and made to feel ashamed of it.'

Dorice took me, one morning, to meet Her Excellency Mrs Maui Short, wife of the Queen's Representative here in the Cook Islands and one of the elders who Dorice most admires. She has fourteen children including two sets of twins and forty-nine grandchildren and great-grandchildren. Like Dorice, she is a hereditary chief and for twenty years was President of the Council of Chiefs, although her diplomatic role now precludes all others. As she is not confident speaking in English she wanted Dorice to be present throughout. We sat on her deep, cool verandah with embroidered cushions plumped on wicker chairs.

Our conversation began in a rather stilted way. Mama Short responded to each of my opening gambits with a short stock answer. She was grateful to her parents who were very hard on her as a child because it taught her the meaning of hard work. Yes, Cook Island women are strong. Nowadays the role of women is very powerful but along with the gains - better healthcare, better educational facilities - there have been losses. She lamented many of the disappearing traditions - supermarket vermicelli and tinned meat replacing freshly grown produce from one's own land. 'Everybody goes to work - nobody left to look after the garden. I don't want us to leave our food for *papa'a* [white man's] food but that is the modern way. A lot of sickness in quick ways of eating.'

She would like her children to learn the traditional ways. 'I like the old ways, no rush, no pressure, just stay home. Today you have to do this, do that, go to a meeting, go to the movies. Too fast! I knew how to look after my fourteen children. No babysitter like these days when somebody else take care of your child and you go enjoy yourself. Today you are changing a nappy and the phone rings - you have to leave the baby, come here, go there. Too much distractions. No time to put the child to sleep nicely.'

I felt Mama Short was trying hard to tell me what she thought I wanted to hear and was unaware of the irony that on the one hand she says the church is the most important thing in her life, and yet all the traditions she mourns have been destroyed by the collision between island culture and the influence of the missionaries.

When I suggested she might feel more comfortable speaking Maori and having Dorice translate, she was much more relaxed and forthcoming. As a tribal chief she is worried about the law courts' erosion of the traditional arbitrator role. 'Formerly, if there was a dispute in the district - marital or land related, for example - people would go to the paramount chief who was very knowledgeable about tribal law, ancestry and inheritance. A meeting would be called in the family marae or sacred temple ground and the matter sorted out.

Now people go to lawyers.'

Of course there is a basic conflict between a democratic system of government and the old autocratic tribal system but Mama Maui believes that they could coexist harmoniously if the chiefs were seen in the role of ombudsmen. 'When things are taken to courts and handled by lawyers who are outsiders, they argue the pros and cons without knowing the people involved. We have given our power away and once it's gone you never get it back.' Historically, the traditional chiefs had always controlled such situations at a family or tribal level and settled disputes without recourse to law books. Using their knowledge and wisdom they sorted things out on a personal basis. 'Rich and poor were treated equally,' said Mama Maui. 'Nowadays it costs a lot of money for our people to take a matter to court and those who can afford to hire lawyers will win the case.'

The Council of Chiefs at Takitumu (Dorice's and Mama Maui's district) is named after the pandanus tree. 'A strong tree with deep roots that grows by the sea and withstands adverse conditions,' said Mama Maui. 'A good symbol of what we are striving for.'

Maui Short has a stone temple in her garden. Her home is part of her marae. Her relatives are buried there. The marae and the tribal chief system are the last remaining things from a once proud culture. 'Our religion is Christian and many of our ways have become modern but this is our connection with our most ancient past. Today we are accused of believing in the old gods if we want to preserve our marae but I say "No". It is the link to our ancestors not to the gods they worshipped. It is the link to our land, to our ancient customs, to the sea, to our myths and our legends. If you don't have something like that in your life you don't know where you have come from.'

The islands, particularly Rarotonga, sit pretty much in the centre of the Polynesian triangle and have been the source of some of the most beautiful art - particularly sculpture - in the Pacific. It was here that classical Polynesian culture reached perfection. Alas, the devastation of the local population by foreign diseases meant that many arts and traditions withered away. Christian missionaries - with the best of intentions, of course - tore down the temples and burned the images of their gods but the spirits still lurk here and even the most upstanding of Christians acknowledge their presence. This fact is accepted and talked about but nobody asks how it fits in with the Church's teachings.

Mama told me this story: 'There is a female spirit that exists in our district. She has been seen at the river and at the bridge and at Black Rock. She is a restless spirit with long, red hair. She protects the traditions, she guards the marae and only shows herself when things occur in the district that go against the interests of Pa Ariki [the paramount chief who inherited the title from her mother]. The spirit likes things to be done in the right way.

'Not long ago she was seen on several occasions when surveyors were doing measurements for a road-widening scheme. This road was to pass through a marae. When the workers were asked to bulldoze a sacred rock, the very rock where she used to sit, they refused out of respect for the spirit but the European contractor, angered by these "superstitious" natives, ignored the warning and drove the bulldozer himself. The next morning he woke up with his face paralysed into a hideous twisted grimace.'

Many supernatural manifestations have been experienced here - a sacred tree, marked for cutting down, 'moved' by itself; a man's son became ill because he allowed his pig to root around in the marae. I find it curious that the so-called 'traditionalists' are such devout Christians when it was the Christians who destroyed so many of their traditions. Nobody seems bothered by the contradiction.

There are conundrums concerning the whole issue of tourism too. A great deal of controversy, for instance, surrounds the building of a 300-bed Sheraton hotel on land sold by one of the paramount chiefs against the wishes of the people. The reason tourists come to the Cook Islands in the

first place is because there is nothing to do. Unlike Tahiti and
Fiji, which are already ruined by discos and traffic jams, there
is no nightlife here, no TV. Yachties don't come here because
you can't sail in past the reef; there's one road that goes round
the island and that's that. You can hike in the mountains, swim
in the lagoon or lie in a hammock. It's wonderful. Nobody
locks their doors at night and people leave their car keys in
the ignition. The Cook Islanders themselves are friendly and
easy-going. Even more importantly, they are in the majority.
They own all the land. There are a few nice crafts to buy and
good places to eat so whoever comes here will leave their
dollars behind them. Whatever revenue comes in from
tourism stays in local pockets. The infrastructure is efficient
enough but amiably amateurish so that you feel like a visitor,
a traveller, rather than a portion-controlled unit.

Being the Marketing Manager for the Tourist Authority,
Dorice is understandably keen to attract as many tourists as
possible. She is also concerned that the growth in tourism
shouldn't exceed the ability of the people to cope with the
changes. 'Our people and our way of life *are* our national
treasures,' she has said. Her husband, Malcolm, who is English
and grows vegetables in his small market garden, loves it here
for all the above reasons. He would rather see the ladder
pulled up and the character of the place fiercely protected.

As an outsider, I'm inclined to agree with him. I hate being
a tourist. I want to be an insider, seeing 'the real thing'. I want
everyone else to stay home so that I can go travelling to
unspoilt places where I'll be sensitive and appreciative and
welcomed. But of course I am part of the rot and the real
thing hardly exists any more because we wiped it out. Take
the fate of the god Tangaroa for example. Missionaries
destroyed all the statues of Tangaroa proudly displaying his
knee-length manhood (except for the ones they pinched
which now live in the British Museum). For ages, poor old
local Tangaroas were neutered. Now the penis has been
reinstated, though not in its original role as a symbol of power
and virility but as a crude joke. In the souvenir shops you can

purchase repellent plastic replicas of Tangaroa with pop-up willies, Tangaroa bottle openers, Tangaroa keyrings. He's no longer a god, he's a prostitute.

It was the arrival of European sailing ships 150 years ago which began the inevitable destruction of these fragile homogenous cultures. Now the jumbo jets and cameras are finishing the job. Increasingly, tourism seems like a form of dreadful pollution. There's practically nowhere left that hasn't been damaged by its impact and I hate the fact that I am a part of it. The dilemma is that the tourism industry is the source of most employment on the island. Without it an even greater percentage of the population would go away forever to New Zealand. They are damned with it and damned without it.

Dorice respects and admires Maui Short. 'People like her are the keepers of the ancient traditions. I look up to her. She knows how to be fair, how to be persuasive and how to speak straight. She can interpret the signs. She knows the history and remembers the stories told to her by the old chiefs before her. She knows the correct way of doing things. I am learning from her so that I, too, can pass it on to the next generation when it's my turn. Old women can best use their influence by keeping the culture alive. It is people like her who hold together the traditional chiefs, and ensure that the mana is not eroded by other influences. It takes an older person to know what all these subtleties are.'

Mama had prepared a wonderful feast for us, with all the traditional delicacies I had come to like so much: marinaded raw fish in lime juice, baked mashed plantains with arrowroot and coconut cream, roast chicken, sweet potatoes and vegetables. We were totally stuffed and feeling merry. The question I came away with was: 'How can we help the "differentness" in different societies to withstand the intrusions?' I don't know the answer but the sharing and goodwill between us as older women felt so lovely and so important. The last thing I would want is for my presence to contribute to the erosion.

The furious wind had died down and the weather had turned very humid and sticky. On a hot, still, overcast day I walked along the beach at low tide watching the small figures of fishermen out on the reef. Illusions and images formed and reformed in my mind. In the end things are what we imagine them to be. Reality is clouded by our search for paradise – both an actual perfect place and a mutual perfect love, a mythical centre, a haven over the horizon where the heart finds meaning and clarity and contentment. I was yearning so deeply for this place to be perfect that I was in danger of inventing it. Just then, out on the lagoon, an outrigger canoe full of children paddled by. It was the definitive Cook Island image that I wanted to take away with me. Little slippery bodies with sleek, wet hair laughing and splashing. A dog in the prow, a fishing line dangling, their radiant smiles as they waved. My first thought was 'Where's my camera?!' But then I said to myself, 'No. Just remember this. Don't try to trap it. It's yours and no one can ever take it away.' Perhaps some things should remain only as fleeting visions.

Dorice had been busy all day helping her neighbour Paddy prepare for a party. In a small place like this it doesn't take long to get to know the social scene – ex-pats, diplomats, artists, the lawyer, the boutique owner, the local Don Juan. It was a nice party but I had an overwhelming feeling of being tantalizingly just out of reach of the 'real' Polynesia. Somewhere out there is my fantasy island life. I don't know what it is – it may not exist. It may never have existed. Probably Mama Moe, with her singing and her quilting and her octopus-catching out on the reef, comes closest to that image.

Tropical rain drummed all night on the corrugated roof and on the banana leaves – perfect sound effects for a scene of rapturous passion and steamy embraces. But I was alone. A curtain of water streamed from the eaves of the verandah, enveloping me in a membrane of melancholy. In the morning the sky was gunmetal grey, the sea a peridot green. Hundreds of delirious squawking birds had invaded the garden and were enjoying the rainwater pools and fat worms on the lawn. It was low tide and the reef rocks stuck up menacingly. There was hardly a ruffle of surf in the still air, the only sound a drip, dripping from all the trees. Another Sunday and I decided to go to church again. I had loved the singing so much I wanted to hear it again. At the door a beautiful child pinned a spray of flowers on my dress and kissed me 'because it's Mother's Day'. Mother's Day and so far from all my babies! I felt even lonelier. A rush of tears filled my eyes and I sat in the pew thinking about love.

This is part of the challenge of my long journey. All the people I love are on the other side of the world. I might never see them again. Can I really cope with the fact of impermanence? Can I just rest lightly in the as-it-is-ness of life? Allowing myself to be warmed and filled with the richness of love without needing to possess and hold on. I want to but it is so hard to let go.

A row of Brownies filed in to the church. Exquisite slender little girls with bare feet and brown legs who wriggled and squirmed throughout the droning sermon. I missed the bodies of my long-gone faraway children – the physicality. Getting older is so arid. Touch-starved, we shrivel and shrink. We become more vulnerable to disease. I yearned to fill my arms and couldn't take my eyes off them in their Brownie uniforms with big straw hats several times too large for them. Another photograph I didn't take.

All through the church service the rain thundered on the roof. It hissed and steamed through the open door. It completely drowned out the minister who was so uninspiring he deserved to be drowned out. (Why are church services so awful?) But then the singing began and the noise of the rain didn't stand a chance. I closed my eyes and was transported. The whole church reverberated like a struck tuning fork. If I were God, I would tune in to the Cook Islands every Sunday. The sweetness of the harmonies opened a direct line to heaven. I filled myself up with it. Like drinking from a mountain stream or smelling a rose, it was pure nourishment.

The knowledge came into my heart of hearts. 'Love is within me. It doesn't depend on the proximity of the love object. When I am alone I am not diminished.' As I felt the impact of those words in my innermost being, my melancholy mood lightened. I have always been afraid to be alone. If I am not somebody's mother, somebody's partner, somebody's daughter, somebody's healer, who am I? But, of course, I am all those things and always will be. Like the untaken photographs they remain part of the sum total of my life. When I am alone I am not diminished.

The rain stopped in time for me to walk home. Dorice and I had been invited by Paddy and her daughter to join them for a special Mother's Day lunch at the best hotel on the island. What I hadn't realized was what a big deal they make of Mother's Day here. It seemed as if every mother in Rarotonga was there to be honoured by her family. From the richest to the poorest, all dressed in flowing muumuus with leis (called *ei katu* in the Cook Islands) of gorgeous flowers in their hair. There was a great feast and a band but by far the most enjoyable thing was the presence of two tables full of venerable old ladies who had come on their own. Maybe their children had gone abroad, maybe they didn't have any, but they were there to have a good time and to celebrate the abstract quality of motherhood. They had a ukelele, a guitar and several bottles of sparkling wine. They set up in competition to the band and sang non-stop the most wonderful songs with inventive harmonies - just like the singing in the church only with saucy Maori words instead. They got merrier and more risqué as the afternoon wore on. Occasionally one elderly gran would spring to her feet and shake her hips in true Polynesian style to whoops of glee and applause from the others. Eventually the legitimate band acknowledged defeat and the old ladies became the centre of attention. They were still going strong when we left. Crone power *par excellence*.

Dorice and I called in to see Mama Maura, a traditional healer of much renown. She had agreed to meet me if Dorice would stay and interpret. Mama Maura, aged seventy-four, is a skinny little woman who lives in a little house by a paw paw plantation down an unpaved back road. She was resting on her bed when we arrived. The bed entirely fills the tiny cabin-like room and is piled high on three sides with all the quilts she has made. There is a torn curtain on a string and a shelf with a Bible and an ashtray. She was resting because she had already been to the 6 am and 10 am services at the church and was just about to go to the evening one. Mama lit up a dog end and coughed furiously until she'd managed to kick-start her lungs, then she settled back on her pillows. 'Nowhere in the Bible does it say you can't smoke,' she informed us, wheezing and gasping.

Mama Maura was born on Penrhyn, the most northerly of the northern group of the Cook Islands and the most remote. Her grandmother delivered babies and made medicines from local plants. The skills have been passed down through Mama Maura's mother to her, and she, in turn, is training a grand-daughter to carry on the tradition. Herbalism is a very ancient family craft stretching back through many generations to long before the coming of the missionaries. Once again no one talks about feeling connected in a spiritual or religious sense to anything pre-Christian. Everyone talks about Polynesian 'culture' and 'identity', which equates mostly with the arts, but there seems to be no interest in challenging the fundamental fact that a foreign faith supplanted their ancient one. Nobody says, 'Hey, wait a minute! We had some profound under-standings too. We had some beautiful metaphors, our creation myth is as valid as yours. Let's be selective.' What sticks in my throat is the wholesale swallowing of the package deal.

Mama Maura never calls herself a healer. The healing, she says, doesn't come from her. Rather it comes from the Divine Source. She never charges but would accept a gift after a person is healed. She began healing after a period of reading the Bible opened her up to becoming a channel. Most often she will have a powerful dream in which the right medicine for a particular ailment will be revealed to her. She also hears inner voices and has visions in which spirit messengers tell her things. She told us how the ghostly figure of a tall man had appeared in her doorway and foretold the death of the previous paramount chief.

Mama Maura has been party to many wonderful healings – a boy who was paralysed, another who was possessed . . . She helps people with whom the hospital can find nothing wrong and yet they are experiencing pain - particularly pregnant women and those with a condition they call 'fallen ovaries'. Mama massages them with special herbs. She makes many of her medicines from the ubiquitous coconut – the inner jelly of the unripe nut, the milk, the water. At one point I asked her if she had any medicine for women who were having a hard time going through the menopause. A blank look came over her face as Dorice translated my question. We tried again with different words. 'What did I mean "hard time"?' she answered, puzzled. 'Why would there be any problems? It's not an illness, it's just the end of the reproductive period.'

I sense that in this society women have no reason to fear growing old. Being fat, being wrinkled or being old does not detract from your attractiveness, sexuality or worth. 'Don't have any children of your own? Bring up one of your brother's.' This is what Mama Maura has done. A lovely plump little three-year-old boy with long black curls climbed onto her bed. She kissed him and stroked his hair and he toddled off again. The place is full of youngsters whom she calls her grandchildren but she never actually had any children herself. Her brother died quite young and she took in some of his children, bringing them up as her own. Watching this and the joyful way in which the old grandmothers celebrated Mother's Day made me conscious of how much we have lost in comparison with a way of life in which family and community ties were still so strong.

I told Mama that I also did healing and was very interested to know how she felt when she was doing it. She said she gets into the right frame of mind by praying and asking for inner guidance. She gets a tingling sensation in her hand (left for a man, right for a woman - often the tingling starts before the patient even turns up at her door) and the healing current feels just like a mild electric charge. She sometimes has a dream about a particular remedy to start preparing several days before the patient with the illness even comes to her. She opens her heart to love the person and the healing flows through. Mama is a deeply believing Christian and yet she feels traditional island spirits around helping her. 'Just presences,' she described them as. Sometimes she sees them but mostly she just senses them.

The ancient spirits of the land are alive and well, and like any earth spirits they will abide. They have never been in conflict with God. They *are* God in His/Her manifestation as love in the human heart. God is love and love heals. Pagan religions were about nature spirits and they understood about respecting and caring for the land and the creatures which give us food. They understood about balance and harmony. Tangaroa is only another name for God. The god of creation, the god of the sea, of fishing, of planting, of fertility. In order to call on a limitless source of power we merely have to align ourselves with it, place the magnifying glass in line with the sun.

Having heard that she was quite a specialist in the field, I told Mama that I suffered from repeated back trouble, a weakness in the lower back that came upon me almost without warning, and I hoped she might be able to suggest something. She knew just what to do, she said, and told me to come back the following day when she would make me some special medicine and give me a massage.

When I turned up at the appointed hour she had me sit on her bed, lean forward and hitch up my T-shirt. Then she proceeded to massage my lower back with pure coconut oil. Her hands were incredibly strong for someone so tiny. She kneaded and prodded with her bony little fingers and I could feel all the muscles relax. She really knew what she was doing and worked on all the little knotted up bits until they melted.

Then she presented me with a whole green coconut which she had taken the top off. The water inside had been mixed with the pounded up fruit of a medicinal tree. Mama said a prayer and gave it to me to drink. It didn't taste exactly unpleasant, rather like regurgitated grass - green and slightly bitter. But there was a large quantity - about a pint - and it was extremely quease-making to drink it all. The treatment was to be repeated every day for three days and on the fourth day the grand climax was to be a special laxative to clear out my system.

I confess I had never thought of chronic backache as being treatable internally but as more of a postural, skeletal imbalance, probably exacerbated by tension and being overweight. It crossed my mind that perhaps all Mama's patients got the same treatment whatever the complaint but I was willing to give it a go. The purgative was unlikely to do me any harm and coconut water is a substance of such purity and life-sustaining qualities that during the war it was used as an emergency intravenous drip. Mama Maura kissed me and hugged me, her little old crone face smiling so sweetly, a frangipani flower tucked into her silver hair. She lives in what, in an urban ghetto, would be considered terrible poverty - a concrete hovel with practically no furniture - but here on an island in the South Pacific, on her own piece of land with breadfruit, coconuts, mangoes, bananas, flowers, herbs, a few chickens and a houseful of 'grandchildren', she is rich. She sells a few hats and a few quilts. She is strong, confident, loved, loving, spiritually fulfilled and useful. I asked myself if we have lost the capacity to live such harmonious lives. No it's a *choice*. I can create, *invent* a powerful, effective old age for myself whatever my outward circumstances may be. The secret is an inward balance.

When I paid my third visit to Mama Maura the medicine was waiting for me on her kitchen table. She showed me the fruit that she had used for my brew - the knobbly, greenish-yellow fruit of the no-no tree with a hard, waxy skin like a prickly pear without the prickles. I had never seen one before.

This time the coconut was twice the size of the last one so there must have been nearly 2 pints of liquid which I could barely force down. She seemed to think it was a good thing that I'd had diarrhoea ever since my first dose. She beamed and nodded and lit another cigarette while her grand-daughter hacked the head off a large fish for supper. My confidence wavered a bit and questions such as 'What am I doing here drinking this disgusting stuff?' kept popping into my mind but I was determined to stick it out.

Ever since I first arrived I had been captivated by the island placenames: Rarotonga, Rakahanga, Manahiki, Aitutaki, Puka Puka. They sounded like the songs of exotic birds – cockatoos, parrots and birds of paradise calling from the treetops, beckoning me to the outer islands. The very words 'outer islands' are almost unbearably romantic so I paid a visit to the director of Air Rarotonga in the hope that I might be able to scrounge a ride. I was in luck! He had an extra flight going to Mauke with some VIPs the very next day and kindly offered me a seat.

Mauke is the most easterly of all the islands. Its original name was Akatokamanava – 'My heart is at rest and at peace'. According to legend, these were the first words uttered by Uke, the founder of the settlement here, when he arrived in the huge canoe Paipaimoana carrying 200 settlers from the distant homeland of Avaiki. I tried to imagine how it must have felt to have sighted land after such a perilous voyage.

Our little plane was carrying the High Commissioner for Canada and some local dignitaries to the dedication ceremony for a new airport terminal building, financed by Canada, to replace the old building which had blown down in Hurricane Sally. What nobody told me was that all 609 citizens of Mauke would be at the airstrip to meet us. Fantastic ei katu were put around our necks as we stepped from the plane and I was automatically included in the official party, as were two astonished tourists who happened to be there.

A huge feast had been prepared by the island ladies, and

teams of enchanting children danced for us in grass skirts. All the behatted matrons and grandmothers were out in force, dressed in their best, so I had plenty of opportunity to sit and talk. Everyone was friendly and the whole event was delightful. The new building was the size of a double garage with two loos and a space for a tiny gift shop. With great ceremony, the guesthouse landlady's crocheted table cloth specially lent for the occasion was tweaked away and a hand-painted board proclaiming 'MAUKE TERMINAL' was unveiled. The High Commissioner's wife cut the blue ribbon and everyone was thrilled.

We all piled into the back of a pick-up truck and swayed off up the road to the guesthouse owned by a relative of Dorice's - four little thatched huts on the beach, each with a bed, a mosquito coil and a light on a string. In the yard was a shower rigged up to a coconut tree. It was perfect, like a child's drawing of a desert island camp. The others wanted to rest but I was too excited. I asked if I could borrow a bicycle and one was found from a neighbour.

The bike was a terrible old bone-shaker with a seat designed to do you an injury. I set off pedalling in high spirits, stopped at a secluded cove, stripped off and had a dip. I was nervous about swimming because there was no lagoon. The island is a large pancake of coral which has been pushed up from the sea. The reef *is* the beach and the surf looked pretty fierce. If I were swept out to sea, no one would know. I wouldn't be missed for ages. They'd find my bike propped up against a tree . . . 'Twickenham housewife disappears in the South Pacific.' I dried off and continued on my way.

After cycling for over an hour I began to get a little anxious. The sun was still on the same side of me so I knew I wasn't even halfway round. My knees got stiffer, my bottom sorer. Too far to turn back, the sun was going down and there were no lights on the bike. I didn't pass a single person. Wild pigs ran through the jungly undergrowth, a herd of goats watched me from the shadows, insects swarmed in the gathering twilight, huge crabs crossed the road in front of me. Coconut crabs – those enormous crustaceans that scale coconut palms and break into the rock-hard nuts with their pincers!

I had stopped feeling like the bold adventurer long since and was thoroughly frightened. I had no idea it was so far. I only knew that if the island was roughly round I would have to come back to where I started eventually. Finally, after two and a half hours riding, I came to the little airstrip and recognized the road. The last mile took me past the dim yellow lights of villagers' homes at dusk. There is no broadcast television on Mauke but the videos sparkle like illuminated fish tanks in the corners of dark rooms – children glued to blurry ninjas and tenth-rate pirate copies of *Dirty Dancing*. Even here! I almost cried with relief when I reached my little hut.

I was desperately hot and thirsty and longing to collapse on my bed but I hadn't reckoned on the famous island hospitality – the most sacred of all traditions here. A guest is seen as an honour and a blessing which is why Cook Islanders are such marvellous hosts. If your home is a speck of land in the middle of hundreds of thousands of square miles of ocean the arrival of a visitor is a very special event and cause for celebration. And now that cannibalism is only a very distant memory, they don't eat you, they feed you! The church ladies had prepared yet another exceptional feast of all the traditional foods: octopus, taro, baked bananas, roast chicken, huge slabs of fresh tuna, sweet potatoes, roast meat, parrot fish in coconut cream, watermelons. They stood flicking the flies away and smiling with generous welcome as the visitors helped themselves.

Dorice's cousin, apart from running the guesthouse, is a farmer, owns the local shop and is the Chief Agricultural Officer. He is also a tribal chief. We sat on his long, cool verandah, while out on the lawn a group of women of all ages gathered to sing. This wasn't a performance so much as a spontaneous happening – that same lovely singing again. The women sat in a circle with some home-brew, a drum and a ukulele, enjoying the music and friendship. One old woman beckoned me over, patted the ground next to her and gestured for me to sit down. I joined in the clapping and swaying for a while until suddenly one of the young men who were standing about watching jumped out of the shadows, stood in front of me and began dancing like a maniac, knees going from side to side like the clappers. The old ladies laughed. 'He's asking you to dance.' So I leapt to my feet and went for it. They were delighted. 'Where you learn to dance Cook Island?' I said I just adored the music and their encouragement gave me heart.

Out at the new airport terminal building a dance had been arranged in honour of the High Commissioner. The ladies piled on the back of a lorry clutching their flower crowns and sped off ahead of us. A beautiful breeze was blowing in off the ocean and a full moon flooded the runway with ghostly silver light. The little terminal was throbbing with the beat and most of the population had turned out for the dance. The band played a mixture of slow 1940s high school prom tunes – 'Harbour Lights', 'Red Roses for Blue Lady', 'The Tennessee Waltz' – and up-tempo, hip-shaking, knee-waggling local songs. No one could sit still for a minute, least of all me. Slight shortage of men? Never mind. The women dance together. No partner? Doesn't matter. Dance on your own. Everyone asked me to dance, both men and women.

I got rid of my shoes, tied a pareu around my hips and for the next three hours had a ball. The fat old Minister of Agriculture soon lost his tie and jacket and looked much happier in a floral shirt with a flower behind his ear. The Speaker of the Cook Islands Parliament who is also the high school principal really cut loose and moved like a house on roller skates. Young guys came over and dragged me to my feet every time I sat down. We, in the West, have lost so much by surrendering all dancing to the young and to a disco setting. These mixed gatherings are so much fun and so natural. Nobody is left out. Even the grandparents well into their seventies were celebrating the sensuality of their bodies and enjoying the wonderful exercise. When the speaker made a little closing speech thanking the VIPs for coming he said, 'and a special mention for a certain Englishwoman who can dance like a local - you're welcome anytime!' I felt ridiculously proud. 'Twickenham housewife given island seal of approval.'

I could hardly move when I crashed into bed. I thought nothing could have kept me awake but, just as I closed my eyes, a really ferocious electrical storm arrived and shook the island like a dog with a rag doll in its teeth. Great jagged streaks of lightning sliced the sky and tropical rain fell in sheets on our little huts, making a wonderful shooshing sound on the woven coconut roofs. The storm lasted for hours and it was impossible to sleep. Running across the yard to the outside loo at 4 in the morning was quite an experience and I hoped my mother was right about not getting struck by lightning if you wear rubber-soled shoes. I was so tired from riding that rattle-trap bike right round the island and from dancing myself silly at the airport, but with the tempest outside and the drum rhythms still echoing in my brain my body was too hyped up to relax. I finally fell asleep at first light.

I had only twenty-four hours on Mauke and I wanted to see as much as I could. I visited the work in progress on the great Mauke canoe being built for the forthcoming Festival of the Pacific. Each island is building one and at the start of the festival they will all be sailed in to the harbour on Rarotonga through the natural opening in the reef where the first canoes arrived from Avaiki. I wished I could be there. It would surely be a magnificent sight. The Mauke canoe is a huge, double-hulled sea-faring catamaran made from three enormous mahogany trees by master craftsmen using only traditional methods. It is all lashed together with plaited coconut-fibre ropes made by the schoolchildren. The whole community is involved in the building. The last great Mauke canoe was built in the 1940s and it is still talked about. No one who has had a hand in this spectacular project will ever forget it. A carved bird's head with pearl shell eyes is at the prow of each hull and carved tail feathers adorn each stern. The children who see it launched and sailed out to sea will always feel proud of their island heritage.

Sitting in her yard among the rituals of a quiet day was Mama Talui, a grandmother who earns a few dollars making pandanus leaf skirts for dance costumes. I had seen her the day before at the dedication ceremony and she was the one who had invited me to join in the sweet music-making on the grass. She waved and I went over and sat for a while, helping her roll and flatten the leaves. Mama Talui told me that she loves her island home but she is lonely because her six children have all gone away. Mechanized travel has altered the pattern of life as surely here as anywhere and because the distances are great and the air fares expensive, once gone it may be years before your children return - if ever. Only three generations ago the only way in or out of these islands was by canoe, hand-carved from a mahogany tree trunk. The old life has gone, swept away by the relentless winds of change, just as the airport building had been blown away by Hurricane Sally. No use regretting it but I couldn't help feeling sad.

Later that evening we flew away from Mauke in the little Air Rarotonga plane, each of us draped in enough flowers to open a shop - exquisite eis that the Maukians are famous for, made of pandanus fruits, single gardenias, flame tree blooms and yellow chrysanthemums. I felt like Titania from *Midsummer Night's Dream* with two garlands around my neck and another on my head. Each one would have taken ages to make and would have been done, not for profit, but just for its own sake. This is an art form so transitory it only lasts a day - just to say 'be safe, come back, you are loved'.

We flew west to Aitutaki into the setting sun. This is the picture you see in all the travel brochures - a big, wonderful lagoon like Peter Pan's Never Never Land, with a couple of flat, sandy islands surrounded by a rim of surf. The sky was aflame as we landed, impossibly, on a microdot of land on the rim of the crater of a submerged volcano. Just a brief stop to drop off a couple of passengers but breathtaking to have seen it from the air at sunset. Finally, back to Rarotonga which suddenly seemed like a bustling metropolis by contrast. No wonder people from the outer islands find it 'too fast'.

'Outer islands' – those magic words. One day I will come back here, I said to myself, and go to all of them by boat, and . . . even as I formulated those thoughts, I knew that the only way to keep the dream unsullied would be to lock it in my heart with the untaken photographs and not try to catch it or repeat it.

On the day I went over for my final visit to Mama Maura, she was sitting on her kitchen floor with a fag in her mouth stitching a yellow and purple appliquéd quilt, bony fingers flying while she watched *Death Wish II* on the video. My medicine was already prepared and waiting on the table. First I was to drink quarter of a tumbler full of pure coconut oil. I made a face. 'Then you eat this,' she said, handing me a pint-sized yoghurt carton filled with snot, or maybe squid entrails. At least, that's what it looked like. 'Dear God! What is it?' I quailed, surveying the grey slime with horror. Teach me to dabble with native medicines! Mama laughed, the grand-daughter laughed, the baby laughed. 'Taste it, it's good,' she urged. I stuck my finger in it tentatively. It was sweet and not nearly as terrible as it looked. 'Green coconut cooked with arrowroot powder and raw brown sugar and mixed with coconut oil,' said Mama, smiling encouragingly. I was to eat as much of it as caused me to have a good clear out. Mama offered a prayer in Maori of which the only words I recognized were 'good shit'. I managed to force down about half of it and felt things were definitely on the move. I gave Mama my red silk scarf from England not knowing quite what sort of gift would be appropriate but she seemed very happy with it and we kissed each other goodbye. I wasn't able to talk with her much but I had a sense of her strength, her knowledge and her usefulness in the community. I also have to say that until this day I haven't had any further trouble with my back!

CHAPTER SEVEN

The Emu in the Night Sky

Where is the Life we have lost in living?
Where is the wisdom we have lost in knowledge?
Where is the knowledge we have lost in information?

T.S. ELIOT, 'The Rock', 1

The person I became closest to during my time in the Cook
Islands was Dorice's neighbour and adopted mother, Paddy.
We swam together most days and some of our loveliest
conversations took place treading water or floating on our
backs side by side in the lagoon where it somehow seemed
easier to exchange the confidences of two grandmothers
trying to come to terms with ageing. We wrestled with the
questions: How can older women best find a role for
themselves? How can they give expression to the power, the
knowledge and the wisdom they have accrued in a lifetime?

Paddy declines to talk about her age, not because of coyness
but because of other people's tendency to make assumptions.
Suffice to say that she is a beautiful, graceful woman with
golden skin and soft hair the colour of moonlight. It is hard
to believe she has a son in his fifties. Paddy is the epitome
of a Pacific woman. Born and raised in Samoa of a Samoan
mother and a New Zealand father, she is the product of two
cultures - Polynesian and European. She brought up her own
children in New Zealand and lived and worked there until
her husband died in 1988 when she came here to Rarotonga.

'I knew when I left New Zealand that I was in search of spiritual growth,' she told me, 'but I wasn't quite sure what that meant. I just knew I had to leave behind the life I had lived which always seemed so busy. Forever *doing* instead of being. I thought I would be relieved when my husband died – relieved for him that his suffering was over after eight years of appalling illness and relieved for me that I would no longer be tied to looking after him. But his death left a deep, deep wound. I was totally numb, confused and without direction. Everything I'd ever done before seemed to hold no interest for me any more.'

After a year, when the worst of the grieving had run its course, Paddy stopped off here on her way back from a holiday in Tahiti. 'Coming to live in Rarotonga had never entered my mind,' she said. 'All I knew was that I wanted a change. I wanted to be able to reach myself. I wanted to understand better how I could reach God. I felt a terrible emptiness – no sense of fulfilment or upliftment and church didn't do it for me. But I found myself here and on that first day as I looked out at the foaming reef and the turquoise sea and the soft breezes blowing the trees, suddenly, on the right side of my head, came the words, "This is it!" I felt very quiet about it as if it were a secret. Two days later I was walking along the beach and came upon someone building a little house. I heard myself saying "Will you let it to me?" '

Paddy had been a City Counsellor in Auckland. She had helped to establish the Pacific Island Youth Leadership Trust which sponsors island students to go to university. She had started an organization called Pacifica, with the objective of giving a voice to island women like herself who had migrated to New Zealand from places such as Samoa, Tonga, Fiji, Tahiti, Papua New Guinea and the Cook Islands. Strong, interesting women with much to offer but no confidence due to lack of formal education. 'I became a professional persuader,' laughed Paddy.

In Rarotonga word soon got around and her talents were pressed into service. Paddy was invited to give a paper in

Thailand at the International Conference of the Pan-Pacific South-East Asia Women's Association. She spoke on the subject of culture as a catalyst for change and creativity. 'I came back really buoyed up,' she said, 'and I became involved.' Now as president of the local branch she sees herself in a nurturing role appropriate to her advancing years. 'We are embracing women and pooling resources from all backgrounds. The international character of the organization is important. It is a vast network of cooperation, a link into the world. We don't feel marginal. Although we are small we have a part to play in something much bigger – not just so-called "women's issues" but peace, disarmament, nuclear testing in the Pacific, environmental concerns. We are trying to bring the wisdoms from the past to our vision for the future and to hold on to the worth of the unique contribution we can make.'

Paddy's move to the island has brought into sharp focus her own need to reconcile the contrasting and sometimes conflicting strands of her own cultural inheritance – the dreamy, mystical, artistic Polynesian side and the dynamic, linear, energetic English side. Learning to feel at ease with the contradictions in her own nature is, as she sees it, one of the tasks of ageing. 'I voraciously read the history of the Pacific, the history of the Cook Islands,' she said. 'I became more and more clearly the Pacific part of me. I am the result of colonialism and I certainly don't wish to disown my European side. I was lucky to have a British education. It gave me the opportunity to be literate. My English grandfather encouraged me to write but my imagination is my Pacific inheritance. Music, movement and the spoken word I see as everything to do with my Samoan side.'

In an attempt to find ways to stimulate cultural pride in schools, Paddy has recently devised a stunningly simple language-based educational programme using song, drawing, mime and the Maori art of dramatic storytelling to bring out the best in children with limited literacy skills. It is a way of using their own traditional legends as a gateway to learning

- to listening, questioning, communicating. She calls this 'The Thinking Child' and it has already been enthusiastically received by primary school teachers throughout the islands.

Paddy has also fulfilled a long-held dream and written the score for a musical based on the paintings of Gauguin. It is called *Where have we come from? Who are we? And where are we going?* and is to be performed at the festival.

Older Pacific women, says Paddy, have always been treated with a great deal of respect so this is as good a place as you could find to grow old in. 'The plusses of ageing are the increased courage to be yourself, feeling that you don't have to be what other people want you to be. I also think I can talk to God much more clearly. Being here, close to nature, that relationship has become more profound, more real. I've learned to be very still, to be very meditative and to read the teachings without feeling that I have to join any particular religion. I pray to the mystery, to the creator. I have an increasingly strong sense of the power of the universe and that we are conduits for that power when we open ourselves. Anyone can channel the teachings. You don't have to conform. You can develop the courage to stand alone. What do you have to lose?'

But getting older is not without its pain. 'I am still frightened at night. I feel very vulnerable, particularly when we have storms and the wind howls and the sea comes surging up. I am far from my children. I miss my grandchildren and I don't have a man in my life. Most of the time that doesn't worry me - or perhaps I choose not to face it - but the truth is that the loss of sex, of touch, of tenderness is a great sadness. To have someone to hold you, to tell you they love you - that's so precious. And, yes, I miss it although this is quite a "touchy" place. Pacific island people hug each other and kiss each other quite naturally so perhaps it is less acute here than in some other parts of the world. Maybe, as one develops a stronger and stronger spiritual relationship with one's concept of God, the human contacts become less significant.'

In my own quest on this journey I have been constantly asking myself, 'What sort of old woman do I want to be?' I asked Paddy the same question. 'The words grace, dignity and beauty have always been important to me,' she answered. 'I value those things and the sense that my mother gave me of my Samoan-ness. I have a concept of 'bigness' that I would like to achieve; big as opposed to petty, generous from the inside, generous of heart. I am learning to be patient but there are a lot of things still to be learnt and lots of backsliding. You have to be very careful when you are older not to be judgemental. I am trying to be a better person. A kinder, nicer, more tolerant person. I don't want to be just a bit of absorbent blotting paper, however, but to have the wisdom to know the right things to say so that my words will be a comfort to people. Every morning I ask God to see that not only my feet go in the right direction but my mouth, my words.'

The Cook Islands is a good place for feeling in harmony. The first time I heard the sublime singing in the church I had the sense that these people were 'in tune' with each other. Six years ago Paddy came very near to death when she underwent major surgery for cancer. Even the doctor prayed for a miracle. 'It was very humbling,' she remembers, 'the agony, the mess, the terribleness, being totally dependent on other people. That whole experience had a great deal to do with my need to change and this gentle place makes it all possible. The simplicity and tranquillity of my life here gives me a sense of harmony and connectedness. Being connected both forwards and backwards in time, both up and down to heaven and earth, and heart to heart to all other beings. As I see it, this is the only way to avoid the *fear* of ageing. If you're growing outwards there's no room for fear because you're expanding into whatever comes next, you're welcoming the change rather than trying to hang on to the past.'

She's right. This business of letting go has to be confronted every minute of one's life: children growing up, relationships ending, death, loss, one's looks, one's health. Gradually everything will go from you until you die. This is a fact of life. Learning to be with what *is* is the only choice we have, and in the meantime we can love.

On my last morning I did my t'ai-chi as usual at the edge of the lagoon and a heron came to keep me company. He stood in the surf a few feet away and watched until the very end when I'd carried the tiger to the mountain, bowed, and said the prayer I always say: 'Divine Spirit, Creator of all things, Abide with me.' Then he lifted off on his huge wings and flapped away into the rising sun.

What really happens at the international date line? 'You lose a day,' people say blithely, but I felt very distressed by the disappearance of Monday the 18th of May. It vanished into a hole in the mysteries of time. It's like the eerie moment when the digital clock reads 00.00 at midnight. I always fear that I could fall into that nowhere, nothing, non-existent minute. The ice floes of time would close over my head and I wouldn't be able to find the crack to get out again. A bottomless crevasse lies in wait for unwary travellers who don't ski fast enough across the international date line.

Once, years ago, when I was on an Outward Bound course, I had to swing on a rope over a slimy bog. All the others who did it first managed effortlessly and sailed across to the waiting nets on the far side. I fell in and the horrid ooze engulfed me. This is how I felt when I arrived in Australia. I had been in an altered state when I boarded my flight leaving the islands, wearing my fairy crown that Dorice made me, my head full of images of my last walk in the enchanted forest of the interior and of my last naked full-moon swim in the phosphorescent waters of the lagoon where my limbs shed droplets of light as I moved and a shoal of flying fish exploded through the surface like submarine-launched missiles. I possibly wasn't in a state to defend myself against the perils ahead, where the time dragon was waiting to swallow me up. I languished in limbo for quite a few days waiting for my soul to catch up with my body again.

In Perth I met up with my beautiful daughter Femi whom

I hadn't seen for three years, during which time she had established a singing career for herself in Australia. I went with a crowd of her friends to hear her solo gig at a nightclub. It was the first time I had heard her new sound and I was so touched and impressed and proud I could hardly stop myself bawling. She had gained so much strength and confidence and looked completely at home on the stage. Femi's friends all seemed to adore me which was very flattering. I felt glad to fit in so comfortably with young people. In fact, most of the time I don't feel any different in age to them. That's one of the reasons why ageing is so hard. The ageless, eternal child in me - the youthful spirit - has remained unchanged but the body gets creaky and the humours get cranky. Traitors both!

I was lucky this time and felt pathetically grateful but I have already experienced the terror of invisibility. One day you're an attractive alluring woman and the next day you become one of the faceless group of old ladies who sit alone in cafés and on park benches. One of the wrinklies, shrinklies, crumblies, old bags, old bats - bewildered at the speed of the descent - dismissed as irrelevant, dying of loneliness. With no recognized rites of passage, we grope uneasily in the frightening tunnel of transition, unsure of what lies ahead, afraid to relinquish what has gone before. Like many women, I have been propelled into conscious choice because of a life-threatening illness. Some do it after a divorce, a bereavement, a job loss. It is an opportunity for reappraisal, a chance to reinvent oneself in time to enjoy whatever time is left. If I make it to old age, I keep telling myself, it is going to be a celebration.

Rites of passage in 'primitive' societies often involve a deliberately induced sense of disorientation, bewilderment, aloneness. They take the form of a vision quest, a pilgrimage, a stripping away of the old identity in order to be reborn. The transition takes place in a twilight zone, betwixt and between, which is what this journey is for me. Life as a mother, a wife, a career woman or whatever else one does in the busy years often does not leave enough time for reflection, or time to distil wisdom from experience. In my quest for wise old role models I want to keep in touch with the beautiful qualities that are essentially female – empathy, sensitivity, surrender, willingness to admit vulnerability – while at the same time discovering new strength, confidence and power. I want to hold hands with the child that I was and the old woman that I will become.

Femi and I went away for a few days to get to know each other again. We drove in her little jeep down to the south-western tip of Western Australia where she had booked us into a lovely old 1920s country hotel in beautiful grounds near the sea. Late autumn weather and we walked down through the valley to dip our toes in the Indian Ocean and watch the brave sleek lads, like young seal pups, ride the crashing surf on fibreglass boards. We walked in the towering forest and breathed in the woody smell. The trees of this land of my birth bring back my happiest, earliest, primary-coloured memories. The blue skies through eucalyptus leaves, the kindly, wrinkly old skin of the huge white ghost gums, the fragrant flowering yellow mimosas, the generous ti-trees with their healing oils, the comical bottlebrushes full of screaming clouds of green parakeets – all flashbacks to my babyhood. The older I get, the more I am moved by the gentle, patient endurance of trees. They give so much and ask for nothing in return. People seeing me must have thought I was batty, leaning my face against the bark, feeling the cool, forgiving, non-judgemental strength, stroking and talking to them. 'Thank you for being here,' I said, and I heard the answering rustle of the leaves.

We were the only visitors to the famous Yallingup Caves on an off-season day, and had the dragon's kingdom to ourselves. I had been wanting to confront the dragon, guardian of the mineral world, since I fell into the time warp. We spent an hour walking through an underground wonderland of limestone formations millions of years old where the rocks are still growing. They felt very alive to me, although the vibrational rate of their mineral energy is so slow and deep as to seem inert. There was a sound too low for the human ear. I couldn't hear it but it resonated in my bones. A sound like the underwater throb of a ship's engines, like the lowest pedal note of a cathedral organ, like the heartbeat of my mother when I was still in the womb, like the pulse of the earth. The cave was hot and humid with dragon breath, the rocks felt warm and visceral. My presence there took on the character of a journey to the underworld to face the fears of ageing and of loss.

I tried, consciously, to ground myself. After all that flying around in the air I still felt scattered and unbalanced. I breathed deeply and drew the dragon energy up through my feet until I was earthed again - soothed and calmed - and the loss of my day and of my youth didn't seem so bad. I knew, as that warm energy flooded me that it would help me with my transformation into whatever phase of womanhood comes next.

As we came out into the sunlight, I was happy to be with Femi and to know the blessed closeness of love with a daughter. I am aware that there has been a gradual shift in our relationship as she has assumed more of the parental role. We were on her territory here and she had made all the arrangements. I thank God for my children - they make it much easier to grow old and to move on.

'We had this camel that was given to us as a wedding present,' said Di. 'If he didn't like somebody he'd put his head through their car window while it was parked outside and eat the seat covers. He'd drag our mattress into the yard and lie on it. He'd stick his head through the laundry window and drink all the water out of the washing machine. He liked warm water and being a camel he could drink quite a lot of it. Then he'd start on the clothes. He hated the colour blue. He'd go to the washing line and if he saw anything blue, he'd pull it down and trample it into the ground. We had to get rid of him in the end.'

Diane McCudden's deadpan stories of life in the Outback

had brought me to Laverton, a remote gold-mining town in the middle of the Great Victoria Desert of Western Australia. She was waiting for Femi and me on the airstrip with Sarah, her four-year-old adopted Aboriginal daughter, and we all squeezed into the front seat of a truck she had borrowed to drive us around while we were there. This is a harsh place to live. Dry as a bone and hot as hell most of the year. People come here to make money working in the mines and the population is strikingly young. There are rows of pre-fab houses, a school, a supermarket, a pub. Scattered about across thousands of square miles of desert are a few homesteads – sheep stations and cattle stations. Woven into this social fabric, although never quite a part of it, are the original inhabitants of this land, the Aborigines. Quite a few live in the town and many more live in the surrounding reserves. The relationship between them and the white mining community is one of barely concealed animosity.

I had come to stay with Di in the hope that she could introduce me to an Aboriginal grandmother or two. They have endured so long and witnessed so much. Were the elders still connected, I wondered, to the thread of dreams, imaginings and deep collective memories of the oldest known human culture? Di is a singularly unprejudiced, open and enlightened person who has lived in the area for most of her life. The Aborigines, or Wongai as they call themselves in this part of Australia, have suffered a lot in their collision with white fence-building, time-keeping, land-owning values. I wanted to ask the old woman what kept them going. I also wanted to journey to the most distant memory of our race. I had felt a stirring in the recesses of my own memory, a sense of affinity with a people who melded so well with their world, a people to whom body and land were one. An Aboriginal woman recently interviewed on television said, 'With your vision you see me sitting on a rock, but I am sitting on the body of my ancestor. The earth, his body and my body are identical.' This speaks directly to that part of me which comes from my own pagan past, the part of me that is descended from the healers, herbalists and witches of pre-Christian Europe.

Just before leaving on my round-the-world journey I went to Stonehenge on a cold winter afternoon. I felt terrible for the stones imprisoned behind the wire which keeps people from touching them. It was like visiting elephants in the zoo. They looked so lonely. Then I read the bit in Robert Lawlor's book, *Voices of the First Day*, where he tells of the time he visited a huge standing rock formation in Arizona with a Cherokee man who sat down and played his flute to the stones. 'They are like lonely old people standing and waiting to be sung to,' he said, 'Our people have always sung songs of admiration to the qualities of strength and beauty and endurance that stones bring to the world . . . they are tired and lonely now because the world has become so blind and selfish. They live in a hollow, unsung world.'

Aboriginal, Native American, Hawaiian, European pagan perceptions all contain the seeds of archaic awareness that I feel lie dormant within me. I want to reconnect with my own dreaming where my inner vision and outer projection are woven in a dance of energy with the natural world and all of creation. 'You should talk to Dimple Sullivan,' said Di. The great-grandmother of Sarah, the child she has adopted. 'She's a lovely old thing and she knows a lot.'

At seventy, Dimple Sullivan is one of the most senior ladies in this part of the world and quite a matriarch, with five sons, one daughter, twenty grandchildren and ten great-grandchildren. A big woman, wearing a vast floral dress and a crocheted hat, she came round to meet me, parked herself at Di's kitchen table and held out her hand. It was to be the first of several conversations where I gained some valuable insights into an all but vanished way of life. She is the head of her household and lives in the town with several members of her family including a five-year-old great-grand-daughter, Azaria, whom she looks after. Nana Dimple has trouble with asthma these days but otherwise she is in pretty good health which is rare. Very few Wongai live past the age of fifty. 'White man's tucker, easy money and grog,' says Dimple. The grog has certainly taken its toll here, as their finely tuned metabolisms which have withstood 40,000 (latest archaeological evidence suggests it may even be as much as 150,000) years of hardship in this inhospitable land apparently cannot tolerate the toxic effects of alcohol.

We talked about the past. Nana Dimple said she remembered, when she was eight years old, going walkabout with her mother and a few other family members. Incredibly, especially for a little child, they walked over 620 miles across the border into the state of South Australia. They carried practically nothing with them – only the basic Aboriginal tool kit of digging stick, shallow wooden bowl, string bag for the women, spear and *woomera* (spear thrower) for the men. Lightweight, portable, easily replaceable. They found all their food and water along the way. They made stone cutting tools as and when they needed them. The purpose of the journey was to meet up with other family group members.

The thing that Aborigines most need and love to do, said Dimple, is to travel up and down the length and breadth of their country weaving a web of kinship and affirming it with ceremony. If ever you meet one when you are out and ask them what they are doing they say, 'Oh just having look round.' They are forever in motion in a huge join-the-dots game. They are the caretakers who, through their wanderings, continually recreate the world. Relationships are everything. Relationships with each other and with the land. In none of the many Aboriginal languages is there a word for ownership.

But as the Europeans began to explore, and later to settle and farm, they dismissed the Aborigines as being simply isolated bands of barbarians and ignored the fact that they possessed an intimate relationship and ultimate mastery over their land. The two cultures had totally different perceptions of the world and man's place in the scheme of things. And now the old patterns are gone and will never be recaptured. They built cities and roads on the sacred sites. The ancient Dreaming pathways were severed and the web of inter-dependency broken.

The Aborigines had evolved a pattern of life that was well-suited to their environment and which was personally satisfying and rewarding to them. They had a story for every aspect of the natural world - their great and beautiful epic called the Dreamtime. The Dreamtime myths portrayed the physical world as a language to be learned - part of the education of every child. Reading the seasons, talking to trees, listening to the emanations of plants, feeling the energy of rocks, being in communication with the elements and with the spirits. The world was a language to be read or interpreted only by those with their ear to the ground, and continual education was a feature of Aboriginal life. Ritual and religious knowledge involved patient learning throughout a lifetime. Continued observation - 'having a look round' - supplemented the survival skills that all children were taught. The Aborigines lived in harmony with their environment because they had developed a capacity to integrate their inner and outer worlds, their waking and dreaming states, their conscious and unconscious minds. They had a sense of common consciousness very difficult for us to comprehend. The visible and the invisible were one.

Money has somehow fatally damaged this fragile equation. Out of guilt for past brutalities and acts of land theft, large amounts of money are now doled out every two weeks by the government and the mining companies in the form of welfare cheques or mining rights. But this has only tended to exacerbate the problem. The spirit of the Wongai is at an all-time low. There is no incentive to work or to hunt their own food. They buy huge Landcruisers, television sets, booze and junk food with the money. Their health has been irreparably damaged. The young people, said Dimple, don't want to listen to their elders any more. Young men have even been known to beat their mothers up. Perhaps further out, in some of the bush communities, something of the traditional respect survives, but not in the towns.

In the Aboriginal world view, everything that happens leaves behind a vibrational residue in the earth. They believe that the spirit of their consciousness and way of life exists like a seed buried in the earth – a seed of knowledge and awareness that will sprout into life when the right fertile conditions come about. I long to believe that somebody carries the flame and that the Dreamtime stories live on in the memories of the old ones, or in the cells of the not-yet-born, memories of the origins of life on earth.

As one tribal elder put it, 'They say we have been here for 40,000 years but it is much longer. We have been here since the time before time began. We have come directly out of the Dreamtime of the creative ancestors. We have lived and kept the earth as it was on the first day.' The ancestors came from the direction of the rising sun, they walked the dreaming pathways of a flat, featureless plain and sang the landscape, the creatures, the elements, the plants into being. These epic journeys were depicted in the stories, the paintings, the ceremonies and the patterns of life that have been maintained for millennia. But the missionaries told them their sacred sites were devil-worshipping places and discouraged their use. They banned the manhood circumcision rites, they took half-caste children away from their mothers by force and put them in homes, and little by little their self-esteem seemed to dwindle. The earth is no longer as it was on the first day and most of the Wongai you see today are pretty broken-down looking.

Dimple's son Gary and his wife Lois do not come into this category. Neither of them drink and they both work and love to go off looking for bush food. While we were talking, they arrived in their Toyota with about eight kids. They had seen some emu tracks out in the bush and were going out to hunt for eggs. They said we could follow them if we wanted to. I was very excited to get this chance to experience a taste of the hunter/gatherer life of our earliest ancestors – the oldest race of people on earth.

Femi, Di and I tailed their four-wheel drive, jouncing out across the red sand and spinnifex vastness miles off the road until we came to a place that, to me, looked exactly like everywhere else. Mulga scrub all around as far as the eye could see. We stopped and got out of the vehicles. There were the tell-tale, giant, three-toed emu tracks and immediately the family dispersed in different directions. We tagged along behind two of the women. They walked fast and kept their eyes unerringly on the bird tracks. I really had to search to spot the higgledy-piggledy marks in the dust but they saw them as easily as if they had been picked out in fluorescent paint. They can tell if the emu is coming or going from its water source by the pattern of the prints. They know that this is the time of year to find the eggs because 'The emu has appeared in the Milky Way in the night sky.'

Try as we might it was impossible to keep up with them. After two hours hard walking, when they had completely disappeared from view, we acknowledged defeat and retraced our own steps back to the truck to find the Toyota had gone. Luckily Di is at home in this country and managed to follow their tyre tracks. It was beginning to get dark. All we spotted were three rotten last year's eggs which had obviously been rejected by the others – their footprints were all around the place. Eventually we caught up with them, calmly waiting for us under a tree. They'd had a good haul and were in excellent spirits. They blow out the egg contents to eat and then carve delicate pictures on the dark green shells which sell to tourists for up to $500 if the quality is high enough.

It was lovely to see these ancient people of the land in their true setting. By and large they are not at ease in houses and towns. They love to camp, to hunt and to sit around under the trees. They are brilliant at tracking, at finding their way across this wasteland, at knowing where the water is, at attuning themselves to the landscape and the creatures. We started back towards Laverton when suddenly a large kangaroo appeared up ahead, caught in the headlights of their vehicle. In a flash they had a spotlight on him and gave chase. A shot from Gary wounded the poor creature and everyone else jumped out of the truck and clubbed it to death with crowbars. I was both horrified at this bloody bit of reality and impressed with the speed of their reactions in catching their dinner. I got out of the truck and walked over. It was very quick. Lois severed the thin skin between the tendons of the powerful back legs and threaded a rope through. They strung the unfortunate animal up to the luggage rack and bounced back to town where Dimple would skin him and make him into a stew.

During my time in Laverton I met quite a few of the older women. Women like Gladys who are still just about managing to hold their broken families together against tremendous odds but who have so little sense of their own self-worth. Generations of abuse and victim consciousness have taken their toll. Gladys turned up on Di's doorstep one day. Her son had just been sent to prison. He was picked up by the police with some bad company, drinking and driving around in a stolen car. She had come to appeal to the local constabulary to get him transferred to a nearer jail where she could visit and keep an eye on him. He knows nobody where he is and is pining terribly. The Aborigines cannot bear to be separated from their kinfolk. In a culture where family cooperation has always meant everything and survival on one's own would have been impossible, ostracism is the worst possible punishment.

I felt so sad for Gladys, a woman of about my age with classical Aboriginal features – round, flat and broad with very deep-set eyes and unruly curly hair. She was patient, enduring and matter of fact but the pain in her eyes was immense. The changes have come so quickly and the dislocation has been enormous. The stark contrast between the simple harmonious life of the past and this wretched present is almost unbearably poignant. For a woman like Gladys, coping with the twentieth century must sometimes seem an impossible task. So easy to fall into the time warp and find oneself spinning out of reach, mouthing out of earshot.

A couple of days later, on the road to Cosmo Newberry where the sky was huge and the bush was endless, we stopped at the site of an old Aboriginal camp ground. Di hunted round and picked up several small rocks which were unremarkable to an untrained eye but were actually stone tools. As soon as she showed me what to look for, I could see where they had been chipped away to make sharp-edged cutting tools for skinning animals. This was a graphic reminder of how recent the Stone Age was in these people's lives. Visiting their campsite, which was probably only fifty years old, was a jump backwards in time of thousands of years. Dimple also showed us the flat grindstones which the women would have used for making flour out of seeds. She told me about the time her mother, who was skilled in the art of native medicines, boiled a special kind of rock for hours in water and gave it to a sickly newborn baby to drink and how the baby recovered and thrived.

Dimple showed us a bush whose twigs you could boil for two hours to make an effective remedy for sore throats, a couple of grasses whose seeds could be ground to make a kind of bread, a low, ground-creeper plant with succulent leaves that can be eaten raw or cooked. She pointed out a tree whose roots retain water so that you will never go thirsty in the desert. We also saw the remains of a bivouac-style shelter or humpy made of bent-over branches. We saw where a mulga tree had been split with a stone hand axe and a piece removed to fashion a woomera. Dimple is a frail old lady and breathless but she really got enthusiastic about sharing some of her bush knowledge with us. It was lovely to see her in her element. She would never be lost in the outback. I would feel perfectly safe if I were with her, no matter how harsh the conditions.

So often in the white community you hear, 'They're lazy, they don't want to work, we're killing them with kindness, they're dirty, quarrelsome, drunk.' And it has to be said that what you see on the surface is a lot of derelict, no-hopers on social security with no pride in themselves and a woeful lack of purpose. But they have been treated so dismissively, and with such a total lack of sensitivity, that it is not surprising.

This is from a book called *In Darkest Western Australia*, written in 1909. Its author, H.G.B. Mason, proposes castration of 'bucks' as the solution to 'the Native Problem':

> Castration has a wonderfully soothing and beneficial effect on all creatures with wild and vicious blood . . . it seems to quieten and cow them once and forever . . . The more a nigger is educated the bigger scoundrel he becomes. If one happens to have bush natives doing fairly well, and one of these educated gentlemen appears on the scene - goodbye to all further control over them . . . Since the advent of the whites, nothing that mortal man can do will prevent the passing of the Australian black within a few decades. Niggers are cut out for the wild and free life . . . thousands of pounds will be frittered away in experimenting [with solutions] . . . and in the end they will remain the same filthy, troublesome, thriftless race.

Many people's opinions were coloured by this sort of appalling propaganda and the scene was set for a fatal collision between the strong, dominant invading culture and the fragile, dreamy, defenceless one. I thought about the survival of the fittest and how we've all been taught that 'natural selection' and inevitable evolution is the way of the world. But even watching the Olympic Games this year I found myself uneasy with the constant parade of winners and losers, national pride and chauvinism. 'It's just a healthy outlet for mankind's naturally competitive nature' is the received wisdom. But is it so natural? Isn't it more natural to be cooperative? Our energy can just as easily be channelled into dance, music, ceremony, carnival, acts of initiation, courage and endurance. There don't have to be winners and losers. Have we been conned for too long by Darwinian excuses for a deadly mutant strain of humans who have led us to the brink of destruction? The fittest are also the strongest, the cruellest, the most devious, the greediest. In a finite world they can only survive so long.

Is our great 'advanced', technological, competitive, Western, white, male-dominated civilization necessarily the peak of human achievement? And has it brought us happiness? A recent advert for a brand of beer shows three men (commodity brokers? lawyers? military strategists?), dressed in rugged outdoor gear, enjoying a weekend of fishing by a quiet, unspoilt lake. What do they do for the other fifty-two weeks of the year? Work at stressful jobs in polluted cities, achieve 'success' in the rat race, fail to have a relationship with their children because they are too busy earning pots of money so they can buy a holiday in one of the few places that haven't yet been ruined by 'progress' and the survival of the fittest.

Perhaps the real measure of the success of a culture is not achievement but relative affluence measured in actual free time and in personal satisfaction. This is from Captain Cook's journal, on his first sighting of the Aborigines:

> They appear to be in reality far more happier than we Europeans, being wholly unacquainted not only with the superfluous but the 'necessary' conveniences so much sought after in Europe, they are happy in not knowing the use of them. They live in tranquillity which is not disturbed by the inequality of condition: The earth and sea of their own accord furnish them with all things necessary for life, they covet not Magnificent Houses, Household Stuff etc., they live in warm and fine Climate and enjoy a very wholesome Air, so that they have very little need of clothing . . . in short they seemed to set no value upon anything we gave them . . .

They hunted for food, and when they had enough for their meals they devoted their time to social and ceremonial pursuits. An Aboriginal man quoted in Robert Lawlor's important book, *Voices of the First Day,* remembers his grandmother saying to him:

> The white men say terrible things about the Aborigines only because we are not farmers, builders, merchants

and soldiers. The Aborigines are something else – they are dancers, hunters, wanderers and mystics and because of that they call us ignorant and lazy. Some day you will see the beauty and power of our people.

The Aborigines still love to hunt and to sit with their families around a fire and to travel freely about the country. Possessions have no value, clothes only get dirty. As well as having no word for ownership, Aboriginal languages also have no word for time. All our thoughts are expressed in past, present and future tenses, whereas Aborigines conceive time as a passage from dream to reality.

The missed opportunities and mistakes are a tragedy too huge to grasp. There is so much we should have learned from these people. I long to step into the Dreamtime, into a vision of humanity reintegrated with nature, to acknowledge once again the feeling, intelligence and consciousness of other aspects of creation apart from our own, to grasp the seed of wisdom that lies dormant. But it seems as if there is nobody left to take me there. People are struggling vainly, like those terrible images from the Gulf War of birds in the oily black sea, drowning, bewildered, washed up on the shores of 'civilization'. We put liquor stores where their wilderness was, multi-storey car parks where the rainbow serpent sleeps.

In the same way that I want to reclaim my ancient pagan inheritance of magic, power and witchcraft from the fear and shame that engulfed it, I feel that just underneath the missionary brainwashing and cultural domination of ancient peoples lies an indigenous mysticism of great beauty and profundity that is also waiting patiently to be reclaimed – the seed which the Aborigines speak of, waiting to take root when the time is right, when there are ears to hear.

Dimple took us to a hill where we could 'speck' for gold. Gary had once found several nuggets in the area. She walked about the stony terrain peering around for the tell-tale glint of yellow metal. But we found nothing that day. When she told me of Gary's success I said, 'How does he know where to look?', imagining that he must use some mysterious Aboriginal knowhow. 'He got real good metal detector,' she said. I had to laugh!

On the road home in the failing light a mother kangaroo with a joey in her pouch sprang across the track with a young one hopping behind. A very large emu broke cover and ran alongside the road for maybe half a mile or more, going as fast as the truck. Magical! I was glad that this time nobody was trying to catch their supper. We got home tired and dusty after 150 miles of being squashed in the cab of the truck with a wiggly four-year-old. But I loved the day. It's not often you go out for a picnic and come home with a handful of Stone Age cutting tools and two shooting stars which had fallen to earth on the desert.

Rosalyn, one of Dimple's grand-daughters, told us she was planning to go out hunting for honey ants the next day and that she would take us. Honey anting is a very companionable activity. This is a time for gossip and songs. The women sit around in the dirt under a tree with their digging sticks and unearth the ants' nests. Honey ants have big, bulbous, distended abdomens and mean pincers. You grab them by the head and bite off the honey sac – instant sweeties! One of the reasons I'd love to go is just to see if I could do it. I've never been particularly squeamish about peculiar foods but popping a live ant into my mouth might require more than the average *sang froid*. Rosalyn told us that you must never talk about honey ants after dark and that pregnant women are not allowed to go out looking for them. I asked her if she obeyed the taboos and she said she would obey Dimple because she respected her but otherwise she didn't take any notice. Divorced from the complex web of Dreamtime Law none of it makes much sense.

It poured with rain all night and was still dripping and steaming the next morning so the honey ant expedition was cancelled, alas. All the nests would have been flooded and I will never know if I could have gone through with it. Instead we decided to drive out to Yamarna, the station where Di lived with her husband for eight years before the marriage went wrong and she left him. She had not been back there since and was apprehensive about the reception she might get. It was a very long way - halfway between Perth on the coast and Ayers Rock in the great red centre of Australia - and in the most desolate part of the Great Victoria Desert. When she lived there the only people she saw were travellers who would stop to buy fuel and food from the little shop she kept. Mostly families of Aborigines on their way through to Warburton in the Central Reserve, sometimes a busload of tourists going from Ayres Rock to Kalgoorlie, occasionally a lone Japanese on a motorbike. It was a very isolated existence but Di loved the life. It was her humorous, vivid writing about the place which drew me here in the first place.

She is an amazingly resourceful and enterprising woman and has become very knowledgeable about the bush, the Aboriginal ways and the history of the region. She has driven a truck, worked at the mines, worked at the hospital, done community nursing, fixed broken vehicles, made stockyards out of old pieces of anything and brought up her adopted Aboriginal kid to be a wonderful child.

When she got married Di already had an idea of how her husband was going to turn out but she ignored her instincts. During their years together he became progressively more abusive and morbidly jealous, hitting her, sapping her confidence, telling lies, getting them into debt. My immediate question was 'Why did you stick it for so long?' which was an insensitive reaction. It's so difficult, as she says, to disentangle yourself from the web of humiliation, loss of self-esteem, fear, guilt, shame and co-dependency (a microcosm of what has happened to the Aborigines). Di suddenly knew that she had to get out, waited for the right moment when her husband was away for a few days, and left.

She lived in fear for quite a while, as he had often threatened to 'blow your head off' and 'punch your face in', but now things had simmered down to an acrimonious court battle about money. Anyway, in preparation for this trip, she had collected his mail for him, bought a few supplies and cigarettes as a peace offering and just asked me not to leave her alone with him. I didn't know what to expect. She'd shown me their wedding picture with her in a white satin gown and gum boots. He looked a reasonable enough bloke. We stopped along the way at the beautiful spot she'd chosen for the wedding ceremony - a natural rock amphitheatre in the 'breakaways' (small elevations in the endless flatness). We were in good spirits when we finally drew up, after three and a half hours driving on dusty tracks. A vicious-looking dog ran out into the yard barking. We sat in the truck. A grizzled, bearded figure appeared in the doorway. 'Whadda ya want?' he yelled.

'We've come to visit.'

'Get off my land!'

'We've brought you some stores.'

'Don't want anything! Clear off or I'll shoot!' He went inside without a word to little Sarah or any acknowledgement to Femi and me. Di turned the truck around and we drove off. She was pretty angry and left his mail in a plastic bag hanging on a tree.

So that was that. We'd driven 100 miles through the bush to be told to piss off. I was still glad to have seen the place and got a feel for the enormity of the isolation even though we couldn't have a proper look round. We decided instead to pay a visit to the shell of another, abandoned, homestead further on. You can't walk two steps out of the truck in these parts without being covered in those awful outback flies which seem determined to fly up your nostrils and aim for the corners of your eyes. I suppose they are desperate for the moisture. I wandered around the old place where you could still see the initials of the last family who had lived there carved into the fence post. I imagined coming here to this heat, this inhospitable land, this loneliness. Trying to raise kids and maintain remembered suburban standards of cleanliness in the relentless dust. Women came out here in their long skirts with their little upright pianos and their Staffordshire bone china tea sets and made homes for the rugged pioneer men. They battled the flies, the snakes, the spiders, the drought, the bush fires. But often the bush won, as it had here, and the people gave up the struggle. The price of wool fell, the cost of living rose and the mining towns beckoned.

We drove on to Minnie Creek, a blessed oasis in this arid emptiness, a rock hole where we refilled the water bottle and washed our dusty faces. Dimple remembers the death of her stepfather at Minnie Creek when she went on that great walkabout as a child. Two days later her mother gave birth to a baby boy down by the water's edge. Dimple found her the next morning lying next to the newborn infant which was covered with ants. She ran and fetched the other women who cleaned the ants off the baby and helped the mother. The child survived and grew up to be the father of Rhys, a nice man who I met in the settlement of Cosmo Newberry and who showed us how to spot the emu in the Milky Way. (Just beneath the Southern Cross is a black shape amongst the whiteness. It only appears in winter when the Seven Sisters go below the horizon. This is the time when it is permitted to hunt for emu eggs.)

We passed the place on the road where a couple of Aboriginal scouts had once saved the life of Di's husband whom they found dying of thirst and dehydration on a day when the temperature was hitting 120 degrees. His vehicle had broken down, he had only a small bottle of water with him and it had been twelve hours before Di realized he had never got to town and alerted the police by radio.

On the long drive home Di told us the sad story of Womblie, a little boy whose sixteen-year-old mother died when he was a baby and whose father died not long after. Di took him in and would gladly have adopted him but the welfare people wouldn't allow it, as mixed-race adoptions are discouraged. Nobody else wanted him so he was sent to an orphanage from which he continually absconded and by seven years old he was fending for himself, stealing from shops (if he only took what he needed each day, he reasoned, the shopkeepers wouldn't miss the stuff).

By fourteen he was arrested for grievous bodily harm and in serious trouble with the law. In an attempt to keep him out of jail, the welfare people approached Di and her husband out at Yamarna and asked if they would be prepared to foster him temporarily or at least try to give him some sort of stability! With heavy hearts they took Womblie in and with enormous forbearance tried to cope with him but by then it was too late. He was too wild, too cunning, too crazy. He set fire to the wool shed to flush out the rabbits that lived under the floorboards, he hid in a cupboard and spied on them having sex, he watched people through a crack in the shower wall, they had to hide the car keys or he took off. He's now in prison for killing a white man.

We were all exhausted the next day and nobody was keen to travel far so I walked over to Dimple's house and invited her to lunch. We made a big plate of ham sandwiches and sat around talking. 'After my husband died I never want no other man,' she said. 'They no good, the lot of 'em.' Then she added as an afterthought, 'Not that the doctor didn't try to have me. I thought about it for a while and said to myself, 'Naaah''. So since I been a widow I ain't had no sex!' She roared with laughter. Although it was a shocking example of the kind of abuse that goes on in consulting rooms I couldn't help seeing the funny side – all 20 stone of her, no front teeth, whiskers on her chin and the crocheted hat pulled down over her forehead, considering the proposition and taking her time to turn him down!

She showed me a book called *A Drop in the Bucket* about the early days of Mount Margaret Mission. Dimple was forcibly taken from her mother and sent there. She remembers the terror of running away into the bush, with the Principal chasing after her in the truck. She was finally caught and dragged off crying and hollering while her mother was paid compensation in the form of some stores. To a little child it seemed as if they had sold her. She remembers being taken once on an outing to Perth where the Aboriginal children were not allowed to ride on the elephant at the zoo.

During one of our conversations I had told Dimple about the Jamaican Memory Bank Project and asked if anything like that was being done here to record the oral history contained in the stories and lore of the Wongai. She said there wasn't but I could tell she was interested. She is full of information on kinship ties and bits of local history. The Dreamtime stories, however, seem to be just out of her grasp, like dreams that fade and evaporate in the morning light. You can still smell them but they're effectively gone. Di has offered to spend some regular time getting her to talk into a tape recorder.

When Dimple came round to say goodbye on our last day she brought me a carved emu egg as a present. I was very touched, knowing how hard it is to find them and how difficult they are to carve without breaking. She was all fired up about the thought of recording her memories and wanted to get started straight away. I have since heard from Di that they have applied for a grant from the Aboriginal Arts Council to finance writing it all up.

It was a stormy afternoon with a perfect rainbow vaulting the airstrip, splashing the greyness with colour. The Aborigines have a profound perception of the rainbow as the symbol of the edge of the unconscious, the place where invisible potential begins to become visible. I thought about the meek inheriting the earth and what an unlikely prospect that seems. Our popular culture is preparing us for destruction. At the little video rental shop in Laverton, as everywhere else, the shelves are stacked with films like *Die Hard, Lethal Weapon, Terminator* – orgies of killing, explosions and smashed vehicles. I looked up 'meek' in the dictionary. It didn't used to mean 'spineless', 'long-suffering', 'submissive', which is how the word is used today. The original, now obsolete, definition was 'gentle', 'amenable', 'likely to listen', 'cooperative'. Surely Jesus meant, 'Those who can hear the voices of the first day and conduct their lives in gentle harmony and cooperation with nature will inherit the earth.'

Femi and I flew away in our little Skyways plane back to the city where we treated ourselves to a farewell meal at a classy restaurant and went our separate ways, not knowing how long it would be before we saw each other again. I gave her the emu egg and boarded my flight to Bangkok on the last leg of the marathon. I was feeling so nervous about India that if someone had said, 'Sorry you can't go', I would have been almost relieved. Half of me was excited by the adventure that lay ahead and the challenge of the unknown. The other half was scared stiff and tempted to stow away as the plane continued on to London. In 'Little Gidding' T.S. Eliot wrote:

> We shall not cease from exploration
> And the end of all our exploring
> Will be to arrive where we started
> And know the place for the first time.

I think he must have written that for me.

At Bangkok I was surrounded by hordes of people all wearing official-looking badges, trying to book me up for special tours and accommodation. I had no idea where to go. I only had a one-night stopover and was torn between wanting to see as much as possible of this fabled, exotic city and cowering in a hotel near the airport. Two tourists had been killed in the recent rioting. Anyway I let myself get hustled into an all-in, pre-paid deal of taxi, hotel and city tour with guide for a price that was probably far too high but time was short and I didn't want to waste it haggling.

It was about midnight when I got to my room and a very long time since the meal on the plane. The kitchen was closed so I had a beer out of the mini-fridge and ate a whole packet of crisps, peanuts and dried squid, which was a mistake. An old episode of *The Saint* was on TV and I sat dumbly watching it, which was another mistake. My brain felt as if it was suspended in pickling solution. If I'd been a man I would have gone out and tackled the night streets, at least had a look at the infamous massage parlours and strip joints. Many years ago, before we were married, my husband had what is euphemistically called a relationship with a notorious hooker aptly known as the Bangkok Tiger. I had half a mind to look her up. She is probably a wise old woman by now if she's still alive. But instead I let myself be overcome by melancholy. The weather was hot and sticky. I was prepared to open the window and suffer the heat for the sake of getting some fresh air but the constant street noise and traffic fumes were worse than the stale air-conditioning. My loneliness and misery were compounded by guilt for feeling miserable in comparative luxury, surrounded by people who struggle every day to survive.

Determined to make the most of my day in Bangkok, I got up at 6 the next morning and swam up and down the hotel pool in conspicuous isolation for half an hour. You need quite a lot of nerve to do this, as the pool is overlooked by both the café and the taxis out front. After a 'continental' breakfast of pretend orange juice and cardboard toast my guide arrived to take me on my little tour. It takes four hours but at least half of that time is spent sitting in traffic jams. Bangkok is famous for these. Building land is so valuable that only tiny narrow streets are left in between. These are not one-way and cars rush each other head-on, horns blasting constantly, each trying to force the other to back down and back out.

Bangkok, laced with an interconnecting network of canals, used to be called the Venice of the East. Now, over two-thirds of the waterways have been filled in to make more building land and the city has virtually no beauty left. It's a dreadful place – galloping population explosion, no urban planning. The combustion engine has all but killed the city with noise, pollution and arterial sclerosis.

The famous temples are besieged islands of peace in the middle of all this chaos and contain many and various representations of the Buddha. There is a huge one made of solid gold which was only discovered in 1965, camouflaged in cement and paint to protect it from the warlike Burmese;

a very large and beautiful sleeping Buddha lying on his side with mother-of-pearl feet; a snake Buddha sitting on a coiled python with an umbrella of cobras over his head to shield him from the rain; and, my favourite, a lovely meditation Buddha in a quiet temple with a red carpet on the floor. Somehow, despite the tourist buses lined up outside, and everyone having to have their photo taken standing next to each Buddha, there was nobody in the temple of the Meditation Buddha. My guide, a psychology graduate who can only afford to go home to see his wife and children once a month, said his prayers and I sat cross-legged for a few minutes in the tranquil sanctuary before another busload arrived.

In the courtyard was a woman with a cage full of tiny birds. For a few baht you could free one for good luck. I fell for it. Good luck for the bird anyway who promptly flew into the nearest tree. They're probably trained to fly back into the cage at night. But I liked the symbolism of holding up the little cage and opening the door in the sunlight. I thought about the work of Amnesty and all the prisoners of conscience in the world and how terrible it would be to be in a cage.

At one temple, the last we visited, a big gathering of Buddhist monks in saffron robes and shaved-headed nuns in white from the northern province of Chiang Mai had come to pay homage to the frail old senior abbot who was celebrating his seventy-second birthday. They were sitting in little groups singing and playing instruments. A big lunch had been laid on for the resident monks by the families of the faithful, and the elderly abbot was led in to take his place at one of the tables. Apart from me there were no tourists here either. A lucky glimpse of something valuable in a city which seems to exemplify the follies of our age. But I shouldn't have been there either; I added nothing and my presence only contributed to the erosion of a nation's individuality – the cultural equivalent of what is happening in the rainforests.

It became starkly clear to me on this trip, taking off and landing over one choked concrete jungle after another, that the 'limits to growth' scenario forecast by ecologists for the last twenty years is already here. If we don't change our ways the planet's days are numbered. We've spread like a dose of shingles round the girth of the globe. There's not much joy left in international travel. Fifty years ago, when my parents travelled the world, it would have been different. Then each country had its distinctive character. There were few, if any, cars, slow sea voyages, no package tours. Of course there are still some unspoilt places left but it's only a matter of time. I used to long to go to Bhutan, Timbucktu, Samarkand, Machu Picchu but now, hungry as I am to see the world, I don't think I really want to be part of that process of destruction - cruise ships to the Antarctic, buff burgers and chips in Kathmandu (being Hindu they don't eat beef but use buffalo meat instead), Inca Cola in Peru, queues to climb Everest.

At one of the temples I particularly liked a large and kindly Po tree under which the Buddha was meant to have sat and meditated. It had been brought from India and planted in the courtyard. Devotees had tied gaudy ribbons around its trunk and left little offerings of plastic dolls, mirrors, lotus blossoms and strings of jasmine round the base. A group of hopeful-looking people with a sign saying 'Experience *genuine* Thai massage' were sitting around in the shade. One came over to give me a free demonstration on my shoulders. 'You can have one hour at your hotel room,' said my guide. It suddenly seemed a good idea, as I had a whole day's flying still to come, so I paid a deposit of a couple of dollars and chose a plump, friendly-looking woman who said she would meet me in my hotel lobby in the evening. Sure enough, there she was with her five-year-old daughter.

Sad that massage in Bangkok, or anywhere for that matter, has come to have such sleazy connotations when it is such a wonderful institution. My lady was all right but by no means the best. The room was hot and she yawned a lot. At one point I think she was nodding off as the action slowed down to almost nil. Her child played on the floor and played with my toes as they hung over the edge of the bed. I was glad that they would have a square meal that night but I didn't much like the imbalance in our relationship. Another problem with being a tourist – people don't see you as a person but as a walking pocket book. What does she care about my quest for wisdom? That the scars on my breasts are from cancer surgery? What do I understand of the struggle she has to feed her kids?

I don't know how men can bear the nature of the relationships, or rather, encounters, they have with whores which must be like that all the time. Pay your money and fuck. Something so intimate with a person you will never know. I suppose tourism is just that on a larger scale. Pay your money and fuck up the country. Take your pleasure and leave a legacy of alienation.

I was still feeling gloomy as I sat in a two-hour traffic jam to the airport but worse was to come.

CHAPTER EIGHT

Travelling in India

. . . For if that which you seek, you find not within yourself, you will never find it without. For behold, I have been with you from the beginning, and I am that which is obtained at the end of desire.

TRADITIONAL: 'Charge of the Star Goddess'
(Starhawk's version)

Delhi railway station is like a refugee camp. Whole families with mountains of luggage wait patiently all over the concourse on every available inch of platform space. Queues for second-class unreserved tickets are fifty deep with everyone shouting and waving their money. It's like the Fall of Saigon – unbelievable chaos and confusion. And this is just a normal day. Fortunately, if you've managed to hear about it on the grapevine, there is the well-kept secret of a tourist ticket office on the second floor for the reserved and deluxe sleeper cars. Here a long queue of exhausted foreigners waits but, hark, there is also a separate window where you can pay in dollars if you have them. An air-con reclining seat to Bombay costs $23 which I luckily had on me so I was able to buy it straight away. In India every such tiny achievement makes you want to crow with triumph.

This had been the latest in a week of wearisome traveller's hurdles which began as I left Bangkok. I suppose it had to happen somewhere. As I flew off to India my suitcase flew off to Hong Kong. This was definitely the low point of the trip so far. I felt very alone and quite scared. India was the big challenge that I had been both longing for and dreading, terrified that I wouldn't be able to cope, that I'd get ill, be robbed, lose my notebooks. And now here I was at Delhi airport at midnight with none of the emergency medical kit, water bottle, cool clothes and other essentials I had been lugging round the world. I also had no idea where to go - my hefty guidebook full of useful suggestions for cheap accommodation was packed in the suitcase.

For one awful moment I thought I was going to burst into tears but then I sat down and made myself think straight. I remembered the name of a place I had stayed at years before in more affluent times, the Hotel Imperial, and took a taxi there. Luckily they had a room. The place was right out of my price range but they accepted the plastic and I knew I could sort myself out in the morning.

Delhi, so everyone kept telling me, was right in the middle of an exceptional heat wave. Instead of the usual searing summer temperatures of 100-110 Fahrenheit, it was hitting as high as 120. Even at night the breeze blowing in through the taxi window was like a hairdryer full on. I suppose on a round-the-world trip I was bound to hit somewhere at the wrong time of year and this was it. All thoughts of travelling on to the desert city of Jaisalmer were abandoned. It is even hotter there. What's more, they have sand storms, dust storms and an acute water shortage . . . Meanwhile, I had a lovely cool room with a bath and high ceilings in the Imperial. I slept naked and exhausted.

I had chosen to come to India because I subscribe to the Adopt a Granny scheme and I wanted to see some of their projects for myself. When I first came across their advertisements in the British press I was greatly moved by the opportunity to have what I'd never had - a grandmother of my own to care about. Alas, in order to encourage people to open their purses, charities, of necessity, have to emphasize the wretched plight of their impoverished recipients. But I wanted to know more about them. Who are these elderly people? What have they seen in their lives? What could I learn from them? I wanted to meet some of them as human beings in context and not just as ragged figures with begging bowls. They may be poor and frail but they have endured, often against incredible odds. They have stories to tell.

The London office of Help the Aged had been very helpful and furnished me with contacts. The next morning I managed to get through to the director of HelpAge India, Maj Gen Pannu (Rtd.), a charming and courteous Sikh who was expecting my call and offered to send a vehicle that afternooon to take me to their headquarters. In the meantime I paid my bill at the Imperial and shifted to the YWCA round the corner - a considerable drop in standards but clean and friendly. A few blocks up the road was an open-air clothes market where I bought myself, for the remarkable sum of 89 rupees (£2), a *kurta pyjama* set, the ubiquitous Indian man's garment of white baggy trousers and loose cotton shirt. The staff at the Delhi office of HelpAge were wonderful and helped me map out a programme that would take in several of their projects. Things began to look up.

It was the hottest weather I had ever known - over 110 degrees Fahrenheit. A blast furnace. At these sort of temperatures the body begins to feel a creeping sense of panic that it won't be able to establish homoeostasis, that the brain will boil, the lungs shrivel and the life-essence evaporate. My eyeballs felt singed, as if all lubrication had dried up, yet all I was doing was sitting in a bus. Outside in the parched landscape there were people toiling in the sun (for an average daily wage of 15 rupees or about 30p), men pedalling cycle rickshaws with the weight of two passengers in them, and women road workers carrying buckets of rocks on their heads. The human capacity to survive and adapt to hardship is astonishing.

On my third trip out to the airport I found to my joy that my bag had arrived. After a mind-numbing few hours spent running the gauntlet of Indian officialdom - collecting six different dockets, passes, tickets and chits, each filled out laboriously by hand in quadruplicate by a different, very slow, clerk and double-checked by a person in a crumpled khaki uniform, and paying a warehouse storage fee to an old babu who had to look the entry up in his ledger and going through customs and security – I was free at last and feeling rather pleased with myself. Another crow of triumph. It can be done!

By now it was evening and the thousands of people who have nowhere else to go had laid their little cots and sleeping mats out on the pavement. It doesn't take long, in India, to feel the extent of one's wealth and privilege. I might be a weary, shoestring seeker of wisdom and truth in my own eyes but here I'm a fat, rich tourist to be beseiged by beggars non-stop. It's a horrible, powerless situation to be in and the scale of it all is too enormous to cope with. It felt awful to walk down a street not heeding the pleas of mothers with babes in arms, ignoring the limbless beggars, shooing away the ragged waifs who plucked at my sleeves, but there are too many. A second's hesitation and you are instantly mobbed. A hundred more appear from the shadows.

Two of India's major film stars were campaigning for political office and the streets were filled with the pre-election hullabaloo. One candidate always plays heroes in the movies, the other, villains, and now they were locked in mortal combat for real. A classic case of life imitating art. The electorate were pretty cynical about the whole thing, treating it as the joke it is, except for the poor who are literally dying to believe that anything could change their lot. Films are the nation's most popular pastime and the doings of the stars are followed avidly. Posters depicting the big, beefy, overweight faces of the two hair-oiled heart-throbs smiled down on the teeming streets. Bands of excited supporters with drums and loudspeakers danced through the streets whipping up followers and handing out leaflets, 'Vote for Bell' or 'Vote for Tree'. The candidates are identified by simple logos for the benefit of illiterate electors. The cows which were wandering about in the traffic during the day were now camped on the grass at the roundabouts placidly surveying the mayhem.

I spent the evening in, talking to some of my fellow travellers: a gentle Dutch student couple in singlets and running shorts on their honeymoon (they baffled the Indians who couldn't tell which one was the girl); and an amazingly naive Australian guy who came out to India on a sudden impulse to volunteer his services to Mother Theresa in Calcutta but ran away after three days because he got too upset by what he saw. He told me a long story about how he was still living on a disability pension after suffering post-traumatic stress disorder from being in Vietnam. It turned out that the stress was caused by his wife leaving him because he caught syphilis off a hooker in Saigon!

There was a large family of earnest, shining Finnish missionaries with five tiny, blonde, sun-burned children; there was also an intrepid English woman in her seventies who travels everywhere alone and has been coming to India for forty years. I thought she would be interesting but she was very grumpy, didn't seem to like the Indians, was rude to the staff and kept complaining that nothing is like it used to be in the days of the British. She ordered soup and mashed potatoes and jelly and custard for her meals every day.

Then there was a pair of pimply-faced American evangelists with neat shirts and ties who wore their trousers pulled up and belted almost under their armpits. I heard one saying in puzzlement to the other, 'The Indians wag their heads politely from side to side when I tell them about Jesus but they just see Him as another God to add to their collection. They can't accept that He is *the* God.'

Finally, number one person to avoid, was a very loud, forty-year-old, completely humourless Australian woman seeking 'self-realization'. She had been trudging the length and breadth of India trying to attach herself to a guru who would tell her how to do it. Meanwhile, a crafty old swami who hung around outside the Imperial Hotel telling fortunes had talked her into a few private sessions and told her about her thirty-six past lives. She was amazed to learn how interesting she was and buttonholed anyone who would listen. Luckily she was just about to go off for a few days to Benares to earn merit by flinging herself into the holy waters of the Ganges.

Sam Oomen, the project director from HelpAge, picked me up early next morning and we set off on the three and a half hour drive to the city of Mathura, the legendary birthplace of Lord Krishna. We were going to visit Dr Sharma whose practice encompasses a very large area including forty villages and 180,000 people. He runs a clinic, a little ear, nose and throat surgery unit, a rural ophthalmic programme, a charitable hospital and drives a mobile medicare van for the outreach programme which also transports poor and needy patients from remote rural areas to the hospital. He is involved in an early cancer detection scheme and is currently trying to raise money to build a cancer unit. And then there is also his passionate concern with deafness, ear infections, hearing impairment and preventative treatment.

HelpAge sponsor thirty Adopt-a-Grans in the surrounding villages and provide funding for Sharma's cataract programme. He gets a bit of Canadian money for a grassroots paramedic training scheme and a small Indian government grant for a handloom weaving project for village women but they are desperately short of money. His dedication and energy are phenomenal and he runs everything practically single-handed with the help of his second wife (his first wife who was also a doctor died tragically young of cancer). We eventually tracked him down in his tiny, cramped office piled high with files and papers. He had been out in the villages all morning and now the electricity was cut off so he did not even have a fan to move the heavy air. The noonday heat bore down oppressively, like a suffocating blanket. The glaring bone-white sky and dusty earth sandwiched us in their merciless embrace.

I asked Dr Sharma about the possibility of talking to some of the old women. No problem. He would send for a couple to meet us there and while we waited he spoke a bit about his own rural childhood and the important role played in his life by his own grandmother who, like many Indian grandmothers, looked after the children while the parents worked. She was patient and impartial, and functioned as a buffer zone or a shock-absorber, he said, between the generations. Things in rural areas, he said, remained essentially unchanged – bound by tradition, custom and caste.

He explained how the caste system worked. I had always believed this to be an iniquitous, unjust arrangement whereby the wealthy and privileged could feel smug and righteous on easy street while the untouchables at the bottom of the pecking order got the shit kicked over them. The way he described it, though, it didn't sound quite like that . . .

Take the occasion of a funeral in the village, for example. The Brahmins, the highest caste, are the priests who conduct the rituals. They will lead the expressions of joy about the luck and good fortune of the departed. The next caste will prepare the food for the feast. The barber caste will make plates and drinking vessels out of leaves, the pottery-maker provides the utensils, the washerman or *dhobi* brings clean sheets to lay the feast out on. These are his property and he is given a small remuneration. Finally, the sweeper and waste-disposal person of the *harijan* caste cleans everything up.

People also have double functions. The sweeper, for instance, would also be the basket-maker and, interestingly, the village midwife. So, even though she is the lowliest member of the hierarchy, it is she who guides the newborn life into the world and puts her 'untouchable' fingers into the babies' mouths to clear the mucus. Everybody knows their place and has their dignity, Dr Sharma said, and were he to meet the woman who delivered him as a baby he would bow and pay his respects even though they would not normally enter one another's houses. His own high caste birth carries with it enormous responsibilities. In any case, as a doctor, he operates outside the strict demarcation lines between castes. 'A doctor is a doctor,' he said. 'My concerns are health-oriented.'

At this point a grandmother entered the room – Mrs Sono.

She was offered a chair but said she preferred to sit on the floor. ('You see, they are the ones who are hesitant,' said Sharma. 'We try to make them realize they are one of us but traditions are still really strong in the rural areas.') Mrs Sono is a low caste woman. When she was given a drink of water by Mrs Sharma she poured it into her hand first rather than touch their cup with her lips. Her family are bonded labourers in the fields but they can also work as weavers, whitewashers or assistants to silver trinket makers.

Like all the other village women I subsequently met, Mrs Sono had no idea how old she was. We tried to establish her age by getting her to recall significant events. She didn't remember Independence or Mahatma Gandhi. Her family doesn't take care of her, she is not well, she doesn't see much of them because she is poor and doesn't have anything to offer them. It was an unremittingly depressing story told in flat, fatalistic tones.

I asked her what was the happiest memory of her life. She had great difficulty understanding the question. Sam had to rephrase it several times. Right from earliest childhood she had seen hard times, she said. Seldom has she seen happiness. There was a whiff of pleasure when her first son was born but *eight of her ten children had died in infancy*. After losing so many babies she has never looked forward to any happiness. I asked her about her religious beliefs. She believes in rebirth, she said, and explained that whatever you are thinking about at the moment of death you will become - rat, dog, person, stone - so she tries to keep her thoughts on higher things.

She had such a sad face, her life so stunted and blighted by suffering. Never before had I met a person who had no concept of happiness. The little pocket money she gets now from her Adopt-a-Granny sponsor provides a small measure of dignity. Thank goodness for it.

When I first thought of a book about old women I had a Utopian fantasy of an Indian village grandmother who despite being poor had a fulfilling and respected role. She would be strong and influential, possessing qualities of stoicism, wisdom, serenity and courage. However in order to achieve an honoured position in old age it is necessary for the society in which she lives to view women as valuable. I had a vision of a people spiritually nourished by the Hindu religion in which the male and female deities stood side by side. Shiva and Parvati, Vishnu and Lakshmi, entwined in carnal pleasure and elevated in divine bliss . . . But far from the exemplary, rhythmic, ancient, harmonious, balanced village life of my imagination, what happens to women in rural India (comprising 75 per cent of the country's 400 million women and female children) is a shocking tale of neglect, exploitation and injustice.

We are still an overwhelmingly male chauvinist society,' said Sam with a shrug. Dr Sharma agreed. Girls are still seen as a curse, he said. They have to be provided with a dowry and got rid of. You have to *pay* somebody to take them off your hands. They then go away to their mother-in-law's house and are treated like skivvies. A son, on the other hand, brings money into the home by marrying, and provides a young, biddable, unpaid servant of a wife to be ordered around by his mother.

It is not uncommon to read about brides being set on fire by their mothers-in-law for failing to bring enough dowry to the marriage. About 600 of these horrible 'bride burnings', as they are called, are reported annually in New Delhi alone, although few cases ever come to court. Most of the women die.

In the light of all this I started to understand why old women in rural India live such wretched existences. It is simply the continuation of a brutalized life. They may well have contributed to the misery of their own daughters-in-law, and in old age, when their power wanes, the tables are turned.

Dr Sharma took us in his car to visit the pile of bricks and sand in the middle of nowhere which constituted the foundations for his new hospital. His facilities are pathetically rudimentary but he says he never gets discouraged. He is trying to do God's work and most of what he needs miraculously comes his way.

He had asked a couple of grandmothers from the nearest village to meet us there. A worn-out looking widow arrived. I asked her what she had learned of value from her mother that she wanted to pass on to her daughters. 'I learned from my mother to look after the whole family,' she said, as if she'd memorized the speech, 'not to fight or quarrel with anyone and to eat when everyone else has finished. Girls from good family have this primary duty.' Dr Sharma asked her if she had ever been tortured by her mother-in-law. She replied that she had been maltreated in ways you would never believe. She was fourteen when she got married and went to live with her husband's family. She was starved and forced to work day and night while her in-laws sat about doing nothing. They were cruel and vicious to her until her husband died, then they threw her out. No wonder there's no love lost when the mothers-in-law become old and frail.

Then a skinny little white-haired old lady arrived, so frail you could have snapped her like a twig. Kishan Devi had been widowed at the age of sixteen after having only one child – a daughter. I asked why she had never remarried. 'My husband had no brothers,' she replied, 'and in our tradition it is not considered proper or right to remarry any other than the husband's brother. It is the Almighty who spoils or improves our lives. I am helpless,' she added with depressing fatalism. The Adopt-a-Gran scheme furnishes Kishan Devi with a few seasonal clothes, a ration of sugar and grain, medicine and 100 rupees (about £2) a month.

The weight of all this oppression bore down on us like the summer heat. I asked Dr Sharma if every old person suffered such unrelieved misery. Weren't there any contented elderly women? Grandmothers who, in spite of their poverty and hardship, had loving families and were not pathetic victims of fate?

Among the illiterate peasants, no, he couldn't think of any offhand. The concept of *dharma*, the obligation to accept one's lot and perform the duties appropriate to it, is fundamental to Hinduism. So maybe the caste system wasn't so wonderful after all if it made people feel powerless to change their circumstances in this life? What about a person from another caste? Someone who had chosen to renounce material things voluntarily for a life of simplicity and spirituality? He immediately thought of Dr Janki, a gynaecologist who had been a colleague of his at the Ramakrishna Mission Hospital. Twelve years ago she retired and had since practised a life of devotion to Lord Krishna. We decided to pay her a visit as night fell.

By now it was 5 o'clock, my head felt like an anvil and I was getting cramp. I knew I was beginning to suffer a salt deficiency from the copious, continuous sweating and I had left my sodium chloride tablets in Delhi. We repaired to our little hotel where the air conditioning and fans were not working due to the power failure. I tried to have a cold shower but the water coming out of the cold tap was nearly boiling. I remembered Di McCudden's Australian outback tip and lay on a wet towel on the marble floor panting like a dog. The evaporation slightly cooled my body but I felt dangerously overheated and slightly delirious. I drank several pints of bottled water and had a couple of aspirins.

Dr Janki lives, along with a handful of elderly destitute people, in an abandoned hospital building in Mathura. It must have been quite an impressive edifice once but is now a dilapidated labyrinth of dark corridors and foul-smelling open drains. We found Dr Janki in a tiny cell furnished with a 25-watt naked bulb dangling on a string, a cot, a table, a bookshelf and a few pictures of her beloved Krishna, the blue god, and his sacred cow. Dr Janki, a serene and beautiful old woman wearing a simple, homespun cotton sari, welcomed us most cordially, found chairs and opened a packet of little salty biscuits. The most remarkable and instantly noticeable thing about her was her luminosity - almost an incandescence. A quality of absolute contentment and peace.

I asked her what chain of events had led her to choose this way of life.

'It has been in me since childhood,' she replied. 'My father was a police officer so it wasn't in the family to move towards the spiritual life. I used to say to myself when I was a little girl, "I'll become a doctor, then I'll serve in an ashram." ' Yes, she said, in answer to my next question, she had had visionary experiences as a young girl growing up in Andhra Pradesh but was reluctant to speak of them because of their sacred nature. Dr Sharma explained that Hindus believe such things to be intensely private and to talk about them would be seen as boasting - as if one saw oneself as special in some way. The true visionary doesn't need to mention any of it. The light just shines within. Well that was certainly true in her case.

As far back as 1945, when she was a young girl of twenty-three, she had been drawn to Ramnamarshi's ashram at Tirivannamali in Tamil Nadu. He became her guru and she was blessed with his *darshan* (teaching) when he was alive. He has now 'left the body', as she says, but continues to guide her devotions. 'Guru is the *principle*,' she explained. 'Not just the body, not just the teacher. Guru and God are one. From internally the guru gives instruction.' When she asked him which one of her callings she should follow, he answered, 'Give your heart to God, your mind to books.' So she became a doctor living in the world, but never quite of it. 'Renunciation amid normal life,' she said, 'is like a water drop on a lotus leaf. Self-contained, complete.'

Years later, when she was pondering whether to move totally toward the spiritual life, she returned to the ashram and meditated with her late guru's photograph. It looked, she said, as if he was smiling a Mona Lisa smile - knowing, mysterious. She picked up a book containing transcriptions of his conversations and dialogues and opened it at random. There on the page before her was recorded the very conversation she had had with him back in 1945! 'You see, the Divine Presence is there,' she said. 'You may think it is your ego or your will in control, but things take their own shape. Since we Hindus believe in rebirth it is much easier to surrender to the greater will. If you love God, everything is for Him and whatever you need you will get.'

When Dr Janki talks about need it is not merely immediate material needs to which she refers but to the whole concept of *karma*, the other core element of Hinduism. Hindus believe (as do Buddhists) that the accumulated sum of all the good and bad actions from their previous lives predetermines the course of their present life. So every rebirth is an opportunity for learning and growth towards the ultimate aim of existence which is to merge with the Oneness and not have to come back. Whatever obstacle you meet this time round is another step on the ladder. You must learn the lessons. Everything is part of the great teaching. A life of prayer and devotion helps to purify you, but it wouldn't suit everybody. As Dr Janki says, 'You will know quite clearly when you are ready for a life of prayer, in fact you cannot resist its call.'

When she found that the urge to renounce the world became overpowering she asked her husband's blessing which he gave freely, knowing how important it was to her. He came with her when she moved in here to make sure she would be safe and now lives in Uttar Pradesh and visits her from time to time. His photograph is on the wall. They never had children.

I asked her one of the questions that bothers me about karma. Isn't it just a convenient way for the privileged classes to feel self-satisfied about their good fortune and keep the disadvantaged in their place? Also, doesn't it excuse a heartless attitude towards suffering ('they must have deserved it')? 'That would be a misunderstanding of the meaning of karma,' she answered. 'We believe that everything - people, animals, birds - has got a soul. Our duty is to show compassion for all souls. Not to add to their suffering but to reduce it.'

So how does she spend her day? 'I do my *puja*, I read my books. It is a life of intense prayer and contemplation. If the Lord sends someone to me I will still help them as a doctor but I don't seek it. I once asked, "God, make my life more useful to you," and my steps have been guided all my life.

I wondered out loud why so many Westerners have sought meaning and enlightenment by coming to India, looking outside their own religious tradition. 'Quite simply, for all its shortcomings, India is more congenial to the spiritual life,' she said. 'It is all around you.' And it is. Every time you walk along the street you pass devotees and disciples and wild-looking holy men dressed only in a loin cloth, carrying a staff and a begging bowl.

Growth, prosperity, development – these Western concepts have brought us much grief. I look in despair at the traffic-choked streets and think of the poor Third World struggling to 'catch up' while we all continue to pollute and rape the natural world with our insatiable greed. And I'm just as much a part of it as anyone. I want the air conditioning, the comfort, the plenty. I eat too much. I must be three times the size of the shrunken little grannies I keep meeting.

Could I ever lead such a life of austerity and renunciation? I'm always very attracted to the strength and certainty of those mystics who do. Maybe I have a few more lifetimes to go. 'Do not forget the aim,' said Dr Janki. 'You will know when you are ready. If you force it too soon the motives will be wrong. Wait for the inner teaching.' She stood in her little doorway to wave us goodbye, her small figure framed by the dim light. In material terms she has no more than the poor village grandmothers I met earlier and yet she is rich. The difference seems to lie in having made the choice rather than having it thrust upon you.

I spent a suffocating, breathless night trying to sleep on my wet towel on the floor of the Madhuban Hotel – my mind racing with a flood of thoughts from the day's lessons. Like all foreigners in this extraordinary land my brain whirled with the paradoxes and contradictions. I felt enraged by the injustices, overwhelmed by the poverty, exasperated by the seething confusion, captivated by the spiritual richness, defeated by the climate, touched by the grace and gentleness, awed by the stoicism, infuriated by the resignation . . .

I was awake long before dawn, headache still pounding, although Dr Janki's salt crackers from the night before had helped a lot. I wrote in my diary, 'I don't know if I'm going to be physically able to bear this heat for another six weeks. I'm trying hard not to be a wimp but I'm actually wilting. My ankles have swollen into little tree trunks and my arms are puffy. My inner thighs are chapped from sweatily rubbing together, I've got a heat rash under my breasts and a thousand flea bites on my feet! How do people live here?'

Dr Sharma and his wife Sunita had invited us to have breakfast with them before setting off for the remote rural village of Akbarpur in Uttar Pradesh. I blanched a bit when I saw the spread but it was actually very delicious: cooked, flaked rice mixed with chopped raw onions, peanuts, chillies and a bowl of thick, sweet sago porridge made with *jaggery* (raw cane sugar) and cashew nuts. All washed down with sweet boiled tea.

We followed their mobile Red Cross clinic out to Akbarpur, a typical Hindu village representing all castes, from the nice, tiled, three-room, blue-painted house of the Brahmin, HelpAge-trained grassroots worker to Mrs Batto, a wizened, toothless, harijan grandmother who threw herself on the ground to kiss our feet, to my intense discomfort. She showed us her house where she lives with her unmarried handicapped son and the baby grand-daughter she looks after. It was a small hut with thick, cow-dung walls smoothed with mud, a thatched roof and a bare earth floor. Inside was as neat as a pin, the floor swept and her meagre possessions stored in the rafters: a water pot, broom, sleeping mat.

As well as being the sweeper Mrs Batto is also the village midwife. She said she was, if not content, at least secure in the knowledge of her place in the scheme of things. People treated her well and with respect and she had no complaints. James Cameron in his classic book *Indian Summer* wrote:

The fatalism of the poor in India is not apathy but dissociation from unhappiness, just as the cruel indifference of the rich around them is not necessarily callous or cynical, but an equal acceptance of the dharma that feeds them and keeps the others hungry . . . This age-old and barbaric philosophy maintains the debased Indian victims in the gutter and most of my well-heeled commercial and official acquaintances in comfort, with the government of India endlessly preaching the betterment of the one and leaving untouched the establishment of the other, and this is why India remains basically a country of the hungry and unhappy.

I asked Dr Sharma to put it to Mrs Batto that if, as a low caste person, she had led a very hard, poor life, what did she hope for in the next life? She failed to understand the question, as with yesterday's question about happiness, and he had to rephrase it. She looked confused and frightened. 'I don't know anything about such matters,' she said as if she were going to be punished for daring to voice an opinion, 'but in matters of delivering babies I am very excellent.' She had delivered many and was proud of her record of helping mother and child safely through. She massages the babies with mustard oil to make their limbs strong and their skin healthy. When pressed she acknowledged that this would be a plus on her karmic balance sheet. She had also once made a pilgrimage to bathe in the holy waters of the Ganges and she hoped God would look favourably on that. Her dear old face cracked into a smile.

A string *charpoy* (bed) was brought out under the trees for me to sit on and dozens of people crowded round to enjoy the welcome diversion. Mrs Leela Wati came to speak to us. She was an elderly grandmother dressed in a threadbare rag of a sari. She kept tugging her veil across her face, as do all married women in the presence of any man who is not a relative, and crouched in the dust at our feet saying she felt more comfortable there. A widow, she had come to this village as a young bride and had had little further contact with her home village. Three of her six daughters had died.

No wonder young girls wail and cry on their wedding day. Everyone told the same story. Little more than children, they are virtually sold off to a family of strangers who frequently ill-treat them. Arranged marriages are standard, the bride has no power of veto. There is a saying in India, 'May you be the mother of a hundred sons'. And, in a country where the birth of a girl child is viewed as a terrible misfortune, when a mother tells you that several of her daughters have died the question of deliberate female infanticide hangs in the air. It happens all the time – from the smothering of girl babies by poor families to the 'sex-selective' abortions in private clinics for those who can afford it.

None of this offers much of a chance to grow into a proud, wise, fulfilled old woman. After a life of tragedy and drudgery the best an Indian wife can hope for is daughters-in-law with whom she will probably perpetuate the cycle.

I asked Leela Wati if she tells stories or sings to her grandchildren. She said she doesn't know any stories but instructs the children in good behaviour. It surprised me when Dr Sharma said that the illiterate poor do not seem to tell stories. I would have thought that an oral tradition would flourish in such a setting but he said that, except for the stories connected with traditional festivals, little apart from superstitions is passed on by word of mouth. Maybe it would be impossible to endure the harshness of this life once your imagination was kindled and they no more weave fantasies and spin tales than do the buffalo yoked in the field. What on earth can be the effect of television on such a community? There is already one TV set in the village.

We talked to several other old women and I sat in on Dr Sharma's clinic. We watched an old man making jute rope by hand, a group of old men sitting in a semi-circle smoking a hookah, a basket-maker loading some winnowing baskets onto his bicycle to sell, women walking to fetch water, women cooking chapattis in the yard, young men decorating cows with streamers and handprints for the forthcoming festival. Despite all the hardship there was a calm, patient, industrious rhythm of life in the village and nobody was starving. The Sharmas' mission to bring health education and better facilities will do as much as anything to improve their lot. As we left I said to the women, 'Take care of your girl children. Girls are good. They are the mothers of tomorrow.' Everybody laughed.

Back in Delhi my two tasks - changing some money and buying my railway ticket to Bombay - took the whole of the next day. India has made bureaucratic confusion into an art form. Only one bank in the city authorizes credit card cash advances. Upstairs, fourth floor, no lift, guards with sub-machine guns searching your handbag. Office like a scene from Kafka. Forty-five employees each sitting behind a desk shuffling papers in slow motion. There is already a queue of twenty tourists who have been waiting for hours with hollow-eyed resignation on their faces. First you hand, to an opaque-eyed clerk with all the time in the world, your card and passport which disappears into a pile on somebody's desk. Then you wait while the requisite six forms are laced with carbon copy paper and painstakingly written out by hand in quadruplicate. Stamps and ink pads must be found. Then you get a disc with a number and queue again at a booth where a cashier laboriously counts out a four-inch thick wad of dirty rupee notes, licking his grubby fingers the while. Leaving feels like being reprieved from death row. Imagine being arrested! Or seriously ill! Please God that will never happen to me in India.

Next the railway station. And now, with my Bombay ticket for the following week safely tucked away, I was ready to head north.

I caught the early morning bus to Dehra Dun from a side street in the centre of Delhi. Very easy to miss. The only instructions I had, scrawled on the back of the bus ticket, were 'DTC (Palika Bazaar – Behind the Metro Hotel'). The bus ('air-con' it was described as, but perhaps that referred to the broken windows) was full to the brim with families of four or five squeezed into each pair of seats, while excruciating, high-pitched, Hindi film music blasted the eardrums at a volume well in excess of the loudspeaker's actual capacity. The driver belted along at top speed for the entire six and a half hour trip as if his manhood depended on it. In India might is right on the roads and long-distance buses see themselves as kings of the highway. Cycle rickshaws, buffalo carts, herds of sheep, blind beggars, all dive out of the way. Goods lorries and town buses offer a little challenge and only swerve from a head-on collision at the last possible second. It's all very nerve-wracking.

I could hardly believe that we didn't hit anybody. The road is never more than just wide enough for two cars to pass each other and runs through many villages teeming with stall-holders, rag-pickers, cold water sellers, fruit vendors, shoe-cleaners, barbers, mechanics. One of the things that can't fail to impress the visitor to India is the industriousness of the people. In spite of the chaos and the crowding and the noise, everybody is going about their business. You never see anything thrown away. Somebody will make a living out of it. I saw a man sitting on the pavement with a little pile of used zip pulls for sale, another with umbrella handles, another with keys for winding up pocket watches.

Our bus made one stop at an eating place by a river and everyone piled off into a great confusion of boiling vats of frying pakoras and samosas, a crush of travellers pushing and shoving, glasses of steaming chai and one of those stand-up toilets which consist of a pair of footprints either side of a frightful hole in the ground slooshed down with a bucket of water.

At last the road began to climb up out of the baking dusty plains into some scrubby hills. It became more and more winding and perilous but mercifully cooler and eventually arrived at the sprawling, hopelessly run-down, jumbled-looking town of Dehra Dun. The bus dropped me by the side of the road and I was wondering what to do next when I was approached by a smiling, courteous Tibetan man who enquired, 'Mrs Taylor?' When I nodded he produced a little newspaper parcel and unwrapped a white, silky scarf which he draped around my neck and said, 'Welcome.'

Ngodup Dorjee is the director of the Tibetan Homes Foundation and he had been alerted to expect me by HelpAge in Delhi. Being met in a strange place is one of the greatest pleasures on earth and was a lovely start to an inspiring time, during which I was fortunate enough to get to know some of the Tibetans who live here in exile while the Chinese occupy their country.

The Tibetan Women's Centre is where Ngodup has his office. The community tries to be as self-supporting as possible from the sale of Tibetan handicrafts, particularly the excellent carpets, both traditional and modern, which the women weave until the age of sixty-five when their eyesight begins to fail. Sponsors in the Adopt-a-Granny scheme UK provide about £16 a quarter for each gran (old men as well as old women) which supplies essentials and a little pocket money. If they work as wool-winders they can earn a bit extra. The centre provides jobs for around 500 employees. Some families are accommodated here and others in nearby settlements. Various Friends of Tibet from around the world have donated buildings and facilities but they are always desperately short of funds.

Tibetans, with their quiet self-containment, friendly natures and gentle strength, are an exceptional people. In spite of all the horrors they have suffered for the past thirty-five years they remain unbroken. Everyone I met was delightful, and the rosy, round babies with their bristle-brush hair must be the sweetest looking in the world.

His Holiness the Fourteenth Dalai Lama has personally taken the initiative in setting up these centres in exile to preserve Tibetan culture, language and pride. As many people said, 'We may have lost our country, our homes and everything we had but we are lucky in one thing - the compassionate kindness of His Holiness.' Indeed, the whole world loves and respects him, a humble and courageous man, keeping alive the hopes and spirit of his people, teaching non-violence, bringing the plight of Tibet to the world's attention. The daily prayer uttered by every Tibetan is that he may live long and one day lead his people home.

The next day Ngodup took me with him to Rajpur to meet Mrs Rinchen Dolma Taring, the beloved mother of the Homes for Tibetan Children. I marvelled at the way so much of this journey has unwound like a ball of string. Without really planning it my footsteps had brought me here, to one of the most impressive women I have ever had the honour to meet.

CHAPTER NINE

A Life of Service

An old age serene and bright
And lovely as a Lapland night
Shall lead thee to thy grave

WILLIAM WORDSWORTH

'When people die the next generation replaces them but when a whole culture is destroyed it can never be replaced.' Mrs Rinchen Dolma Taring, eighty-two years old, her fine intellect undimmed by the years, was talking to us in her pretty garden. The little house in which she lives and the modest comforts she now enjoys are provided by a regular monthly pension sent to her by a devoted English friend.

For over thirty years she has dedicated her life to keeping both the next generation of Tibetans and their unique culture alive. Her story has the epic quality of some great legend. Born into one of the oldest families in Tibet and brought up in the timeless, close-knit world of Lhasa nobility (a feudal, Buddhist society virtually untouched by the West), she can directly trace her paternal ancestry back to a celebrated eighth-century Tibetan physician who wrote several classical medical works still in use today and on her mother's side to the Tenth Dalai Lama.

But calamity came early into her life. Her father and older brother were brutally murdered by ruthless political opponents and her mother died a few years later. Rinchen

Dolma Taring remembers, 'Before Mother died I used to tell her that I wished to go to the place where oranges are grown. She replied that that place is India and to get there one must cross a great snow pass like a wizard's home.' Not long after her mother's death, a visiting British trade agent, the first European she had ever seen, suggested that she should come to India and attend the British school in Darjeeling with his own daughters. Her imagination was fired. 'I notice that all through my life I have had a very bad habit of getting my own way – even to this day,' she said, raising her eyebrows in mock innocence. 'I have to watch myself all the time to try and correct this fault.'

Her family agreed and preparations were made for the journey. Three weeks on horseback to Sikkim, across the lonely Kharola Pass, through the valley of the glaciers, eating noodles and powdered yak meat, through remote mountain regions infested with bandits. In her autobiography *Daughter of Tibet* she describes what happened in the ancient temple of Jokhang:

> by the light of the Lord Buddha, I took a vow never to tell a lie or to harm anyone. This vow was taken on the anniversary of my mother's death in return for her kindness as she brought me into the world and in memory of the love and worry she spent on us. I renew it every year.

Thus, at the age of twelve, Rinchen Dolma became the first Tibetan girl to go to an English school and learn to speak and write English. Jigme Taring, the young Sikkimese Prince who would one day become her husband, beloved life's companion and father of their nine children, was the first boy.

Back in Tibet, with her knowledge of English and talent for astrology (which enabled her to select auspicious days for certain events, she became secretary to her brother-in-law, Tsarong, a wealthy nobleman who had an import-export business in Lhasa. She eventually and somewhat reluctantly, at the age of sixteen, agreed to become his fourth wife and gave him a daughter. He was twenty-five years her senior but polyandry was just as common as polygamy in Tibet and he assured her that she could marry again when she came across a suitable young man.

When the Prince of Taring, eldest son of the Raja of Sikkim, her former classmate at school, wrote asking for her youngest sister's hand, her first husband suggested it would be a better match if the Prince married her instead as they both knew English and could work together. 'He added that since there was such a difference in age between himself and me he would very much like to see me married to a nice young man for the sake of my future happiness.'

I loved her description of the elaborate engagement ceremony when trays of gifts were carried through the streets from the groom's to the bride's family – the most important offering being the nurin or 'breast price', always paid to the bride's family even if her mother was dead, symbolically thanking her for having breast-fed the bride as a baby.

'I took a vow, right from the beginning that I would serve Jigme's parents most lovingly, since I had no opportunity to serve my own mother and father,' said Rinchen Dolma. 'We believe there is nothing more meritorious than to serve one's parents, especially one's mother – who suffers so much to bring up her children and gives us the best love we ever get.' Tibetans earn religious merit by their gentle thoughts, she explained, by practising non-violence, doing good deeds, spinning prayer wheels and offering gifts to lamas. Religion is a constant practice, life is an endless cycle and a meritorious life guarantees a good reincarnation.

To hear these words or see them written down makes them sound rather pompous and calculating but somehow, coming from a Tibetan, they are not at all like that. There was an unselfconscious sweetness and innocence about them – entirely devoid of sanctimoniousness.

'Lord Buddha found the truth by contemplating the realities of life and recognizing the transience of our existence,' she said. 'I wanted to study Buddhism and try to understand the false or illusory nature of things.' She invited learned lamas to her house in order to gain a better understanding of the central Buddhist doctrine of the eightfold path. 'We are taught,' she said, 'that by oneself alone is evil done; by oneself alone is one defiled; by oneself alone is evil avoided; by oneself alone is one purified. No one can do these things for another. The teaching is concise but understanding is difficult and practice still more difficult. Eventually you find God, or truth, in yourself if you study. Mind is very important; if we do not cultivate our minds there can be no spiritual advance.' *Kindness* is the key, she said. Not only does it develop compassion but it sharpens intelligence itself. Kindness was the word that most characterized all the Tibetans I was to meet. It seems to be woven into the fabric of their being like a thread of gold.

She remembers how, in the 1940s, she and her husband Jigme often visited a saintly hermit woman known as Ani Lochen. She lived to the age of 130 and was believed to be the reincarnation of a deity. 'From the age of six,' said Rinchen Dolma Taring, 'she preached by singing of religion in a wonderfully melodious voice and whoever heard her found their hearts coming closer to God. As a child she rode through the streets of Lhasa on a little goat preaching from door to door. Many girls became nuns and followed her. At the age of forty she made a vow to live in a cave in the mountains and meditate.' Holy lamas and ordinary folk from all over Tibet would walk for many days to pay their respects and receive her blessing.

Once Rinchen asked her to pray that she, too, would one day be able to live in the mountains and lead a religious life. 'She said it would never be possible for me to do this, but explained that a true religious life consists in *watching your mind*. "There is no need to isolate yourself," she told me. "There are truly religious people among people everywhere. If you practise the teaching of the Lord Buddha in your daily life it is not necessary to go into the mountains. Be kind to all living beings, then I'm sure you will achieve what you wish." ' Prophetic words.

In the years that followed, the Taring family enjoyed a happy and privileged life. Babies were born, children were brought up; Jigme, a close associate of His Holiness the Fourteenth Dalai Lama, became an architect. He designed and supervised the building of the Summer Palace in Lhasa. But there were increasing signs of the Chinese threat. Rinchen Dolma Taring became quite a prominent, outspoken figure in Lhasa public life. She led the delegation of Tibetan women to the All-China Women's Conference, she travelled to Mongolia and Korea, she spoke in public.

'Tibetan women have always enjoyed equal rights and status with men,' she told me. 'They shared in all the social activities of men and a wife had to be consulted on all matters. Women could do all jobs except working in government offices or being carpenters. They could also shoot and fight - there have been several women soldier heroines in our history. Women could take part in religious ceremonies and some nuns became famous scholars.'

She once said, in a speech to 400 Chinese women soldiers and officers' wives, 'We Tibetan women are known to be very capable and have always had a most enjoyable life. We have never been subjected to submissive or degrading practices such as the foot-binding of the Chinese, the purdah of the Muslims or the suttee of the Hindus. Men do the hardest work, yet we believe that without women nothing can be done as they are considered *more intelligent* than men. The husband provides the effort and his wife the intelligence!'

As the Chinese presence in Tibet became more menacing, much of the dissent came from the women. 'Our women were more fierce than our men,' remembered Rinchen Dolma. 'They made anti-Chinese posters and shouted slogans in the street - "China Must Quit Tibet".' The regime became more and more oppressive. One of her relatives, a mother of six, who spoke out publicly, was arrested, beaten and lost an eye. To this day no one knows if she is still in prison.

In March 1959 Chinese tanks rolled into the streets of Lhasa. She remembers the terrible last night during which she and Jigme talked and talked about what they should do. The Dalai Lama was making secret preparations to flee into exile in India. Jigme felt it was his duty as the only official who spoke English to accompany him. Rinchen felt she should stay to take care of her aged mother-in-law, four small grandchildren whose parents were on official business in India, and two other daughters and their babies. Following months of ghastly anxiety and indecision, knowing that at any moment she might be imprisoned and tortured by the Chinese who didn't trust her, not daring to anger them for fear of reprisals against her family, they said goodbye at the Summer Palace. Rinchen Dolma gave Jigme her ring as a keepsake in case they never met again.

She was making her way back home when the shelling of Lhasa began. In the chaos and confusion she became separated from her family and was, herself, forced to flee across the border to Bhutan alone, accompanied only by a faithful family servant. It was to be twenty years before she saw her grandchildren again.

At the time of the Chinese invasion Rinchen Dolma was the age I am now. All the time I was talking to her I kept thinking: What if this was me? My family? What if I had to leave my home and everything I loved? What would I have to sustain me if I couldn't see my children and grandchildren again for twenty years? Would I be destroyed? Could I bear it?

It is hard to conceive of the suffering the Tibetans have endured. The Jewish blood in my veins helps me to empathize in a small way with what it must be like to lose everything including your homeland but you could never know unless it actually happened to you. How do people find the strength to go on? What stopped her going crazy?

During the weeks of waiting in Bhutan, until she got permission to cross the treacherous, high, snowy passes into India, Rinchen Dolma was comforted by a beautiful book lent to her by a woman who gave her a place to sleep in her little storage room. It was called *The Will of Kunsang Lama*. 'Reading it made me very happy,' she said. 'It taught me all about life and how every living being has to suffer. I was reminded again that one cannot escape one's sorrows – "Whatsoever is originated will be dissolved. All worry about self is vain." The teaching was based on the Four Truths: the existence of sorrow; the cause of sorrow; the cessation of sorrow; and the way which leads to the cessation of sorrow.

'I appreciated what a great time this was to realize the teaching of the Lord Buddha through the grief I was enduring. Now I could see for myself that all things are impermanent. I thought of all our beautiful possessions and of how hard we had tried to accumulate wealth. Yet when the time came, according to our karma, for us to part with everything – including the children – it happened just like that.

'Now the pain was making me think much and I understood that one must come to the state where one is meant to be. Although children are born to us they each have their own karma and must bear it alone. I feel that parents are like fruit trees from which the fruit is separated when it ripens.

'In Bhutan I experienced the reality of the Buddha's teaching that only love can conquer hatred, that goodwill towards all beings is the *essence* of religion and that we must trust in the truth, though it may be bitter and we may not be able to understand it. I saw that *self* is a transient vision and that the real way to happiness is the path of unselfishness. I found that my own suffering lessened by thinking of the suffering of others.'

Her husband reached India before her and she had no idea what had happened to him. He had had an even worse time making the arduous crossing but, miraculously, they found each other again. By now she had resolved to lead a religious life wandering the plains but Jigme urged her to think again before making such a decision, reminding her of the old holy woman, Ani Lochen's teaching that anyone can lead a religious life anywhere through the practice of mindfulness.

He said he felt she could achieve her aims by giving service to others.

By this time refugees who had followed the Dalai Lama into exile were beginning to pour over the border in a piteous state. They had come straight from the cold weather high in the Himalayas in early spring to the plains of India at the height of summer. Many children had become separated from their parents. There were hundreds of children without families. Many died of heat and exhaustion. 'His Holiness was deeply distressed by the death and hardship of his people,' Rinchen told me, 'and felt his first priority was to open schools, nurseries and homes to care for the increasing numbers of orphans.' So she and Jigme were asked by him to organize the Tibetan Homes Foundation in the old hill-station of Mussoorie. The only stipulation was that the children be cared for kindly and brought up in Tibetan ways. 'When the first seventy-five children arrived I wept,' she said. 'They were in such a state of shock and so undernourished, with bloated tummies, skin diseases and eye infections.'

Writing in her autobiography (published before their reunion) of her grief for the grandchildren she had to leave behind, she said:

> I remember every day the last kisses I gave them but also every day I try to remember and practise the difficult teaching of avoiding desire or hatred. Whenever I feel unhappy or worried I look into myself and find the root of my unhappiness hidden in a dark corner of my selfishness. I try constantly to avoid the sorrow of selfishness but my love and longing for my own children is always there. I miss them when I have good food to eat and nice clothes etc. but especially when I see the pale moon I miss them for we all can see the moon yet we cannot meet.

When she wrote her book she had no idea of what was really happening in Tibet. She had heard that her former home had been turned into a prison for Tibetan women but had had no news of her family. The hundreds of destitute children became a substitute for her own and for the next twenty years she dedicated her life to caring for them. While Jigme was appointed Education Director of the Tibetan Government in Exile, Rinchen Dolma rolled her sleeves up and petitioned relief organizations from all over the world for funding. She found old deserted houses formerly owned by the British which she converted into emergency accommodation for the destitute families, into orphanages for lost children, into education and literacy centres. Employment was also a problem so in 1963 she formed the Tibetan Women's Centre. There are now twenty-seven homes all over India belonging to the Tibetan Homes Foundation, in which a generation of children has grown up, adapting as well as they can to the new world, while keeping the best elements of the old – above all their Tibetan identity, individuality and self-respect. It is inspiring that so much of the initiative, the administration and the energy has come from this lovely, quiet woman with her deep humanity and her unfailing faith.

One day in 1979 she heard the voice of one of her grandsons on the radio from Lhasa saying they were all alive. Gradually the Chinese began to allow visits and she is now reunited at last with several of her grandchildren and great-grandchildren. Her elder daughter (now in her sixties) lives here in Rajpur with her. She is the little girl in the picture on the cover of her mother's book, dressed in silk brocade, looking like a little doll. 'She suffered so much,' said Mrs Taring. 'Her husband was imprisoned for fifteen years and tortured by the Chinese. He lost an eye in prison. When he finally got out and escaped across the border he was a sick man and he died a few years after.' One son-in-law who became separated from his wife and baby during the bombing of Lhasa suffered from mental illness for the rest of his life and died in a residential mental hospital.

But there is no trace of bitterness in Rinchen Dolma Taring's voice when she speaks. 'The practice of my religion gives me more and more confidence in myself and I pray to overcome weakness. Until our weaknesses are overcome we have to be born again and again into suffering; only enlightenment frees us from rebirth and to reach nirvana we must try to improve our understanding in each lifetime. Lord Buddha himself has said that, whether we have great teachers or not, the truth is there and no one can alter or improve it. This truth is sought all over the world and if you compare religions you will see the principle of truth is the same in each one.'

I asked her what the mood was like among the young people in the refugee camps. 'You know, our gracious leader has full compassion and is exceptionally kind,' she answered, 'but nobody can compare with him. The young people are very angry. They know the Chinese have done terrible things and been very cruel. The government of India have done their best and have generously given us asylum but when we cried for help the UN didn't hear us. If they had taken notice this situation would never have happened.'

Was she optimistic at all about the future? 'One of the good things that has happened is that, since we Tibetans have been forced out of our isolation, the West has come to know our culture. Our lamas are travelling very widely. It is wonderful how quickly Europeans and Westerners have come to understand the core of our religion, the *essence* of the teaching. In some cases they understand even better than our own people who learn by rote without grasping the true meaning. In Tibetan thought the word "crisis" also means "opportunity".'

Before I left she showed me her beautiful little prayer room with its photographs of the Dalai Lama, of her late husband who died last year, and of the Potala, the famous landmark palace in Lhasa, with the snowy peaks of the roof of the world in the background. She kissed me and gave me a book of Tibetan folk tales. I often think of Rinchen Dolma Taring holding her newest great-grand-daughter and standing beside the shrine she built for Jigme in his cherished garden. 'He had a beautiful death,' she said, 'so I'm not sorry, I'm happy.

I think of sixty-two happy years together. Yes he died beautifully and I'm ready to go at any time.' She spun the prayer wheel. 'Now it's very important to practise non-attachment.'

We returned to the Women's Centre where Ngodup's wife had prepared a delicious lunch of Tibetan food and yak butter tea. Then we went round to visit some of the residents in their homes. Everyone made me feel welcome. Housing is allotted according to seniority: one small room for new arrivals, one bigger room after eight years, two rooms after sixteen years. They share a common bathroom and toilet. In one room a family of six were living. Mother, the breadwinner, works in the carpet-weaving shed; father, an unemployed ex-serviceman from the Tibetan Unit of the Indian Army, does labouring work when he can get it. They have four children. The place was neat and clean – a few belongings stacked on a high shelf, three beds, an altar and a corner to cook in.

Ngodup wanted me to see the huge, nearly completed Drigung Monastery at Kulhan so we drove over there. It is built around an enormous open courtyard and garden. Inside the main temple are three lovely golden Buddhas brought from Ladakh, some beautifully painted *thangkas* of the Four Protectors and some books and treasures miraculously salvaged. Hundreds of such monasteries, the backbone of Tibetan culture, were destroyed and defiled, and the loot was shipped to Shanghai and Beijing.

The monastery has been built with great love and devotion, with residential quarters for the 120 monks, guest accommodation and a big communal kitchen and wash house. It is a strictly all-male environment but there was no objection to me being there. It is open to everyone for worship. I was asked if I would like to meet His Holiness, the Abbot. I said I would be honoured. One of the monks made us comfortable with tea and cakes until His Holiness, who was having a snooze, was ready to receive us. I was anxious not to disturb him but he insisted that, since I had come so far and was concerned about the Tibetan people, he must welcome me. Actually he had recently arrived on a six-month visit from Tibet especially for the inauguration of the monastery.

He received us in his private chamber and talked a little about how terrible things still are in Tibet. If I wanted to see for myself, he said, I should visit the rural areas and not just the places the Red Chinese point you towards. People are suffering very much and there are countless abuses of human rights – mothers are forced to have abortions, even nuns are raped and tortured, and people are afraid to speak out. He and all Tibetans are grateful for continued concern from the West. The audience was over. I asked him for his blessing, imagining it would be some Tibetan equivalent of the sign of the Cross, but instead he gave me his own white silk scarf, a sacred thread to tie around my throat, a little key ring, a tiny tin of scented medicinal balm and some special little pills wrapped in yellow paper. I was quite overwhelmed. When we parted, His Holiness's last words were, 'Until we meet again in Tibet.'

At the end of a long day I finally fell into bed at Meedo's Grand Hotel which wasn't very grand. There were no sheets on the bed and I was glad I'd brought my sarong. My head was swimming, my throat dusty and sore, feet tired. All the television documentary programmes and colour supplement stories in the world are no substitute for the real thing.

The next day was the start of the Full Moon Festival of the Buddha's birth – one of the most important festivals of the Tibetan year. All the looms had been moved aside in the weaving shed and the space turned into a communal prayer area where for two days the holy books would be continuously read aloud by both men and women in a singsong chant. Whoever can read does, whoever can't sits and listens, twirling their prayer wheels and fingering their beads. I had just received news from home of the tragic death of my husband's younger brother in a motor-racing accident and I wanted to say my own prayers for his spirit so I asked if I could sit with them. It was a wonderful atmosphere and, amid the droning, chugging sounds of the melodious Tibetan prayers, I thought of Ian and of his family and felt a deep peace and comfort.

Ngodup had arranged for me to speak with one of their HelpAge-sponsored resident grans - sixty-seven-year-old Tsering Pema. Shy and hesitant at first, she sat peering through her thick-lensed glasses, fiddling nervously with her prayer beads while I asked her some questions and Ngodup translated. 'Please tell me what happened,' I said. 'Most of us in the West know so little.' Slowly she relaxed a little and related her story. It was tragic but not at all uncommon. Nearly every Tibetan of her age would have a similar one to tell.

Her family were peasant farmers from Dako, about four days walk from Lhasa. They were employed by the large monastery there to collect wood and yak dung for fuel and to look after the flock of monastery sheep. They also had their own piece of land where they grew beans, grain, barley and vegetables - enough for their own needs and a small surplus to sell. They lived in a three-room house in a beautiful mountain valley and kept a number of goats and a cow. They were neither rich enough to lend money nor poor enough to need to borrow any.

Tsering Pema was one of eight children whose father died at the age of forty-two. When she got married (a love match, she said, not an arranged marriage) she and her husband moved into the small house next door to her mother and the younger children. 'We were hard-working and happy,' she said. 'We served the monastery and had our land.' Spring and summer were for planting and tending the crops. Autumn was a favourite time when they would make the four-day trip on foot to Lhasa to sell their surplus produce and exchange it for tea and other things which they, in turn, sold on for a modest profit to nomads from even more remote areas who came as far as their monastery. On spare winter evenings they would weave cloth for clothes and trade.

On every occasion people got together for singing and dancing. Local musicians were skilled at playing the flute and a kind of banjo. About 100 families lived in the area and there would be horse races. Tibetan doctors with a fine, ancient tradition of medicine and an extensive pharmacopoeia of remedies and herbs kept them well. Lamas and magicians would be called to give blessings or to get rid of evil spirits. There were also oracles – unmarried women who lived as hermits in the mountains – who would be summoned to homes if there were problems.

When Tsering Pema was thirty-five the Chinese invaded Tibet. She had four children and was pregnant with the fifth. Like many others they decided to follow their beloved Dalai Lama into exile and set off on the terrible journey through the very high mountain passes, walking all the way through snow which was sometimes chest high. Where Rinchen Dolma Taring's high-born connections sometimes smoothed her path, Tsering Pema had no such advantages. Many people died on the way by falling into crevasses but she managed to find two sticks and made her way slowly, feeling the ground every step of the way. Sometimes they only had boiled snow to eat. The journey took a year. They would walk for a week, then rest for a few days. After crossing the mountains she gave birth to the baby but it died after two months.

When they finally arrived in India her children were starving. There was no choice but to swallow her pride and go begging from door to door. 'What could I do?' she said. 'We lost our country, all our property was left in the house, we came empty-handed. It was so hard for me to be a begger but seeing my children hungry I had to do it. Many days they didn't eat. I did it for four years.' She also worked as a coolie, labouring on the roads for a year. Then someone told her about the Tibetan Women's Centre and she luckily got admitted. She's been here for twenty-eight years and as one of the oldest inhabitants she and her husband qualify for the two-room accommodation which is quite a difference from the one room they shared with three other families when they first arrived.

Of the twelve children she has given birth to, only four are still alive. Tibetans, on the whole, are not keen on family planning and who can blame them in a climate of genocide. Only the more educated see the value in smaller, healthier families with a better chance of education.

Tsering Pema worked as a carpet-weaver until her eyesight worsened and now she winds wool. 'Gradually, by the grace of His Holiness and the good efforts of the people here, I lost my fear,' she said. 'Now I feel happy and safe. No need to beg ever again.' She sees it as her main duty to tell her grandchildren about the homeland so they will never forget they are Tibetans. Although, as a child from an agricultural family, she had no chance of education herself, her surviving children are educated and her daughter is a teacher in the Children's Home at Mussoorie. She only has one hope – every day she prays for independence and her last wish is to die in Tibet. Her eyes filled with tears.

I heard the same words again and again. 'I want to go home before I die.' Such a modest request – 'Home' – to have the right to be in the place where you belong. I tried to imagine what it would be like to try to start a new life and learn a new language if my own country was occupied? Could I beg in the streets?

It was with these thoughts that I left Rajpur with two Tibetan women and Ngodup's driver for what should have been the pleasant one-hour drive up to the hill-station of Mussoorie where the Tibetan Homes Foundation is. The 14 miles in fact took four hours. In the light of the story I had just heard, this hair-raising experience was of no consequence but it deserves a mention as the Worst Car Journey I have ever taken.

Ngodup's regular driver had recently been selected as part of a Tibetan resettlement programme in America so our driver, newly appointed, was neither very confident nor very experienced. At the best of times he was extremely nervous and sat hunched forward over the steering wheel, white-knuckled, with an anxious look on his face. He rarely ventured out of second gear and had an alarming habit of slipping into neutral whenever he finally got up enough courage to overtake a tractor or a bullock cart. Every time someone honked at him he jumped and slammed on the brakes. Often he lost his nerve in the middle of overtaking and whizzed across the oncoming traffic to the other side of the road where he then had to wait, mopping his brow, for the stream of consistently unchivalrous drivers to let him back in.

The road to Mussoorie is a perilous zigzag of hairpin bends with sheer drops to the valley below and huge jagged gaps in the guard wall where buses have gone over the edge. Far beneath us on the hillside could be glimpsed a scattered graveyard of rusty, twisty, metal skeletons. About 6 miles from the top, at the steepest part, a lorry was skewed across the road, blocking one side and teetering on the precipice. A shouting, gesticulating mob of people were all screaming contradictory advice. Rather than any orderly attempt to control the traffic, everybody charged up the wrong side of the road trying to queue-jump. The result was total stalemate. Fights broke out, someone's engine caught fire, people scraped each other's vehicles trying to jostle for position. Clouds of black exhaust fumes choked the air and everybody kept their finger on the horn just in case we hadn't noticed that they were in a hurry. Every time our driver tried a hill start on the steep incline he stalled the motor and slipped backwards. Everyone shouted at him and he got more and more flustered and nearly reversed over the cliff by mistake. I was desperate to take the wheel but it would have been unthinkable to make him lose face.

Lots of people had told me how lovely Mussoorie was – 'The Queen of the Hills' – a delightful peaceful place. It used to be an elegant summer retreat in the days of the Raj but now it is just another run-down dump, dirty and dilapidated. The reason for the traffic chaos was because it was a summer

Sunday and Indian holidaymakers like to come up for the weekend. When we eventually reached the town it was stuffed with large, noisy, colourful families doing what families on holiday like to do - eating things from little stalls, riding on the bag-of-bones ponies which throng the streets and getting pulled around in rickshaws by emaciated coolies.

The Happy Valley Tibetan Homes Foundation and the SOS Tibetan Children's village is a half-hour walk beyond the town. We arrived exhausted, and poisoned by fumes, and the staff member in charge gave us a welcome dish of noodles and some tea. I had kindly been given accommodation in their guest block - a small bare room with no mosquito netting and a communal toilet with no water. Water is the big problem here in the summer when the hotels in Mussoorie demand a twenty-four hour supply. The children have to walk into town to the stand pipe and trudge up the hill carrying the 5 gallon cans on their heads.

On the second day of the festival in honour of the Buddha's birth all the Tibetans go to the local monastery. Men and women, young and old, sit together on the floor reading aloud and turning over the pages of the narrow, unbound sacred books. I again sat with them for half an hour or so, letting the ocean of chanting voices and banging gongs carry me along. I didn't know what the words meant but the atmosphere was holy and I concentrated my thoughts on asking that my life be meaningful and useful. Outside, people were walking in a big circle around the courtyard, turning the prayer wheels as they passed, lighting the wicks of the little butter lamps. Old women, schoolgirls arm in arm, tiny brothers and sisters holding hands, people chatting - there was a lovely relaxed yet devout, very natural feeling about the proceedings. Prayer flags fluttered in the breeze, 'that the wind may read them in countless multiplications'.

All that night a thousand-voice chorus of howling, barking, yapping dogs poured their hearts out to the full moon, making it impossible to sleep even with ear plugs. In the morning they were all collapsed in positions of relaxed repose under the shade of the trees and I felt like crashing some Tibetan cymbals in their ears. A large, beautiful, dangerous-looking, woolly grey monkey was sitting on the branch of the tree by my window peering in. He was lazily scratching his bollocks and eating a lychee at the same time, and I was glad I had listened to the housekeeper and kept the window shut.

I asked a young woman in the office to act as my translator and we spent the day talking with a few of the old residents. I had to come to the reluctant conclusion that either I was being singularly unsuccessful in drawing them out or their minds had been somehow cauterized by their terrible suffering and I was treading on very dangerous ground. We tried about six or seven of them, sitting together on their balconies or over a cup of tea. All welcomed us cordially with smiles and 'namaste'. When they told their stories it was in a matter-of-fact way as if they were talking about somebody else. They could all relate the stark facts of their escape from Tibet: one had a husband who was shot and killed by the Chinese; one escaped with two tiny children when she heard that the Chinese were taking children away from their mothers by force; one lived in such a remote hamlet that it took her a month to walk to Lhasa. Her husband had been in the bodyguard that accompanied the Dalai Lama and she never saw him again. But beyond that there seemed to be a void.

I asked each one if they recalled happy times as children in the old days. They all answered that they couldn't remember their former life. It was as if I'd asked them about a previous incarnation. Did they remember any old stories or songs? No, they didn't. What did they hope for for their children? They didn't know about such things. It was as if luxuries like memory, imagination and hope were too dangerous. Perhaps, like children who have been terribly abused, there is a mechanism in the human mind that shuts off the pain of memory for the sake of survival. Total recall would be unendurable. Then again, maybe that is a Western, psychological projection. Since the Buddha teaches that all suffering comes from the refusal to recognise the fact of impermanence, perhaps they had already let it go.

They all said they now feel safe thanks to His Holiness and just spend their time praying for his long life and repeating, 'Om Mani Padme Hum' ('Hail to the jewel in the heart of the lotus'). I thought of some lines from Rilke:

> . . . But the deadly and violent days
> How do you undergo them, take them in?
> I Praise.

They certainly looked amazingly happy considering the extreme poverty they live in. Their toothless, leathery old faces creased into smiles each time we greeted each other. There is a strength learned from suffering that cannot be learned any other way. They seemed emptied by their pain but perhaps from that void they had achieved a true non-attachment. This was wisdom in a different guise and I was in awe of the endurance of the human spirit when it is sustained by faith. They had lost neither their identity nor their self-respect and they were being cared for in their final years as part of a real community. Now, as always, their primary concern was not with transcendence but with existence. They may not have had the ability or inclination to put their experiences into words but their endurance was eloquent testimony to the triumph of kindness over tyranny. The jewel in the heart of the lotus was still there.

The next day I got a lift in a jeep down to the bus terminal in Dehra Dun. A place called Wedding Point (a favourite spot for marriage receptions), it consisted of a roller-skating rink and a scruffy concrete space with disintegrating plastic chairs under a tin roof. The bus was, of course, delayed so I had a one and a half hour wait enlivened by the spectacle of turbanned Sikhs and ladies in jewelled saris whizzing round to the music of the Gypsy Kings on terrible old skates tied on to patent leather slippers with bits of string. I bought a whole *branch* of succulent lychees from a man with a cart and had luckily brought three bottles of mineral water with me. The 'air-con' bus was certainly a con, though there wasn't much air in evidence. It should perhaps be renamed the Sauna Express. Six and a half hours of suffocation and stupefaction. The only thing to do was sink into a trance and pant. Maintaining homoeostasis was a full-time job – pouring water down my throat as the sweat trickled into my eyes, soaked my clothes, stuck me to the seat. Returning to Delhi's inferno from the cooler mountain air was a torment. It was only when I got off the bus that I realized it *had* actually been cooler inside than out, although it felt like being locked in a cupboard with an electric fan heater. NEVER COME TO INDIA IN THE SUMMER.

Back at the YWCA I was glad to see the friendly face of Barry, the soft-hearted, stress-disordered Aussie who had been stuck in Delhi because his money hadn't come through. In the meantime he had 'adopted' one of the street urchins, a remarkable little Oliver Twist character called Deepak. He was one of the flock of beggars that Barry had given money to one day and then was surprised to see this kid outside the hostel that same evening handing him back the 20 rupees saying, 'Sir, you give me too much by mistake.' Nothing could have been calculated to work better on Barry's psychology. He was moved to tears, gave the kid twice as much, and told him to go and buy some clothes.

Deepak turned up the next day in a sharp white denim outfit with his hair combed and Barry could see a real way he could make his contribution to alleviating India's misery without having to work with Mother Theresa in Calcutta. He decided to open a bank account for Deepak and pay for his education. Needless to say this had proved to be easier said than done, with Deepak's Fagin-like uncle trying to appoint himself trustee. Deepak, who is smart as a fox, made the suggestion that Barry should put the money aside for him in Australia and then send for him.

Today they'd been out to the indescribable shanty town by the railway tracks where Deepak's family live. His father is dead and his mother, the usual crushed drudge with no initiative, is unable to feed her kids from the few pais she gets as a rag-picker so Deepak, aged twelve, who speaks remarkable English, acts as head of the family. He was the most beautiful twelve-year-old boy I had ever seen and quite exceptionally bright. Barry had gone with him to purchase some bricks, cement and roofing material with which to fix up their little slum dwelling. It all came to about £50, for which they will virtually have a new house. Deepak wouldn't take a penny more than it came to and said to Barry, 'You have spent so much. Now you must not send any more money for one year.' Barry was touched to the heart.

It would be wonderful to believe in a Little Orphan Annie happy ending and that Daddy Warbucks will be able to rescue this deserving kid from the gutter who will eventually grow up to be the Prime Minister of India and Save the World. Stranger things have happened and I'm rooting for them.

I was on my way to Bombay that evening and Barry was leaving for home. We all hugged each other goodbye. 'Don't worry Auntie,' said Deepak, grinning. 'I will make him proud of me.'

CHAPTER TEN

Bombay Contrasts

> In the middle of the journey of our
> life I came to myself within a
> dark wood where the straight way
> was lost.

DANTE ALIGHIERI, *The Divine Comedy*

The Rajdhani Express, billed as 'India's Most Prestigious Train', left promptly on time. A miracle. A pearl of efficiency in an ocean of muddle, and we were served with cheese straws and dear little individual thermos flasks of tea. Trains are the way to see India. It was like watching a film and being in it at the same time. Hindi music piped into the carriage accompanied the diorama of white-hot, biscuit-fired landscape that slid past the train windows for hour after hour until, gradually, the fading paprika sunset seen through the dusty haze turned to night. There is an arid beauty in the spice-coloured plains, in the throbbing vistas of saffron and cinnamon, but I don't know how anyone can wrest a living from such a harsh environment.

Seventeen hours after leaving Delhi we arrived in Bombay Central. All along the tracks as you approach, cheerfully smiling folk, *dhotis* gathered up, are squatting down for a companionable morning crap. This phenomenon has been noted by other travellers to India and, as James Cameron remarked, 'One would not have to be especially fastidious to feel that this, as a public relations gesture, is whimsical indeed.' It is certainly not the most salubrious view to accompany one's breakfast.

My generous hosts, Rasheeda and Anees, friends of friends whom I had never met before, greeted me with the news that, alas, they had to leave that very morning for London but I would be welcome to use their apartment. They had enlisted various friends and relations to show me around and their four servants would look after me! I was wafted into another world.

Up to this point, from my conversations with Indian women, I had gained an impression of the mother-in-law as a dominant and frequently forbidding figure. After the lifetime of powerlessness she eventually comes into her own when she can terrorize her own daughters-in-law. Now, one of Rasheeda's friends was keen for me to meet an exception to this stereotype, the matriarch of a top drawer, multi-generational family successfully living under one roof.

A Gujerati of the Mafatlal family ('one of the ten largest industrial families in the country'), Mrs Mahadevia reigns over her extended family in a luxurious complex of two adjoining apartments in one of Bombay's most exclusive residential areas.

Mrs Mahadevia greeted us cordially. A handsome, elegant woman in her sixties, she was dressed in a gorgeous shot-silk sari of purple and peacock hues with gold thread embroidery. I felt a frightful frump in my cotton jersey parachute pants and cheap *kurta* from a Delhi street bazaar. We sat in her temporary drawing-room while the main one was being redecorated. It overlooked the bay on two sides and was spacious and cool. An enormous St Bernard lolled by the air-conditioning unit. Eight servants live in the place ('not all at once, of course, sometimes one or two of them are on leave'). One of them brought delicious cold buttermilk to drink and freshly made tasty, fried savoury puffs and bowls of home-made mango ice-cream. The daughters-in-law came in and kissed her on the cheek, the three grandchildren came in to be stroked and tousled and they all plainly adored her. One son came in from playing golf, the other was a polo ace away on a tournament.

Her own mother-in-law had lived with them for forty years until her recent death, making it a four-generation household. 'I wouldn't say it was easy,' said Mrs Mahadevia, remembering those days. 'We used to have a lot of conflicts, mainly about the servants. She was much less tolerant than I but then I had been spoiled rotten ever since childhood. We had servants to tie our shoe laces, brush our hair, put out our clothes. We never had to do a thing.' In the end she and her husband's mother always made up their disagreements and made a pact 'never to tell tales – we never involved the males!'

She, herself, had a patchy education and left school before matriculation. She married in what would have been her final year but feels she made up for any shortfall in formal education with voracious reading. I asked her if she had ever had a desire for a career outside the home and she told a rather wistful story. Her brother was a social worker who conducted eye camps in rural areas. For six weeks every year she used to join him and help out. She became so competent at assisting the doctors that one of them, incredibly, asked her if she would like to try her hand at doing a cataract removal operation since she had watched so many of them. 'I said I would love to and actually performed a few before this was discovered by a higher authority who put a stop to it.' Her hands fluttered gracefully, describing the vanished possibilities. 'I never missed my education,' she said, 'because I always felt I could hold my own but when they stopped me from operating because I was not qualified, then I was sorry.'

Mrs Mahadevia had been brought up in a very sheltered environment. 'It was also very strict and traditional,' she said. 'I thought marriage would mean freedom, but it was right from the frying pan into the fire!' Very daringly for her time she openly had an affair with a man who was also married. 'I tried to grow wings but I decided it was not worth it. Too many people to fight. Anyway, I loved my husband. I was brought up not to cause trouble or to hurt people and there are so many people involved in an Indian family. The pressures are too much. Ultimately you either stay in the family set-up and abide by the rules or you leave. I stayed and have not regretted my decision for one single moment.'

Now, as matriarch, she presides over the family with firmness and diplomacy. 'There is no coercion,' she says, 'but I generally get my own way.' She had three sons, the eldest of whom died tragically at the age of thirty-four from a mysterious illness. His widow and children live nearby. In her immediate household are her husband, her two other married sons, her two daughters-in-law and three grandchildren. I asked if the young wives had been hers or her sons' choices. 'Their choice but, naturally, with my complete approval,' she answered emphatically.

The elder daughter-in-law, Mona, is a stunning, languid beauty with waist-length glossy hair and a flawless complexion of golden honey who used to be a model for Helena Rubenstein. Mona had confessed to her mother-in-law after the wedding that her new husband had given her an ultimatum – if she wanted him to propose to her she would have to give up her modelling career. He did not want a working wife. 'What if I give up my career and you don't propose?' she had asked him. 'That's a chance you will have to take,' he answered. They all found that very amusing. 'You see! My boys are such chauvinists,' laughed Mrs Mahadevia indulgently, adding with a shrug, 'although I, myself, was proud of the girls and would have liked them to go out in the world.' I asked Mona if she missed the fashion world. 'Not at all,' she answered, popping a date into her mouth. 'I grew out of that a long time ago.'

'In most Indian families the birth of a girl child is an occasion for weeping and wailing – a rather depressing way to be received into the world, don't you think? Whereas a baby boy is a time for celebration. People send sweets to all their friends to share their joy.' Mrs Mahadevia told me what I had already heard before in the rural areas I had visited. 'I am proud to say I broke with tradition by doing the reverse! After having had only sons myself and three grandsons, by the time the first grand-daughter came along I was absolutely delighted and I made sure that everyone knew it.'

In the joint household there is only one kitchen. Everyone is vegetarian (except the dog whose food is prepared out on the balcony and his mouth rinsed out before he is allowed to come and breathe his carnivorous breath all over people) but mealtimes are very flexible. They eat at separate times to suit themselves. Mrs M. always waits and has lunch with her small grand-daughter who tends not to eat properly and needs a little companionship and encouragement. Her life, she says, is completely full. She prays for an hour and a half each day in her special little shrine. She visits people in hospital. She plays bridge every day and, twice a week, all day. She writes poetry, paints and sculpts.

'In a joint family of course you sometimes tread on each other's toes,' she said. 'It's very important to be able to say you're sorry if you've been unreasonable.' So who is responsible for keeping the whole ship afloat? 'I am,' she said firmly, 'but a lot of credit goes to the girls. Gujeratis have a reputation for being an aggressive lot so it's a good thing neither of them are! You have to be tolerant and easygoing and not let your ego get in the way. I admit I'm a bit of an autocrat,' she smiled sweetly. 'In fact my sons always said they didn't want to marry rich girls because they had seen what a bully I was!' Of course only a velvet bully ever admits to being one at all and Mrs Mahadevia is so charming and persuasive that she always ends up getting her own way through diplomacy rather than dictatorship.

She described herself as a religious woman and when I asked her what that meant to her she answered, 'Religion is a philosophy. I don't believe in all the rituals but regular prayer gives me peace of mind. Every religion basically says the same thing and teaches the difference between right and wrong. It makes you into a better individual. Instead of wasting time with rituals I believe you should do good deeds on holy days.'

Mrs Mahadevia lives a life that has all but disappeared in England but would have been quite common before the Second World War. 'I'm still living in my ivory tower,' she says with disarming frankness. 'I'm pretty ignorant. My interests are aesthetic rather than political. I'm not interested in what's happening in the world if it doesn't directly affect me. You'll be amused to hear,' she laughed merrily, 'that when I was young I actually got very interested in Marxism, until I realized I would have to give everything up!'

Her family, the Mafatlals, own not only the entire apartment block but all five apartment blocks in the exclusive development. When she was first married she lived with her parents-in-law and children in one of the flats. Then when the flats were offered for individual leasehold sale, the next-door occupant couldn't afford to buy, 'So my brother kindly helped me out and we were able to acquire it.' They now have oodles of space for living and entertaining without getting under one another's feet. 'Naturally I am consulted on any major decisions,' she said, 'but my sons now make up their own minds and they put me in my place if I try to interfere too much.'

I have to say there was a most attractive warmth and stability in their home and a real lynchpin role for the grandmother. There was an ambience of charm and tranquillity, cohesion and loyalty that we have all but lost in the West. I love the idea of living surrounded by my family in a situation where each member has their own space yet much is shared and I am queen! If it works, and there is love, tolerance and respect, it must be one of the nicest ways to live. I am also aware that having eight servants helps considerably to oil the domestic wheels. Meals appear at the ping of a little bell, clean laundry arrives in your room the same evening (when you left it strewn on the bedroom floor that morning), the driver smooths your shopping trips and visits to the bridge club by depositing you from air-conditioned car to the door of your destination. When Mrs Mahadevia says 'I would not trade my life for anything in this world,' who can blame her?

When we left the lap of luxury and descended to earth, Disha, my companion for the day, took me to visit some of her favourite little shops selling textiles and suchlike. The monsoon had arrived that morning with a vengeance, bringing a welcome drop in temperature but also streets awash with unsavoury bilge, dead furry things and muddy puddles. Disha picked her way delicately in her pale yellow, Swiss-embroidered *salwar kameez* and high-heeled sandals and I trudged along behind with my glasses steamed up, perspiring like a pig. My hair had gone totally out of control and resembled a bush. I really envy the classic elegance of Indian women and wish I knew how to achieve it.

I was whisked off to tea by some young friends of Rasheeda's daughter – this time a Parsee family. I was quite overwhelmed by the hospitality and kindness of everyone I met – aunties, cousins, friends. Somehow I can't imagine, if a total stranger came to stay in my house in London, that my family and friends, particularly my *children's* friends would take the slightest interest. This was another big, multi-generational family with a place for everyone. I am sure that, like the archetypal Jewish or Irish family, there is abuse and suffocation, emotional blackmail and restriction, but the arid isolation and fragmentation of families in the West seems a very poor alternative. So many people I know experiment with living in communes and ashrams, join groups and workshops, look for gurus. They are literally dying to belong somewhere. Dying of loneliness.

There is a very low divorce rate in India, not least because a couple have a lot of emotional support. It's not just a marriage between two people but between two families, between two grandmothers. And yet, sadly, the erosion of the family is taking place here too. Due to economic pressures and lack of housing, young people move into small flats on their own. They need two salaries to live on, there's no room for grandma, the kids go to a childminder . . . the hard-won freedoms ring hollow. I don't think human societies have come up with a better unit than the extended family.

In the evening Rasheeda's elderly parents treated me to dinner at the famed Willingdon Club, named after Lord Willingdon, a late Viceroy of India, and frozen in an Edwardian time warp, with its huge airy verandah, card room and billiard table. The sahibs and memsahibs have gone now but their Indian impersonators dream on, caricatures down to the last detail, nursing little pegs of whisky in their club chairs, watching Wimbledon on the television and shouting, 'Oh jolly good *shot!*' Rasheeda's father was chivalry itself and must have been a devilish lady's man in his youth. He told me of his days as a passionate ballroom dancer and of the time he won a competition on an ocean liner with an Australian girl for a partner. It must be agony for him to be so incapacitated now. He walks with a stick and takes a man-servant everywhere but he still dresses very elegantly and his beautiful old eyes still shine at the memory of days on the polo field and nights of the Viennese waltz.

So there it was. A whole day of Bombay high society! Accident of birth is such an unfathomable mystery.

I read in the paper that 45,000 millionaires live in Bombay and it's not hard to believe, though one does wonder why some of the money isn't channelled into building a drainage system, for example, which would prevent the city turning into a vast, open sewer every time it rains. Enormous wealth and privilege coexist quite openly with rock-bottom destitution. The slums are among the worst in Asia and whole families live in cardboard lean-tos right outside the posh apartment buildings. Tiny, ragged children come and scratch on the windows of the air-conditioned cars that wait at the traffic lights and leprous beggars thrust their stumps at you as you pass.

Another newspaper story concerned the recent discovery by the authorities of a colony of about 1000 people living like rats *underneath* the labyrinth of platforms at Calcutta railway station. Side by side with these horrifying aspects of India are all the paradoxes; they have some of the finest writers, poets, mystics, scientists, musicians, philosophers and entrepreneurs in the world, yet in the country where Mrs Gandhi ruled, most women lead wretched lives and only 10 per cent can read and write. Like most foreigners who come here with romantic notions, longing to love India and penetrate its complex psyche, I can only scratch the surface and be overwhelmed by the enormity of its problems. Loath as I am to admit it, I can't really cope with India – the contrasts are so confusing. Spirituality and heartlessness, idealism and fatalism, culture and corruption, sophistication and squalor.

When I was in California with Cecelia Hurwich she had made me promise to look up her good friends Madhu and Gopi Mehta if ever I got to Bombay. Now I found to my amazement that their house was next door to the flat I was staying in. I walked round there one morning and stepped into yet another India, the India of idealism, art, culture and intellect. Madhu comes from a very wealthy family who lost all their money on a misguided business venture so he had to start from the bottom which gave him, as he says, a much greater understanding of the needs of ordinary people. These days, although he still has a hand in the running of a successful embroidery business, he pours most of his passion and energy into Lok Swaraj Andolan (People's Freedom Movement), a 'people's parliament' where prominent or not so prominent men and women, fed up with the parlous state of Indian politics today, have a forum for debate and policy-making.

Madhu tirelessly rounds up idealists and thinkers from every state and now has probably a million supporters all over India. He is a deeply ethical and spiritual man and says he has learned not to be obsessed by the concept of success in his mission but just to work patiently to the best of his ability, trusting that enough people 'of substance and character, committed to change', as he puts it, will join him until a network too wide to ignore will have been created.

Gopi, his wife, is a model of Indian feminine subtlety. While he blusters and holds forth she appears to allow him to dominate but she will often sum up everything he's said much better when he's finished or dismiss a point of his with a wave of her hand. They were enthusiastic about my research and immediately began suggesting older women for me to meet.

The first of these was Mrs Kumud Patwa, the sixty-five-year-old retired Principal of Home Science College, whom they rang up immediately and invited round to tea. A very impressive, articulate woman, now a widow, Kumud Patwa is still deeply committed to making education more widely available. And not just any old schooling but inspirational teaching – giving poor children a childhood, feeding their imaginations, equipping them with a bank of memories and ideas that they will carry with them throughout their lives. 'I suppose my main crusade has been to teach in an enlightened manner,' she said 'I am very fond of teaching and very fond of my students. I was always interested in their extra-curricular activities and wanting to expose them to as many mind-broadening ideas as possible.'

Kumud Patwa spoke candidly about the personal conflicts and difficulties she had faced in wanting to pursue her career while simultaneously trying to please her very traditional husband. At a certain stage she found it necessary to give everything up for a period of several years in order to stay home and take care of her family whom she felt were suffering.

'Traditional expectations put a tremendous strain on the Indian wife,' she said. 'Husbands have been brought up to expect a woman to be there constantly for them. I was always feeling slightly guilty about not giving enough time to my family. I could not reduce my involvement in my work so, in the end, I chose to leave. I noticed the difference immediately in my children – they never looked back. My husband was shocked when I gave up my job. He couldn't believe it. He knew how devoted I was to the work but I said "No. I care more for peace in the family and happiness. I would rather leave it on one side and be contented without extra money." I said, "If I carry on like this I will be bringing up children with a lot of tension." '

I asked if she had felt a sense of defeat. 'Listen, I had fought all my life for the right to make my own choices. I rebelled early in my childhood. If my brother could ride a horse, swim in the river, go on an expedition so could I. I challenged my father a lot and in the end I think he was proud of me. He had only wanted me to get married. He held the view that once a daughter gets married she belongs to her husband's family and the father's duty is over. It was my mother who was the real influence and from her I inherited my strength and what wisdom I have. She wasn't highly educated but she was a very wise woman, fortunately for me. My mother, who was so submissive on the surface, but very independent-thinking, provided the energy for me to fight. She was the backbone. Softly, softly she gave me the strength. She was the one who encouraged me to apply for a place at an American university and to tell my father only when it was all fixed up.

'She was very kind and she was a mother to everybody. A symbol of motherhood. I identify with her a lot and my own mothering instinct is very strong. I feel that the mother instinct takes you a long way in life. If you can love people easily you can solve a lot of conflicts. You can help people to calm down faster. You can be a mother to a person who is older than you also and to children who are not your own. In our Indian custom we don't speak with language so much – saying "I love you, I care for you" to a person – as much as we do by little fondling with hands. If a child is upset I might caress her feet and convey a lot that way. Especially if a person is not well, talking is not enough. Use your hands! Touch is so important. It says so much more than words. Modern women who are working sometimes forget little softness here, little softness there. I personally feel we should be careful not to lose the mothering instinct. It can help to solve so many problems.'

So Kumud Patwa made a rational choice, as she explains it, to take a detour from her career. She doesn't really like the concept of sacrifice to describe a mother's role. 'Maybe a combination of duty, love, compromise, and a philosophical approach to life would be a better way to sum it up.' Motherliness, she believes, is true wisdom, a way of being, even if you are not a mother - a thoughtful, loving, kindly way of interacting with others at work and at home. It's so easy for this beautiful quality to become lost in the struggle for equal opportunities.

Her ideas on education include teaching boys how to share the responsibility for childcare so that women can be freer from the torments of divided loyalty. 'If you want to bring on women, you need to educate men, and it is the women who bring up the boys to be pampered and spoiled. Even in my home when I was a child, if my brother came into the room my mother would say, "Go and get water for your brother, get this, get that." Then when he grows up and gets married a husband will complain to his wife, "My mother used to give me hot chapattis every day and you have no time." It has been a tragic legacy for Indian women but things are changing.'

Hers was an arranged marriage but she gradually grew to love her husband. 'It wasn't a *very* successful marriage,' she said, honestly, 'because I had this conflict of being a career woman but he was a gentle and cultured man and our values were the same. I could make it work because the home and family are worth more than anything.'

When her husband died and her daughters left home, Kumud Patwa immediately returned to her first love, teaching. Even now she is still involved in the crucially important area of municipal primary education for poor children and in teacher training. 'Actually this suits me the best. I want to do a small job in a small place. I like to be at a grassroots level. These children have no exposure to anything and the teaching quality is also not good. I am concerned with input of culture, input of right attitude, countering the cynicism and corruption which is all around them.

'A woman of sixty-plus can contribute so much to society. She is very powerful, balanced, sensitive and no longer has the same conflicts. My sister who all her life has been a housewife is now, at sixty-seven, voluntary president of a

college. Be patient! You can do anything. You have to find your
own interests and not be dependent on your children. They
have their own lives to lead. There's always someone who
needs you and, in India, so much that needs to be done. I
have taught my house servants to read, for example. They
were completely illiterate. How else will they have the
opportunity to learn anything? I told them, "I will not give
you a rise unless you give some time to study." Now they are
delighted and proud.'

Kumud Patwa was born a Jain but has adopted Buddhist
meditation. 'It is simple and easy to practise and I like it very
much. I meditate regularly for half an hour or maybe one hour
a day. It helps me to observe myself. It has made me much
more temperamentally cool. Everything is impermanent and
the continued thought of impermanence helps you to guide
your behaviour in the right way. To be able to steer your way
with serenity is a must. Meditation helps you to get over your
unconscious mind's prejudices which you have collected for
years, or maybe, according to Indian culture, for *lives*. I wish
I had started it at thirty. If I had learned at a young age maybe
my life would have been much happier and smoother than
it was.'

Talking to women like Rinchen Dolma Taring and, to a
lesser extent, Kumud Patwa has underlined, painfully, that I
haven't learned about impermanence and non-attachment at
all. I am too undisciplined. Without being too fanatical about
things, I would like to make some changes. I know it is time
for me actively to pursue a regular spiritual practice. I really
believe that true peace and happiness are only possible within
the framework of a humbler, simpler life. An Indian sage,
Swami Chinmayananda, once said, 'The tragedy of human
history is decreasing happiness in the midst of increasing
comfort.' This is true, but I fail all the time and my eyes glitter
with desire for this scarf or that pair of earrings.

A few days later, Madhu dropped me at Mani Bhavan,
Gandhi's old Bombay headquarters, now the Museum and
Research Institute for Gandhian thought and rural

development, where I was to meet his friend the Hon. President, Dr Usha Mehta. A tiny, bird-like figure dressed in khadi, the plain cotton homespun cloth that became a symbol of Gandhi's moral leadership, she received me in her little book-lined study surrounded by old polished-wood, glass-fronted shelves filled with volumes on Gandhi, Aurobindo, Vivekananda, political philosophy and religious thought. I was thrilled to meet her and again amazed at the way my footsteps had been guided to yet another life-enhancing encounter.

Usha Mehta was born in 1921 into a traditional but enlightened family. Her father was a judge and insisted from their childhood that his daughters should know what was going on in the world around them. 'During the vacations instead of taking us out to some posh places and hill-stations he insisted on our going to the villages,' she said. 'He wanted us to see the conditions for ourselves.' Her earliest and most profound influence, however, was her own grandmother who, along with hundreds and thousands of women, was transformed by the civil disobedience being preached by Gandhi at the time.

She remembers, at the age of nine, seeing her grandmother, a simple, uneducated, Hindu woman, outside in her yard lighting a fire to boil seawater and make illegal salt in defiance of the unjust salt tax which Gandhi was exhorting people to oppose. 'Here was an old lady, completely traditional, completely protected, who had never gone outside her home, doing something so uncharacteristic. "Grandma, what are you doing?" we asked in amazement. "Bapu [Gandhi] has asked us to do this so that we shall cease to be slaves," she replied. You know, under Gandhiji's leadership there was hardly any section of society that was not touched, from the poorest to the richest families, and since that time I also felt that it was everyone's duty to do something for the country and for the freedom of the nation.'

From then on there was no stopping the young Usha. She got involved in a children's protest movement. 'Mostly it was boys but I felt the girls should not lag behind so we formed ourself into the "Cat Corps"!' she remembers, smiling, 'We marched in processions, we sang songs, we demonstrated against the Simon Commission, we shouted "Up with the National Flag, down with the Union Jack". I don't know where my mother got her strength but she said to me, "You must do whatever you feel compelled to do. As far as your father is concerned, he will say he is not willing but at heart he also has sympathy. If there's any trouble, I'll manage it." She was an inspiration.'

Committed to non-violence, she and the other children were often beaten up by the police with sticks. One little girl carrying a flag was knocked to the ground unconscious and the flag fell in the dust. That night, with the help of their mothers and grandmothers, they stitched themselves costumes out of khadi cloth dyed in the colours of the flag. 'Now see if you can bring down the flag,' they said.

As a student she got interested in constructive social reform, gave literacy classes, went into harijan colonies. She became deeply committed to the freedom struggle. During the Quit India movement in '42, when the free press was banned, it was she and a few friends who initiated and ran, at great risk to themselves, the clandestine radio station 'Congress Radio Calling' that transmitted news bulletins from a secret location in Bombay. Every ten days or so they had to move headquarters to avoid detection. Eventually they were betrayed by their own technician. She was arrested and sentenced to four years in jail. She was still in prison when independence came.

Having been a brilliant student and a Fulbright scholar with a degree in philosophy, she became attached to the Women's University where she taught for the rest of her working life. She never married and has pursued a celibate life the better to follow her chosen path. These days her energies are divided between administering the two memorial trusts at Mani Bhavan. 'One is concerned with preserving this building as it was and looking after visitors,' she said, 'and the other is the Research Institute into Ghandian Thought which is also preparing students by giving training in rural development leading to an MA degree recognized by Bombay University.'

I was humbled by such tireless strength in such a tiny, frail frame. It is a mammoth task. Did she ever feel discouraged? 'Peace is what Gandhiji lived for and died for so we mustn't lose heart but we do have to face the fact that what is happening in India is not on Gandhian lines,' she answered, sadly. 'As a matter of fact, sometimes we feel it is absolutely in the reverse direction - that this, certainly, is not the freedom we fought for. Unfortunately our government is trying to imitate the West and our concept of "development" is completely topsy-turvy. Government, Gandhiji taught us, does not mean merely material development. After all, unless the individual himself is changed, unless he has some compassion, some feelings for the downtrodden, this "development" will have no meaning at all and we will only descend into greater inequality and disparity of income.'

I asked her, as a wise older woman, what advice she would give to the younger women of today. 'You know we have become so crushed, in India, by the corruption of politicians and so *lost* along the way. We can no longer claim to be fit for spiritual leadership, we have forfeited the right. Women are still imprisoned and tortured in their own homes. After more than forty years there is still so much illiteracy. And the *poverty!* Going for miles just to fetch a small bucket of water. I have seen the trend for our young women to want to imitate the West. I say, "Let's develop our own personality as Indian women and use it for the good of society." Peace lovers of the world unite and do something to save the world. My advice is this: Understand the real meaning of the term development. We must not just go after consumer goods. We must put a limit to our greed. Secondly, have some aim, some purpose in your life. See that the country progresses without losing the old values and, thirdly, do not look down on physical work.'

I felt privileged to have met such an outstanding woman, using her experience and mental agility, influencing the

young, presenting such a quiet, sterling example of courage
and devotion. Before I went on my way, Dr Usha Mehta,
freedom-fighter, showed me round the lovely old house - the
place where Mahatma Gandhi used to stay whenever he was
in Bombay: the very books he read in prison (Ruskin,
Shakespeare, the Bible); his room with his plain white sleeping
mat and little spinning wheel; some beautiful photographs of
him from childhood through to the shocking sight of the gun
that killed him, the blood-stained clothes and the final
funeral pyre.

I know aesthetics aren't everything and there are many ways
to God but beauty is high on my list of helpful aids. A Thomas
Tallis motet, the voices of the Cook Island singers, or the
sublime architecture of the Jain temples at Dilwara, and I am
instantly transported into the arms of God. For me, the
trouble with the Brahma Kumaris was not their philosophy
or their deeply sincere spiritual aspirations but their taste. I
found it difficult to take the place seriously or be affected in
the deepest recesses of my soul by an ashram which looks like
Celesteville. The different buildings have names like Hall of
Happiness and Tower of Peace. The representation of 'The
Supreme Soul/God-Shiva' is a bulbous piece of red plastic
which lights up from the inside and looks like a Comic Relief
false nose. It was hard to be moved by the garishly painted
charts and still-life tableaux in the Spiritual Museum showing
unhappy people caught in the grip of vices and happy people
leading blissful lives.

And another thing: God is meant to be 'incorporeal' and
yet giant photos of Baba, the founding father, dominate every
room even though, in his lifetime, he was said to reject any
guru status. I love meditation and I can see the virtue of a
devotional object to focus on but I was not drawn to Baba's
self-realized likeness at all and found the accent on the Father,
once again, even though the place is run by women, quite
oppressive. The reason I had come here, to Mount Abu in
Rajasthan, was to experience an ashram where the spiritual

head is an old woman. First impressions were disappointing.

All the teaching and administrative work of the World Spiritual University is done by the *dadis* (elder sisters). They are the ones who travel and preach – a fact which distinguishes them from nuns. In other respects there are similarities: the 'marriage' to God, the renunciation, the celibacy and the obedience. The Brothers do the heavy work: kitchen service, laundry, maintenance, and so on. But for all their insisting that Shiva, the four-armed, male/female, father/mother, supreme being beyond gender is God on High, he is always a HE and Baba is a MAN (who, once he had changed from a rich diamond merchant into a celibate visionary, made his own wife into a 'child' by calling her his daughter).

Anyway, shame on me. I hadn't come here to pass judgement but to learn. Sister Shilu, one of the meditation teachers, kindly spent a long time answering some of my questions. This was Baba's home, she explained, and his spirit is still very much around. People find his image inspiring although he is not worshipped for himself. I asked if I might make an appointment with Dadi Prakashmani, the senior dadi, to talk to her about older women and wisdom. It would be arranged. I was generously given a room and invited to eat with the senior staff.

The next morning a recorded voice singing a cheery good-morning song blasted over the PA system at 3.30 am, calling the faithful to the first meditation sitting. I managed the second session at 6.30. This is called Godly Pursuits, or Murli, a daily class presided over by the elderly, white-haired Dadi Prakashmani, the charismatic, grandmotherly presence who is much revered and loved by everyone. Her classes include a bit of teaching, discourse, audience participation and stories in the Eastern style of guru instruction. This morning her theme was the rain of knowledge making us pure and taking us home, as a river to the ocean. Sex-lust, she said, is the greatest enemy. Forget about your body and wake up to soul-consciousness.

At the appointed hour I went along to her office with a tape recorder and a list of questions. Sister Shilu acted as interpreter. I realized that my views about the potential for beauty and joy in the act of sexual union were going to be in opposition to hers. Was it not possible, I asked, for sex to have a spiritual and mystical dimension?

'No, this is impurity. Physical love is the distorted form of true love,' she answered. We need to give up all attraction for anything which is physical, converting this energy into spiritual power. Women can show the way here. 'We don't hate the body, we appreciate the body. Like a good cassette player you have to look after it and maintain it and it will give you good service. It is only an instrument.'

Soul-consciousness, she said, takes us beyond differences of gender, class or race, thereby removing oppression and discrimination. In this state we are all equal. 'A woman can teach this to society. She can be a guide to the understanding of the equality between men and women if she has the inner power of truth which follows from the realization that she is a soul. This is not passivity, this is choice and strength.' According to Dadi Prakashmani, the root of all our problems is sex-lust and this, in turn, has led to the global population crisis. Because we are weak and 'too much body-conscious', men do not respect us. 'If a woman can remain pure and simple and understand her true value in a spiritual way, man will respect her.' The need of the hour is purity and transformation. As things stand, the planet is heading for destruction by the turn of the century and unless we mend our ways only a few pious souls will survive.

Dadiji's message to the women of the world was: 'Oh woman, you are a Shiva/Shakti. You have the power of God within you. You can give strength to your creation with the help of your power and your love. You can maintain the balance between love and law. You can transform the world.'

In the context of India, and the wretchedness of the poverty everywhere, I can see how celibacy might seem to be a good idea. It is certainly a valid choice, although personally I feel that abolishing sex entirely is a cop-out. We are born into this life with bodies and there is a great challenge in trying to achieve intimacy with the opposite sex, to merge with the 'otherness', to celebrate and respect the differences and know the bliss.

Later that day I was invited to visit their recently opened Global Hospital and Research Centre. I was filled with a whole new respect for the organization when I saw this aspect of their work. The hospital would be magnificent anywhere. In India it is miraculous. Imaginatively designed, and with an impressive range of facilities, it is committed to a holistic view of healthcare which incorporates, most importantly, meditation. The use of a meditation room in a hospital – to lessen anxiety, quieten and focus the mind, and help the patients participate in their own healing process – seemed a wonderful thing. And not just for the patients. Staff members, whenever they need a quick recharge, can retreat to a still and peaceful place. In fact, at regular intervals throughout the working day, a three-minute piece of meditation music is played over the PA and both doctors and patients stop what they are doing and observe the silence.

By providing a first-class facility, absolutely free to the poor and needy and at a nominal charge to those who can afford it, they hope to introduce some of their other ideas. The staff are all Brahma Kumaris (the organization attracts a large number of professional people worldwide) and they cater to all the Brothers and Sisters as well as the locals. I went out with Dr Vinay Laxshmi, the consultant gynaecologist, to visit a poor village where they are beginning to establish contact. Initially the villagers were suspicious and hid in their houses, but by the third or fourth visit they were bringing their children out. This was the fifth visit. We parked the minibus in the middle of the parched, dusty village. Immediately the women, like frightened small animals, pulled their filthy saris over their faces and melted into the shadows. Gradually they started trickling back, carrying snotty, scabby babies with flies stuck to their eyelashes. Vinay examined them, showed them how to wash their hands, doled out some medicine. The mothers looked so young and so exhausted.

'This is the beginning,' said Vinay, 'of Dadi Prakashmani's vision in action – reaching the women and showing them that they can be the spiritual power in the household, that they can control the health and become the real strength of their families.' Only by these means, she feels, is there the remotest chance of reversing the massive catastrophe that is otherwise India's unavoidable fate. The population statistics are horrifying – fifteen million more Indians every year competing for the already scarce water, food, housing. The Brahma Kumaris may be a drop in the ocean but they, at least, have a strategy and it is one of self-empowerment rather than coercion.

I was touched by all the kindness and selflessness I saw and astonished by the organizational miracle and self-sufficiency they have managed to achieve. Everybody goes smilingly about their business, dressed in white. They beam at each other with long eye-to-eye transmissions of brotherly/sisterly love and greet each other with 'Om Shanti' (I am a peaceful soul). Having said all that, it is definitely not for me. Four days of Celesteville and I was ready to go home.

By the time I took my last Indian train journey I had found out how to get it right. My mistake on the previous occasion was to book an 'A/C Chair Car' which had all the charms of flying to Australia in a hovercraft. The secret is to ask for the very reasonably priced 'Reserved Second Class A/C Sleeper' – less than £12 from Udaipur to Delhi. It took twenty-two hours but there were only four people to a carriage. You can hire a clean bedroll for 20p and have a delicious freshly cooked dinner of hot chapattis, dhal, rice, two types of vegetable curry and yogurt for 25p. Another secret is a small hand towel and a flannel soaked in cologne in a plastic bag done up with a rubber band. This means you can even eat a mango in a train compartment. Plenty to read, plenty of mineral water, a supply of toilet paper and you're laughing.

I felt inordinately pleased with myself for having cracked it. I even daringly got off to have a glass of steaming, sweet, boiled chai on the platform when the train stopped at Jaipur Junction.

It would have cost three times as much to fly so I could also justify indulging myself with one night in the Lake Palace Hotel, Udaipur. Twenty-four hours of pretend, tourist India – the land of Maharajas and elephants, of red-turbanned flunkies and happy folk-dancers. I ordered tea by the lily pond and watched through filigree marble screens as the sun set behind the sable hills across the lake. It was an exquisite fantasy island where the real India could be kept at a safe distance. A little sybaritic detour from the path of Righteousness.

On the flight back to London I remembered how tearful I had been when I left and how scared. As time went by I had felt less lonely and more at ease with my own company. I had found it easy to make friends and quite peaceful to be alone with my thoughts. My sense of myself as a person separate from my family had been strengthened. All the time I was away I held them, my beloved and precious ones, in my heart like a glowing fire – the source of my warmth and my joy – but I also learned to be apart from them. The two things I missed the most were laughter and passion – both hard to achieve without a companion. Like all journeys, mine was essentially a solitary quest. For what? For clues. For God, I suppose, whatever that means. For union with the Divine, for enlightenment. A pursuit of truth and the courage to stay with it. I want to become more tolerant, more self-disciplined, less voracious, more content. I want to grow into a wise old woman.

I feel so grateful to have been given this time. It showed me so many new perspectives, it tested my resourcefulness, broadened my experience, it forced me to be alone in a way I've never had to before. It made me aware of my blessings. It was a rite of passage. As Matthew Fox wrote, in *The Original Blessing*:

With the naming of our spiritual journey, we are able to realize that beyond strife and loneliness lie common origins, parallel journeys and a communion of saints.

CHAPTER ELEVEN

Looking for My Grandmother

> Grow old along with me
> The best is yet to be
> The last of life for which the first was made
> Our times are in His hand
> Who saith, A whole I planned
> Youth shows but half: Trust God! See all!
> be not afraid
>
> ROBERT BROWNING, 'Rabbi bin Ezra'

As the big engines of the night flight to Tel Aviv hummed me to sleep I wondered at the gentle forces which had brought me so far. I think this part of the story undoubtedly began in the unlikely setting of a teepee in Wales last summer, at a Mother Nature camp where I had gone to learn about 'magic in the European tradition'. For the last meditation of the week, the idea was to journey in your mind to a place where you might meet your 'guide' - perhaps a wise spirit or animal with knowledge that could help you in your life. This is a magical technique which assumes that deep down inside ourselves we know everything that has ever happened or will happen. Spirit guides help us to access this wisdom. Although, of course, we create them, they can sometimes take on surprising personalities. I had tried this before and was always amazed at the results. So much lies hidden just beneath the surface of the conscious mind waiting to be summoned up.

This time, meditating at the summer camp, I travelled a long way, through a tunnel, a gate, along a path, through a labyrinth, but instead of coming to a sunny meadow or a hill with a little temple on the top which is where such meditations often take you, I came out by a deep, bubbling pool which looked like the spring at the source of a river. My guide appeared at once and said, Lalushka, I am your grandmother Sara.' Only one person ever called me Lalushka and that was my father - her son. As she spoke, mist swirled around her and her face disappeared from view. 'It will not be easy for me to reach you or for us to communicate because I am very far away but I will find ways. Know that I love you, care for you and watch over you.' Then the mist covered her up and her voice became fainter. 'Before I go I will give you a gift - a token of faith,' she said, and put into my hand a very unusual shell carved into a spiral. A cone-shaped, smooth, beige shell - quite large. Then she was gone. The scene faded, the meditation was over and I returned to everyday consciousness - to my body curled up on sheepskins and wrapped in a blanket.

Grandmothers had been on my mind so there was a rational explanation for this vision. But that didn't account for the incredible clarity of the message, or the symbolism of the setting and the gift. What did the shell mean? An image of rebirth? Of self-containment? And the source? A connection with the most ancient part of myself? I was puzzled and yet suffused with a sense of happiness. It really felt as if I had made contact with her.

The next day it poured with rain but I wanted to walk along the cliffs. There was nobody about and I shouted and sang in a cheerful mood - hollering out the goddess chants we had been learning. Even though they are rather tuneless drones, they're actually very invigorating to sing round a camp fire with other women and lovely to yell to the ocean and the wild wind. After about an hour's walking I descended to a windswept, bleak and cheerless little seaside village, deserted by the usual throng of holiday-makers. There was an empty café where I had a cup of tea and warmed myself for a few minutes and a sad little bucket and spade shop with a rusting 'Walls Ice Cream' sign swinging in the wind and spray outside.

I went in to buy a packet of biscuits and absently looked at the tacky souvenirs and postcards of sunnier days. Suddenly I saw it, unmistakable, lying there on a shelf - a smooth, beige shell carved into a spiral, the only one in the shop - the very shell my grandmother had given me!

The shell now sits in a basket on the table in my sitting-room. So, what did I know of her, Sara Tennenbaum, my grandmother? Only one photograph of her exists - a round-faced Orthodox Jewish woman dressed in medieval black with a rather stiff wig covering her shaven head. As far as I knew, she had died, along with all the other members of my father's family whom he left behind in his home town of Tomaschov Mazowiecka, in October 1942 when all the Jews were rounded up and sent to the death camp at Treblinka. I hoped one day to make a pilgrimage to Poland as part of my attempt to find out more about her.

'Hello, is that Allegra?' said a deep, heavily accented woman's voice when I answered the telephone a few weeks later.

'Yes it is.'

'My name is Janka Hochland. Your grandmother was my great-aunt which means that you and I are second cousins. I have been trying to trace any surviving relatives. Would you like to meet me while I am in London?'

I was so excited I could hardly speak and rushed off to the rendezvous at her daughter's house not 10 miles from where I live. Janka lives in Manchester and in the past few years has begun to feel passionately about putting together a family archive before time runs out and all the witnesses are dead. I had thought they *were* all dead. She had traced me through my brother's surname in the London telephone directory. She told me that in Israel, still alive but in her late eighties and very frail, is the oldest surviving relative, also named Sara Tennenbaum! A first cousin of my father's and also of Janka's

mother. I knew that, come what may, I must try to visit her
- to physically touch the last remaining link with my
grandmother. The problem was that she spoke no English so
I would need to go with someone who spoke Yiddish or
Hebrew.

A few months passed, during which I struggled to come to
terms with my second bout of breast cancer, wondering what
riddles I should be trying to solve, which voices I should be
trying to listen to more acutely; wondering if I would be
granted a life long enough to complete this quest and this
book. Then one day I heard that Levana, an Israeli friend, was
going to Tel Aviv, so I asked her to call the old people's home
where Janka thought Sara Tennenbaum was living, having
taken shelter there during the Gulf War. She was there and
Levana managed to speak to her directly. Yes of course she
remembered my father, yes of course she remembered my
grandmother, yes she would like to meet me. Her daughter,
Malka, was arriving from America that week so we would be
able to converse through her. I knew this was one more
journey I had to make.

I rang my travel agent who managed to book me on a flight
the following day. Now for the next miracle . . . That very
evening I met Sari, an Israeli woman, at a dinner party. When
she heard I had nowhere to stay she immediately offered me
the use of her apartment right in the centre of Tel Aviv. A
total stranger! On the eve of my departure. Thank you,
guardians, guides, angels and spirits. I rang Janka. She was
going to be in Tel Aviv too.

Everything went according to plan: the airport bus dropped
me at the corner of my road, the key was there, the door
opened, Sari's mother had left me some bread and some fruit,
I was in Israel.

I had brought with me my father's manuscript of his
unfinished memoirs, *The Wonderings of a Wandering Jew*, which
I had skimmed through years before when I was too young
and too preoccupied with the present to be interested in the
past. This time I hoped it would fill in some of the missing

bits of the jigsaw. I read for a bit, then walked down to the beach at sunset. I knew it was important to take things gently and let the story unfold of its own accord. I stood in the Mediterranean in the warm twilight air, marvelling at the way the wave of events had suddenly picked me up and brought me here.

By now, because it has always happened before, I really do trust the process of putting things out to the universe and knowing that when I need them, so long as I do whatever I can to help myself, my helpers will appear. I said it out loud. To whom, I have no idea. To the goddess? To the divine spirit? To the winds of fortune? 'Thank you again for bringing me here.'

I had a day to myself before the historic meeting so I walked around Tel Aviv. I found myself in Hacarmel, the street market, a feast for the senses. Piles of melons and almonds, coriander and olives, sticky Middle Eastern pastries and vats of creamy cheese. Biblical foods. I bravely bought two mangoes, a pickled herring and some onion bagels, using fractured Hebrew from my phrase book. I stopped spellbound outside a stall selling music cassettes, mesmerized by a rich baritone voice singing those heart-rending Yiddish songs my father used to sing. I wandered down Nahlat Binyamin, a pedestrian street filled with cafés, craft sellers and street musicians, soaking up the heady mix of smells and sounds: a violinist and an oboe player making exquisite seventeenth-century chamber music, a mournful sax and trombone playing 'Autumn Leaves', two fiery Rumanians fiddling a passionate rhapsody fit to bust. So many places in the world have become synonymous with violence and hatred – Israel, Lebanon, Northern Ireland. It was good to be reminded that normal life goes on, that artists still create beautiful things, and that most people just want to be happy. I bought a little silver ring depicting a woman and a tree – the last time I was in Israel I had planted two trees for my parents in the Jerusalem Peace Forest.

I sat at a café in the shade and read some more of my father's tragic manuscript - the bit where, as an eleven-year-old boy, he witnessed his father's murder by ruffians on the Sabbath eve. The horror of seeing this beloved, gentle, good man fall soundlessly with only the small round hole in his temple and the trickle of blood on the floor to indicate that he was dead. The terror, the screams of his mother, the German police arriving and sealing off the house, leaving the body inside all alone - these mental images were to haunt him forever.

I knew the story, of course, but I read it this time with more awareness and receptivity. I have always tried to protect myself from my father's pain. Its unspoken presence was so overwhelming in my own childhood - in the sound of his terrible, shouting nightmares echoing through the house and my mother's voice, 'It's all right darling, it's all right'; in the sight of him suddenly convulsed with weeping, sitting in his study when he didn't see me standing there - that I never wanted to hear about it. It was too enormous for a child to deal with. I wish he had lived until a time when I could have let him talk. Now I want to know everything. I want to know what happened to all of them. It's my turn to be the witness.

I walked along the shore with a bag of plums. Couples strolled with their arms around each other. Gorgeous young women with mahogany tans and impossibly tiny bikinis made out of what looked like dental floss kidded around with beefy lads on the sand. There were enormous Russian peasant women, white as lard, with skirts tucked into their bloomers, standing in the surf. Ethiopians, American Jews with 'I Love Israel' hats and ridiculous nose shields, Oriental families packed like sardines under one umbrella playing their radios and cooking huge feasts. The Baltic, the Middle East, the Mediterranean, North Africa - people of every conceivable ethnic origin come together to make one nation.

As I'd already discovered, a stark feature of middle age is solitude. Not that I mind it, but it's different. At any other time in my life, from the age of eleven onwards, I would have had to deal with the attentions (welcome or unwelcome) of cruising Romeos. This time the only man who approached was a young gigolo. He was oiling around, looking for a meal ticket, and thought I might be grateful for company. He was rather put out when I declined his offer. It made me feel quite melancholy. I went back to the flat, changed for dinner and ate my herrings alone.

The next day I met up with Janka and we caught a taxi over to B'nai Brak, the Orthodox Jewish suburb of Tel Aviv where Sara lives. Her daughter Malka had just arrived from New York and immediately decided that Sara should leave the old people's home where she was desperately unhappy and come to live with her in America. If I'd left it another week she wouldn't have been there.

Malka, a warm, attractive woman of my age, was waiting down on the street for us, feeling as emotional as Janka and I about all this new-found family. She took us upstairs to meet Sara and there she was, a tiny, bemused little woman with a headscarf tied under her chin in Eastern European style, my father's cousin, daughter of my grandfather's sister Rachel. The only one left of that generation. I wept as we embraced each other. She hadn't quite understood who it was coming to see her but when she realized I was Rachmil's daughter she wept as well. I had brought her photos of my dad as a small boy, of his father and mother, of my dad as a young man, a middle-aged man and an old man shortly before his death. Her eyes kept overflowing as she remembered the stories.

She remembered their great-grandmother, Lipke, who lived to 106 and could thread a needle without glasses, their grandmother Chana, the Aunt Leah and her husband Moshe Aaron who took care of my father when he was orphaned. She remembered that my dad had been a miracle child, born after eighteen years of marriage when his mother was forty-six. He was a brilliant child, she said, a *yeshiva hasid* – destined to be 'a spiritual leader of the Jewish people' by all accounts. She remembered how his parents, in gratitude and joy, had commissioned a new Torah to be handwritten at his birth – a very expensive and rare event taking several years to complete. She recalled as if it were yesterday, the murder of my grandfather (her uncle) - a saintly and pious man.

When I told her that my father had finally turned his face against God and all the narrow repressive restrictions of Jewish ghetto life after the murder, Malka refused to translate it. She wanted her mother to be left with her comforting memories and to tell her only things that would make her happy. She also didn't want her to know that I had married a non-Jew. Sara held my hand in hers and stroked my face, shaking her head in disbelief and blotting her eyes. 'Rachmil's daughter, Rachmil's daughter,' she kept repeating. I don't know what she made of the photographs of all my Aryan-looking and African children.

One astonishing piece of news was that my grandmother had not perished in the concentration camp. Sara remembered her - Mimisura as she was affectionately known - remarrying after her husband's murder and 'passing away' from 'natural causes' about two years later. Amongst Jews of the older generation words like 'death' and 'cancer' are too crude and cruel to be spoken out loud and the accepted euphemisms are used to soften the reality but cancer is what it seems to have been, possibly liver cancer. She went completely yellow, 'as yellow as lemons', and died at the age of fifty-nine. At least I had found out that she hadn't died in Treblinka as I'd always feared. It seems awful to be glad she died of cancer. And only just in time. Within a few years the entire Jewish population of Tomaszow Mazowiecki died in the gas chambers.

My grandmother had been a sharp, shrewd woman who ran her own delicatessen and was clever and resourceful with money, enabling her husband and her only son to spend much of their time studying the holy scriptures. Learning and education (for men only, of course) were valued above all things, so much of the income had to be generated by the women.

I had been fantasizing about tapping into some ancient Jewish crone wisdom rich in folklore and tradition but what I found was a sweet, gentle old lady who had left Poland as a young bride in 1933 and never seen any of her family again, believing them all to be dead after the war. She had never spoken about it to her own children because they couldn't bear to hear any more than I could. If ever she tried she became hysterical with grief, so eventually her husband forbade her to speak of the past and the pain was locked behind closed doors. But of course it didn't go away. It is etched in the lines of her face and the expression in her eyes to this day. Nobody thought there might be any survivors. Sara's three children were born in Israel and all of us second cousins grew up scattered to the four winds, not knowing of each other's existence.

Now, here we were, all grandmothers ourselves, weeping with joy at rediscovering each other. The power and the wisdom were not in the past where I had been looking, but with us - building, networking, chronicling, travelling thousands of miles to repair the fragmentation and mend our family. We put our arms around each other in a bond of common blood and I felt a great sense of contentment and completion. I had brought with me a tape recorder in order to do an interview with old Sara and get it translated but it wasn't appropriate. Rehashing the pain of the past is not what she needs now. What matters is that the family lives on. We rose from the ashes of the Holocaust but there aren't just bones to look back on. There are new babies - our grandchildren - growing up and a future to look forward to.

Israel must be full of stories like ours, people looking for their kinfolk, piecing together splinters of broken lives. Janka and I, feeling very happy and pleased with ourselves, went off to celebrate in the seedier part of town where the best Middle Eastern Jewish food is to be found. We had a wonderful meal in a Yemenite restaurant - freshly baked pitta bread cooked by slapping the flattened dough onto the roof and sides of the little arched ovens, aubergine slices fried and marinated and dripping with fragrant olive oil and garlic, melt-in-the-mouth goose liver kebabs, and cool, sweet slices of watermelon to finish.

That night I woke up having had such a powerful dream that it seemed important to write it down: I was pushing a child along a very long, dusty road in a rickety, broken-down pushchair. She was chatty and good company but I was impatient with the slow pace. In an effort to speed things up I gave the pushchair a shove, hoping it would free-wheel a bit but it ran over the edge of the road and tipped up. The child fell out and to my horror I realized that the field was like a bog or a rice paddy and she disappeared under the surface. Lying at the place where I last saw her hand go under, I fished about, trying to keep calm. At last I managed to grab her hand and haul her out. I woke up wondering who the child was, as she didn't seem like either my daughter or my grand-daughter. Then I realized she was me.

I read some more of my father's writings which gave me a very vivid picture of the little Polish *shtetl* in which he grew up and the narrow confines against which he rebelled. He describes an incident in his teens of a terrible fire at his home which started accidentally when a barrel of oil caught light. The Chassidim, who ran from the synagogue to help, began throwing his precious collection of books into the flames, saying that it was because of these godless, subversive, blasphemous volumes that the fire had struck. It made him hate them even more for their fanaticism, bigotry and closed minds. He resolved to flaunt his 'godlessness' and his 'epicureanism' more than ever. To dare to be a free thinker and a non-believer took a lot of courage. In an act of revenge against the Chassidim he stole back from the synagogue the Torah scroll that his father had had written at the time of his birth and hid it in a cupboard. He was threated with *hairem* (a combination of excommunication and ostracism), the ultimate punishment the Rabbinical Court could impose. In the end he argued his own case successfully, got a hefty sum in compensation for his destroyed library, replaced them with more 'godless' books and returned the hostage Torah.

He comes across, in his writings, as a very precocious, disturbed youngster – brilliant, conceited and courageous. It was no wonder, given the peculiar mix of his upbringing. Total adoration followed by the catastrophic loss of his parents and normal family life at a young age, and extreme religious orthodoxy coupled with innate intellectual curiosity.

Convinced from an early age of his own specialness, he didn't have to try very hard to empathize with other people. The women and girls in the family indulged him and the men he exasperated and outsmarted with his sophistry and cleverness. He read voraciously all his life, collecting knowledge like ammunition. His relationships with people often consisted of firing this knowledge at them, scoring points, delighting in being able to tell them things they didn't know. I can see him setting forth, cockily, from this fish pond to conquer the world of letters outside, completely unprepared for real life. And as the flames engulfed the world he left behind there was literally nowhere he belonged.

In the manuscript he writes movingly about how, as he moved further and further away from religion and the 614 *tariag mitzvahs* ('do' and 'don't' commandments that governed their lives), the more devoted he became to an inexplicable feeling of Jewishness. It was not Zionism or Jewish nationalism, which to his mind was as bad as any other nationalism, but a kind of universalism, a cosmopolitanism, an intellectualism. I always felt he was the most Jewish of men in his gentleness, wit and love of learning, but as with any suffocating tradition, it was necessary to break away before he could choose what he wanted to keep.

I long for rituals and ceremonies in my life because I was brought up without them. I am seeking to reinvent them because I grew up lacking a sense of tradition and a sense of the sacred. I don't want to invent a prison but to live in celebration, freely chosen. I think the whole neo-pagan movement is based on this desire and grows out of a total disenchantment with the tyranny and moral bankruptcy of most organized religion. I, like many other women I know, am strongly drawn to the women's spirituality and goddess movements but, at the same time, extremely wary of joining anything. Movements have a habit of developing 'correct' ways of doing things and before you know it there are 613 do's and don'ts again.

On my last day in Tel Aviv I walked along the shore to the old city of Jaffa which has been tastefully restored and looks like a cross between a Biblical film set and a shopping mall of boutiques and galleries. I watched the sun go down and read the last bit of my father's memoires. He describes going to his favourite place - a famous local beauty spot on the outskirts of their town. People used to come from miles around to marvel at it:

> It was a walk through the woods to the River Pilica and its blue, effervescent source . . . A place called Molieskie Zrodla where you could look to the bottom of the clear sky-blue water several metres down and see the very place, deep and mysterious, where the water bubbled up out of the sand.

I thought my heart would stop it was so uncanny! It was the dreamscape of my meditation where my grandmother had chosen to meet me - the source.

My visit to Sara Tennenbaum in Israel was something of a turning point. Not that she herself was the fund of spiritual wisdom I might have hoped to discover but she sparked off in me a longing for something much older, something ancient and timeless to which I am connected through my grandmother Sara - my Jewishness. But what did that mean? I have always considered myself to be racially Jewish but estranged from the religion. I know practically nothing about Judaism except that, as one of the great wisdom traditions of the world, out of which sprang the stories, jokes, songs and other elements of Jewish culture which I love so much, it must be a path worth exploring. However the forbidding, unwelcoming, patriarchal nature of Judaism has always seemed like a men only club, with the women, relegated to second-class status, hidden behind screens.

I feel deeply wounded and cheated by all the centuries of exclusion and I know that these sentiments are echoed by a growing number of women - Jewish, Christian and Muslim - who are trying to find a way to visualize anew what religion is and what we may be. In turning to the myths and stories of the ancient goddesses, in exploring the witchcraft tradition, in searching for something meaningful amongst the sacred traditions of other cultures - women are recognizing that the Divine is not only 'out there' but is in us and that we can reclaim it. The word 'religion' means to re-tie the bonds, to reconnect with the source.

I read an essay by Rabbi Sheila Shulman entitled 'A Radical Feminist Perspective on Judaism', in which she writes:

> Both Judaism and Jewish culture will sooner or later have to come to terms with the full weight and complexity presented by the lives of women - our particularities, our differences, the specificities of our experience with each other, with God and with men. None of that can be articulated for us, understood for us, judged for us, defined for us, or explained to us by men.

This must also be true for Christianity and for Islam.

A rabbi once said that it is a monstrous error to translate the four-letter name YHWH (usually pronounced Yaweh) as 'Lord' or 'Father' when what it actually represents is 'That which was and is and will be, formless and genderless, being and becoming - oneness.' The divine name is deliberately unpronounceable. It symbolizes union and wholeness by its combination of masculine consonants and feminine vowels. So what has happened to the feminine aspect of God? Was it ever there? If it was, can we reclaim it and come in from the cold?

Feminist theologians, with dedicated scholarship, have been exploring ancient texts in order to pinpoint the time in the history of religions when the powerful goddess figures of the ancient world were banished by an exclusive male priesthood. One of the most lucid books on the subject is Asphodel Long's *In a Chariot Drawn by Lions*. She points out that when you know what to look for, the goddess is clearly there in the personification of Hochma, the wisdom figure of the Bible. She also appears in the form of the Shekinah, a Hebrew word, feminine in gender, which is the name of the female, indwelling spirit of God. This beautiful concept represents the female part of God who manifests as both the Torah (the Holy Scroll) and as the Sabbath Bride.

Gradually the solely patriarchal nature of Judaism forced a swing away from an acknowledgement of and a veneration for the female in the Divine, but although she was eventually banished and exiled she inevitably remained in the racial memory, the Jewish collective unconscious, and in folklore. This is what I wanted my grandmother to tell me about, and although she has been dead for longer than I have been alive, I like the notion that my connection with her will guide my steps on the road to discovery.

These thoughts led me to sign up for a weekend workshop in New Age Judaism given by the visiting American Rabbi, Zalman Schachter, and his wife Eve Ilsen – leading lights in the Jewish Spiritual Renewal movement (as distinct from the rigidly orthodox fundamentalist Jewish Revival movement). The Renewal movement claims the right to question and reinterpret the tradition in ways that allow people to integrate their secular learning and experience into their spiritual life. It is a movement for radical transformation where men and women are equally involved and valued. As one woman explained to me, 'We feel free to stand in a circle facing each other rather than facing east, because we aspire to see the Divine in each other rather than somewhere else.' It incorporates an ecological awareness and a reverence for nature. Members, both men and women, wear prayer shawls coloured like the rainbow, symbol of peace and inclusiveness.

The workshop began on a Friday night, the Sabbath eve,

with singing together, breathing, connecting, attuning with one another, in preparation for lighting the Sabbath candles – the most beautiful ritual in the Jewish tradition. The candles are lit and the light gathered in by a sweeping, circular motion of the arms followed by covering the eyes – bringing the light within. The mood changes. The Shekinah, the feminine face of the Divine, the Sabbath Bride, God's consort, enters the sacred space we have created. She spreads her wings in protection and peace descends with her blessing.

This simple ritual brings together the four elements – the blessing (the song, the air), the candles (fire), the bread (earth) and the wine (water). Interacting with the elements brings us closer to the place where the Divine resides, said Reb Zalman; and I felt very comfortable with that symbolism, knowing that it is shared by so many ancient spiritual traditions. Only when we acknowledge and pay homage to the natural wonders that sustain us can we begin to see the invisible.

Through all the centuries of persecution, and wherever they found themselves in the world, Jews kept their weekly appointment with the Sabbath Bride. And as the Jewish people kept the Sabbath, so the Sabbath spread her wings over the Jewish people. It was the first time I had ever lit the Sabbath candles and it was so wonderful I felt I wanted to do it for evermore.

It was a lovely weekend full of laughter and stories, songs and dances and refreshing insights.

We talked about the meaning of ritual: 'To trap angels.'

We talked about the meaning of angels: 'Divine energy focussed on a particular task. Angels are created by our deeds.'

We talked about the meaning of prayer: 'The work of prayer is to offer attention, to attune oneself to the divine name. Prayers are to travel on. They are your carrier wave.'

We talked about love: 'If I love myself the way God loves me then I am in the best condition to serve. Harmonized, reconciled, healthy.'

We talked about 'spiritual eldering' as an important way of

concluding our incarnation in the harvest time, the October, November, December, of our lives. Seeing it as a sacred duty to pass our wisdom on.

I asked Eve Ilsen: 'How can a woman, discouraged by the misogyny of most religions, begin to find a meaningful spiritual path? How can we reclaim and reinvent a spirituality that includes women, that teaches us what we may be?'

'Look for it in your body,' she answered. 'The goddess must become a gardener! Plant your feet in the earth, bend your knees a little. Loosen up. Dance. Wear more flowing clothes. For most women, their spirituality is centred in physicality – in love-making, pregnancy, breast-feeding, nurturing, making things grow, preparing food. It is in making celebrations and rituals.'

As she spoke I knew that what she said was true. All the things I love best have been with me all along. The earth is sacred. The sexual is sacred. The female is sacred. Life itself is sacred. The goddess is in all these things. Not a deity *per se* but a personal relationship with love and wisdom. As Alix Pirani writes in her stimulating book *The Absent Mother*:

> Denial of the body, loss of contact with it, severely limits our spiritual creativity and evolution . . . to call the body 'sinful' is surely a sin against the God who created it and the Goddess who dwells in it.
>
> Patriarchal religions (and male ways of doing things) take pride more in controlling people and their bodies than in surrendering to the divine purpose and to the inevitable cyclical changes and mortality of the feminine way which is rooted in bodily cycles of creativity, menstruation and pregnancy.

My father called himself a 'wondering Jew'. Now it's my turn to wonder: In what way am I Jewish? And where does my spiritual identity lie? My Jewishness has indeed become very diffuse and dissolved through intermarriage and cultural mixing. I have a sense of having had past lives that are African,

Celtic, Aboriginal, Etruscan! I have had to travel all over the world to collect fragments of myself and try to fit them together into the wise and spiritual elder I hope one day to become. When I discovered the Shekinah I recognized her. She is a concept I can relate to, healing, flowing, ecological, whole.

Reading Asphodel Long's book made me very much want to meet her so I wrote a fan letter care of her publisher and was delighted to receive a reply. On a fine, cloudless September day I drove down to Brighton to visit her. In fact, many roads had joined together to bring me to her door. She is much loved and respected in the women's spirituality movement. Her name had repeatedly come up in conversations and I had been lent a copy of a privately printed book, a collection of tributes, poems and reminiscences called *A Garland at Seventy*, put together by a group of her friends and admirers as a present for her seventieth birthday. I knew she was going to be special.

Asphodel was born in England to Yiddish-speaking Orthodox Jewish parents who had come from Poland. They died when she was young and although she was a clever child who loved learning she had to leave school at sixteen. In contrast with most of the women of her generation, Asphodel lived her adult life as an independent, self-reliant woman and a single mother.

Always an active feminist, it is particularly in old age that she has found her true voice as a vital and inspiring role model. 'The thing about age is that it's not bad,' she says. 'And the thing about the menopause is that it releases your energy. I think younger women should know that there's a wonderful time coming when they're over fifty.' After spending her working life as a business journalist, she was finally able to go to university after she retired and took a Bachelor of Divinity degree with honours in theology at the age of sixty-two. Her first book, *In a Chariot Drawn by Lions*, was published when she was seventy-one. I wanted to ask her about what Judaism meant to her, about the difference between spirituality and religion, about finding a voice and a role in later life. We sat and talked in her pleasant flat by the sea in her sitting-room full of photos of her children and grandchildren and statues of goddesses.

'I was a secular Jew,' she recalled. 'I proclaimed my Jewishness very loudly, my heritage, but I was anti-religion. I became an atheist. I didn't think Judaism was worse than any other religion but I wasn't interested in religion. I was interested in justice for all.

'I'd never heard the word spirituality – didn't know what it meant. Religion meant going to synagogue and hearing all the men downstairs mumbling on while women did all the work. I thought Passover was a terrible time – women scrubbing everything with carbolic soap, then the man of the house coming to see if there were any crumbs left. I remember, when I was about eight, rebelling; thinking he was like the taskmaster of the Egyptians and we were like the slaves. Men did nothing and had to be treated like God. God was a man and the man was God and so I had nothing to do with religion for years and years.'

Idealistic, passionate, independent, bringing up her two sons on her own, Asphodel became very active in left-wing politics and in the women's liberation movement. In 1975 she joined the newly formed Matriarchy Study Group who wanted to refute the idea that there was something in the nature of women that made them, *a priori*, the subordinate sex; that there was an *inevitability* about patriarchy. Their explorations uncovered more and more evidence about the goddesses and the way that the female aspects of the Divine had been suppressed and distorted.

Studies of the goddesses of the ancient world led to visits to old temples and stone circles and the political suddenly became personal. 'My spirituality grew out of the sacred sites,' said Asphodel. 'We started celebrating the seasons, the solstices and the equinoxes at these places and it was as if the channels were becoming unblocked inside me. I was enormously moved. I cannot explain it in rational terms.

From being a confirmed atheist I moved to an awareness of a new dimension. I felt She was there and I opened up to feelings that I had never before experienced. These goddesses had been murdered, wiped from the earth and from our knowledge, and yet their ancient monuments still remained, waiting. Their sacred places are in the shape of the Great Mother; the stone circles are in the shape of a woman's body and you enter it by the vagina. When you go to such a place you can't remain merely political. Your heart or your stomach or something moves and the emotions are there. You really begin to feel.

'I felt an enormous sense of oneness with our foremothers. It went with a feeling of awareness of union with a universal force that contained a powerful female element, divine and cosmic, made out of heaven, earth, the oceans, rivers, trees, animals and all natural objects and all those that had gone before and were yet to come.

'The female aspect of God is in all of us. She was put down as we were put down. In raising her we raise ourselves, and in raising ourselves we raise her. And this is my religion. Because I am Jewish and that is my inheritance, I'm particularly interested in rediscovering the female side of the Jewish deity.'

So Asphodel decided to study theology at university - Christian theology at that - and bearded the lion of patriarchy in his den. 'I decided to look for the goddesses in the Bible and I met the Wisdom figure. It's a huge subject, very difficult and daunting, in that everything you touch leads to something else but I decided to have a go. And now I've produced the book but the work still goes on - writing, teaching, giving lectures and talks. Reclaiming Wisdom, seeking her, rejoicing in her and understanding her ways seems to me vital if changes are to be made so that not only relationships in society but also the world itself can be renewed safely and harmoniously.

'I see my task in life as more than just work. It is somehow taking part in the Divine Whole. People often ask me what

I believe in. I'm never prepared to say that I believe *in* anything but I believe *that* . . . The whole is more than the sum of its parts. I am finding out, discovering and helping other women with the process.'

We talked about the challenges and difficulties of growing older in our culture. 'There's a lot that's positive in being older,' she said, reminding me that the word 'crone' comes from the Greek *chronos*, meaning 'time'. 'You don't have to be or do anything you don't want. You can be cantankerous. You can say what you like. You don't have to be a sex symbol, supposing you ever thought you had to be. You can be yourself. You can feel the ground under your feet. But,' she went on, 'the other side of this, of course, is that society doesn't have a role for the older woman. One of the talks I give is about dragons. What is a dragon but an older woman that men don't like? The dragon, like the witch, like the wicked stepmother, is a symbol of older women's power.

'Our power as crones is associated with being strong, with knowing how to do things, with not being frightened, not being under men's thumbs, not being a sex symbol. This terrifies men. They don't like women to be out of control.'

I asked Asphodel if she felt there was a gathering groundswell of confidence among the older women of her generation. Were things changing?

'I wish they were but women of my age group are so put down they don't realize their strength. The idea that the older woman is meddlesome is terribly ubiquitous. I've learned not to give anybody any advice. It's always seen as interfering which is sad because you want to share what you know.

'A lot of women in my age group do voluntary services, in fact the voluntary services would collapse without them. They run Help the Aged shops and Meals on Wheels but they really don't feel they have any status. We are assailed at every turn by the younger age group. I meet it all the time - an assumption that youth is best.

'Things are even harder today. People in my age group would have expected our mothers to give advice. You could learn from your mother. Just bringing up her family earned her respect. This is no longer the case. The older person feels totally rejected. Her opinion is not sought. She's only wanted as a baby-sitter but not allowed to be a person in her own right.

'The danger is that old women, denied a voice, begin to use their power negatively. They become trying grandmothers, bossy, manipulative. They become cornered victims, professional invalids. Their wisdom isn't required and there's nowhere for them to put themselves.'

A turning point in Asphodel's life came when she was in her fifties and she changed her name. She talks about it in the book *Generations of Memories - Voices of Jewish Women:*

> I realized that while I saw myself as a person, I was seen by some others only as a mother figure. They saw my age and not myself.

Then, after one particularly upsetting incident, she remembered the myth of Persephone who returns from the Underworld wearing a wreath of asphodels. 'An asphodel is a small, quite undistinguished, lily-like flower that grows in profusion in the Mediterranean,' she says. 'It grows on the graves of the dead in the Elysian Fields. No matter what the weather, an asphodel is there, so it's the symbol of immortality, of revival and regeneration. And I thought, "That's my name." At that moment I changed. I left Pauline behind and as Asphodel I was renewed. I could be older, but I could get strength in being old. I could celebrate my age. It made a huge difference to me.'

So how can we reclaim granny power? 'Well for a start you don't have to earn it,' said Asphodel. 'It's yours of right. You are who you are. You have the wisdom and experience of your years of living. Let's put it into practice. Be not afraid! Speak out! Stand on your own feet! Don't let the bastards grind you down. You can sit and knit a bit if you feel tired but don't limit yourself. Get around. Meet other women. *Do* things!

Celebrate your birthdays. I had a big one at fifty, a bigger one at sixty and a huge one at seventy. These are our rites of passage.'

Asphodel is still out in front, where she's always been, fighting injustice and apathy with her fierce intellect, carrying the cause of women forward with courage and commitment, living proof that it's never too late to do what you want to do. She lectures widely and gives slide shows on women of the past as symbols of our power. 'The reason for doing this,' she says, 'is not only to reclaim women who have been lost and bulldozed out of history, but to re-inspire ourselves for today's struggle.'

I asked her, finally, if she felt there was something ageless and eternal about the human spirit. 'I don't know about reincarnation as such,' she answered, 'but whether or not we come back in another body there is an essence of something, somewhere that's never gone. It's part of the universe, part of the whole.' And then she quoted T.S. Eliot's lovely words from 'The Dry Salvages':

> Only undefeated
> Because we have gone on trying
> We, content to the last
> If our temporal reversion nourish
> (Not too far from the yew tree)
> The life of significant soil.

'I think I contribute to the life of significant soil and I think that satisfies me,' she said.

FURTHER READING

ACHTERBERG, Jeanne, *Woman as Healer,* Shambala, Boston, 1991.

ADLER, Margot, *Drawing Down the Moon,* Beacon Press, Boston, 1981.

ALLEN, Paula Gunn, *Spider Woman's Grand-daughters,* Ballantine, New York, 1989.

ALLEN, Paula Gunn, *Grandmothers of the Light,* Beacon Press, Boston, 1991.

ALLIONE, Tsultrim, *Women of Wisdom,* Arkana, London, 1984.

ALPERS, Antony, *Legends of the South Seas,* Whitcombe and Tombs Ltd. New Zealand, 1970.

ANDERSON, Lorraine (ed.), *Sisters of the Earth: Women's Prose and Poetry about Nature,* Vintage Books, New York, 1991.

BANCROFT, Ann, *Weavers of Wisdom: Woman Mystics of the Twentieth Century,* Arkana, London, 1989.

BELL, Diane, *Daughters of the Dreaming,* Allen and Unwin, Sydney, 1983.

BIRD, Isabella, *The Hawaiian Archipelago . . . Six Months Among the Palm Groves, Coral Reefs and Volcanoes of the Sandwich Islands,* John Murray, London, 1875. Republished as *The Hawaiian Archipelago: Six Months in the Sandwich Islands,* Kegan Paul International, 1986.

BOLEN, Jean Shinoda, *Goddesses in Every Woman,* Harper and Row, New York, 1984.

BUDAPEST, Zsuzsanna E., *The Grandmother of Time,* Harper and Row, New York, 1989.

BUMILLER, Elisabeth, *May You*

be the Mother of a Hundred Sons, Penguin, India, 1990.

BURLAND, C.A., *The Magical Arts: A Short History*, Horizon, New York, 1966.

CAMERON, James, *Indian Summer*, Macmillan, London, 1974.

CHAMBERLAIN, Mary, *Old Wives Tales*, Virago, London, 1981.

CHEEK, Larry, *Arizona*, Compass American Guides, Oakland, California, 1991.

COMFORT, Alex, *A Good Age*, Pan Books, London, 1990.

DAVIS, Tom, *Island Boy*

DUDLEY, Michael Kioni, *Man, Gods and Nature*, Ne Kane O Ka Malo Press, Honolulu, 1990.

EATON, Evelyn, *The Shaman and the Medicine Wheel*, Theosophical Publishing House, Illinois, 1982.

FOX, Matthew, *The Original Blessing*, Bear and Co., Santa Fé, 1983.

GRAVES, Robert, *The White Goddess*, Farrar, Straus and Giroux, New York, 1966.

GREENWOOD, Sadja, *Menopause the Natural Way*, Optima, London, 1984.

GREER, Germaine, *The Change*, Hamish Hamilton, London, 1991.

GUILEY, Rosemary Ellen, *The Encyclopaedia of Witches and Witchcraft*, Facts on File, Oxford, 1989.

HARDING, M. Esther, *Women's Mysteries Ancient and Modern*, Harper and Row, New York, 1971.

HARDING, M. Esther, *The Way of All Women*, Rider, London, 1971.

HEMMINGS, Susan, *A Wealth of Experience: The Lives of Older Women*, Pandora, London, 1985.

THE HEN CO-OP, *Growing Old Disgracefully*, Piatkus, London, 1993.

JEWISH WOMEN IN LONDON GROUP, *Generations of Memories: Voices of Jewish Women*, Women's Press, London, 1989.

LASLETT, Peter, *A Fresh Map of Life: The Emergence of the Third Age*, Wiedenfeld and Nicolson, London, 1989.

LAWLOR, Robert, *Voices of the First Day*, Inner Traditions, Vermont, 1991.

LOFGREN, M.E., *Pattern of Life*, Western Australia Museum Information Series, WA, 1975.

LONG, Asphodel, *In a Chariot Drawn by Lions*, Women's Press, London, 1992.

MANKOWITZ, Ann, *Change of Life: A Psychological Study of Dreams and the Menopause*, Inner City Books, Toronto, 1984.

MARIECHILD, Diane, *Mother Wit: A Feminist Guide to Psychic Development*, The Crossing Press, New York, 1981.

MARLOW, Mary Elizabeth, *Handbook for the Emerging Woman*, The Donning Company, Norfolk, Virginia, 1988.

MOON, William Least Heat, *Blue Highways*, Ballantine, New York, 1982.

MORGAN, Margaret, *A Drop in the Bucket*, Mission Publications of Australia, Lawson, NSW, 1986.

MOSS, Richard, *The Black Butterfly: An Invitation to Radical Aliveness*, Celestial Arts, Berkeley, California, 1986.

MURRAY, Margaret, *The God of Witches*, Anchor Press/ Doubleday, New York, 1960.

NOBLE, Vicky, *Motherpeace*, HarperCollins, London, 1983.

PAINTER, Charlotte and Pamela Valois, *Gifts of Age*, Chronicle Books, San Francisco, 1985.

PIRANI, Alix (ed.), *The Absent Mother*, Mandala, London, 1991.

PENNICK, Nigel, *Practical Magic in the Northern Tradition*, Aquarian, London, 1989.

ROBERTS, Elizabeth and Elias Amidon (ed.), *Earth Prayers from Around the World*, Harper, San Francisco, 1991.

RUSSELL, Jeffrey B., *A History of Witchcraft*, Thames and Hudson, London, 1980.

SAMS, Jamie and David Carson, *Medicine Cards*, Bear and Co., Santa Fé, 1988.

SCOTT-MAXWELL, Florida, *The Measure of My Days*, Allen and Unwin, Sydney, 1983.

SIDHE, Wren and Daniel Cohen (collected), *A Garland at Seventy*, Wood and Water, London, 1991.

SJÖÖ, Monica and Barbara Mor, *The Ancient Religion of the Great Cosmic Mother of All*, Rainbow Press, Trondheim, Norway, 1981.

SJÖÖ, Monica, *New Age and Armageddon*, Women's Press, London, 1992.

SLADE, Paddy, *Natural Magic*, Hamlyn, London, 1990.

STARHAWK, *Spiral Dance*, Harper and Row, San Francisco, 1979.

STARHAWK, *Dreaming the Dark*, Beacon Press, Boston, 1982.

STARHAWK, *Truth or Dare*, Harper and Row, San Francisco, 1987.

TARING, Rinchen Dolma, *Daughter of Tibet*, Wisdom Publications, London, 1970.

TULLY, Mark, *No Full Stops in India*, Viking, London, 1991.

VEARY, Nana, *Change We Must: My Spiritual Journey*, Water Margin Press, Honolulu, Hawaii, 1989.

WALKER, Barbara G., *The Women's Encyclopaedia of Myths and Secrets*, Harper and Row, San Francisco, 1983.

WALKER, Barbara G., *The Crone*, Harper and Row, San Francisco, 1985.

WOOLGER, Jennifer Barker and Roger J., *The Goddess Within*, Rider, London, 1990.